The Tourism Encounter

The Tourism Encounter

Fashioning Latin American Nations and Histories

Florence E. Babb

Stanford University Press
Stanford, California

Stanford University Press
Stanford, California

Printed in the United States of America on acid-free, archival-quality paper

Library of Congress Cataloging-in-Publication Data

Babb, Florence E.
    The tourism encounter : fashioning Latin American nations and histories / Florence E. Babb.
        p. cm.
    Includes bibliographical references and index.
    ISBN 978-0-8047-7155-9 (cloth : alk. paper) — ISBN 978-0-8047-7156-6 (pbk. : alk. paper)
    1. Culture and tourism—Latin America. 2. Tourism—Political aspects—Latin America. 3. Collective memory—Latin America. 4. Latin America—Politics and government—1980– I. Title.
    G155.L29B34 2010
    338.4'7918—dc22
                                    2010013020

Typeset by Bruce Lundquist in 10/14 Minion

*To all those who made this work possible
in Peru, Nicaragua, Mexico, and Cuba*

And, once again, to Vicki and Daniel

Contents

Illustrations

Preface

Anthropologists notoriously worry about being mistaken for tourists, and this is particularly so for those who study tourism, conducting research in places where tourists gather. While carrying out the research for this book on tourism in contexts of change in Latin America, I was sometimes happy to blend in with other travelers, to see as they see and interact with them freed of the trappings of my trade. Nonetheless, conversations soon turned to what we do back home and our travel plans—or to what I was recording in my notebook—and I quickly revealed the ulterior motives for my repeated sojourns to Cuba, Mexico, Nicaragua, and Peru. Moreover, my internal checks had me constantly monitoring myself to be certain that I was working hard enough on a research topic that involved leisure and travel even if it also frequently involved tourists' (like anthropologists') desires for knowledge of culture, heritage, and politics in foreign lands.

To be sure, I was just as interested in the other side of the tourism encounter, the experience of those local populations that were toured in postrevolutionary and postconflict societies in Latin America and the Caribbean. In that regard, it was easier to feel in my element as an ethnographer and in touch with my subject position as a U.S. researcher as I considered the active ways in which those of culturally different backgrounds sought opportunities to make good on tourism. With both tourists and toured as the focus of my inquiry in fairly equal measure, the methods of cultural anthropology were indeed useful to exploring the terrains on which all of these actors came together.

Like some others who have come to appreciate the importance of tourism for understanding the co-construction of cultural identities, histories, and nations, I would say that tourism found me as much as I found tourism as a research subject. As I describe in the Introduction, I had already spent time and carried out research in all four nations before I came to view tourism as a particularly useful prism for considering questions that emerge in places marked in recent times by conflict or revolution. At first I noted the erasures of past histories that might be unsettling to tourists, but then later—and more significantly to the argument advanced in this book—I discovered more subtle ways in which these nations, often despite ambivalence, look to tourism to continue processes of social transformation begun during earlier times. This often presents surprising contradictions, as nations that have embraced revolution now adopt practices more common to neoliberal capitalist societies. National tourism industries may account for the turn toward marketing their peoples and cultures in terms of broad efforts to rescue economies. Or industries and nations may reference deep histories and cultural heritage in order to salvage a claim to greater valor in tourism development. In regions such as Chiapas in southern Mexico, a recent history of rebellion may be invoked to capture both economic and political support through solidarity tourism.

The experiences of tourists and toured have been captured in literature by such well-known writers as Graham Greene, a British novelist whose work was inspired by his travel to places like Mexico (*The Power and the Glory*, 1940) and Cuba (*Our Man in Havana*, 1958) and whose left-leaning sentiments were informed by politics in these "remote" destinations. Fewer writers have explored the experience of being toured, but West Indian writer Jamaica Kincaid, in *A Small Place* (1988), offered a quintessential and searing critique of the tourism encounter from the vantage point of the small Caribbean island where she grew up. My use of textual material more often calls on travel writing, guidebooks, and advertising, but the literary turn toward travel in fiction and memoir signals how profoundly global tourism has marked contemporary lives.

In an anthology of ethnographic work in contexts of dramatic change, Kay Warren writes that "anthropology has increasingly become the study of instability and fragmentation, of systems caught in contradictory currents of change" (2002:380). Of course, we are drawn to examining instability and change in large measure because this is the state of the world today. I share with contributors to that volume (Greenhouse et al. 2002) a commitment to an engaged anthropology that explores historical processes in order to shed light on transitional societies, transnational currents, and efforts to support a more equitable balance of power across nations. Part of this critical exploration is to question representations of the "Other" in periods of abrupt political change, including tourism's quest for the exotic and different, and the occasional (often strategic) complicity of the toured in marketing their cultural identity and "authenticity." In the work presented here, I propose that even if regions' and nations' ambivalent tendency to trade on nostalgia—whether for revolution or cultural heritage—is a product of neoliberal capitalism, it is often carefully calibrated as a way to interpret the past and anticipate the future, to stabilize governance and save economies. Thus, we need to view tourism as far more than a selling out to global interests and to understand it as fundamentally linked, for better or worse, to the refashioning of histories and nations.

In much of my past work, feminist analysis of gender relations in Latin America has been central. It is no less important in this work, though I do not shape my argument entirely around the connection between tourism and gender. Nevertheless, I keep gender and other forms of social difference, including race, class, and national identity, at play throughout. One of the three main sections of the book examines the particular gendered consequences of tourism for local populations, including those who are marked by their racial difference, and how women in particular respond to both the challenges and opportunities presented by tourism. While some women in tourism destinations enter the world of sex and romance tourism, others are centrally involved in forms of cultural, eco-, and mainstream tourism. There is no single or unilinear outcome of tourism development for the women and men discussed here, whether they are tourists or toured.

Tourism in postsocialist, postrevolutionary, and postconflict areas has become trendy in recent years. In the *New York Times* 2007 Fall Travel supplement, articles touted Europe's postcommunist capitals as "totalitarian chic." Whether the areas of Latin America and the Caribbean that are the subject of my work are likely to become ironic *post*tourist attractions is unclear, but it is evident that many find captivating their improbable mix of radical past, contradictory present, and uncertain future. For my part, I have found tourism research to offer fertile ground for thinking through the diverse, often unexpected ways in which transitional societies work to further processes of social transformation and, as they do so, fashion themselves anew.

Florence E. Babb
Gainesville, Florida

Acknowledgments

I am indebted to many more individuals than I can name for their generous assistance as I carried out research and writing for this book on tourism in four nations. As I ventured into new areas of academic inquiry as well as new geographic terrain, I was grateful to those whose long-term expertise guided me and often saved me from the pitfalls of heading too far out from more familiar scholarly ground. This project marks my first experience with a broadly multisited approach, and I am humbled by those who kindly showed me the way to deepen and extend my understanding. The colleagues and friends I mention here are of course in no way responsible for any shortcomings that remain.

For my work on Cuban tourism, I was fortunate to have guidance from Daniel Balderston, Ruth Behar, Amalia Cabezas, Luisa Campuzano, Carmen Diana Deere, Jorge Duany, Nadine Fernandez, Marta Núñez Sarmiento, José Quiroga, Helen Safa, and Joseph Scarpaci. On Nicaraguan tourism, Josh Berman, Jennifer Burrell, Claire Fox, the late Grant Gallup (who often played generous host in Managua), Karen Kampwirth, Rosario Montoya, Ellen Moodie, and Aynn Setright offered keen insights and collaboration. For my work in Peru, Jeanine Anderson, Marisol de la Cadena, Jane Henrici, Michael Hill, Billie Jean Isbell, Jessaca Leinaweaver, Jason Pribilsky, Mary Weismantel, Annelou Ypeij, and Elayne Zorn read parts of my work and gave valued counsel; as always, my compadres Socorro Sánchez and Vicente Camino, my goddaughter Magaly Camino Sánchez, and their family in Huaraz provided a welcome home and much support for my work. In Chiapas, Mexico, my newest site for research, I benefited from the advice and support of Christine Eber, Armando Hernández Gonzalez (research assistant in 2009), June Nash (gracious host for two visits to

San Cristóbal de las Casas), Elizabeth Paris, Norma Pérez López, Peter Rosset, Jan Rus, Richard Stahler-Sholk, and Lynn Stephen.

Others who have worked on tourism and related subjects in Latin America, the Caribbean, and elsewhere have helped inspire my work and provided needed guidance. I am most grateful to Walter Little, who read the entire manuscript and shared valuable insights from his long-term work on cultural tourism in Guatemala. Those who read parts of the manuscript or commented on conference presentations include Kathleen Adams, Dina Berger, Andrew Canessa, Carla Guerron-Montero, Matthew Gutmann, Faye Harrison, Mark Padilla, and Tamar Diana Wilson; all have set a high standard with their own scholarly work.

Several of my students (and former students) at the University of Florida have played a significant part in moving this book toward completion. Joseph Feldman read all of my work in at least two versions and offered critical intellectual and editorial support; Traci L. Yoder read a near-final version and provided suggestions for improving its clarity; Diana McCarley came on the scene just in time to give the work a final, careful reading. In fall 2009, as I write, students are taking my new course on gender, travel, and tourism, giving me an opportunity to try out some of my ideas and to share with them my passion for the subject.

The Tourism Encounter had its beginnings while I was at the University of Iowa, where I benefited from research support and colleagues' responses to my first writing on tourism in Nicaragua. In 2003, I was fortunate to have a residency at the Bellagio Center in Italy, where part of this book was drafted and presented to fellow scholars. Since 2005, I have made many trips to my four research sites with the support of the University of Florida; I am especially grateful for the support available to me through the Vada Allen Yeomans Endowment. Other institutions, research centers, and travel organizations throughout the Americas too numerous to mention have provided vital assistance to me as I pursued this work. Finally, Stanford University Press has been a wonderful place in which to publish this book, as my work has received the close attention that any author might hope for. My editor Joa Suorez, production editor Carolyn Brown, copyeditor Cynthia Lindlof, and an anonymous reader have been enormously helpful in seeing this book through its final and critical stages.

My son, Daniel Babb, spent some of his earliest summers with me in Nicaragua and Peru well before this book was conceived, and as I complete it, he is embarking on his graduate studies. Daniel has always been an inspiration to me as I have sought to find a balance between family and work.

One more person has been valuable beyond words in this writing project, from start to finish. Victoria Rovine and I have worked side by side over the years in carrying out our research and writing and, although her own work as an art historian takes her to Africa, she has accompanied me on several research trips I made in preparation for this book. Vicki has lent my writing her unfailingly thoughtful and editorially precise attention with grace and good humor. I could not wish for a more delightful partnership in my personal and intellectual life.

The Tourism Encounter

Introduction

The Tourism Encounter

ONE HAS ONLY TO PERUSE a few issues of *Condé Nast Traveler* or read the *New York Times* Travel section for a few weeks to be persuaded that tourism in post-conflict "hot spots" is very much in fashion. Over the years that I have carried out the research and writing of this book, I have clipped newspaper and magazine articles on the pleasures of travel to postrevolutionary and postconflict nations, so that I now have folders stuffed with the material. Many pieces describe the joys of travel to postsocialist Eastern Europe and to recently communist Asian nations that are now looking to tourism to build their economies and lend stability to young democracies. Even in the midst of the war in Iraq, that nation's tourism ministry and entrepreneurs stood ready to build new hotels and other attractions to entice tourists and economic development.[1] In Latin America and the Caribbean, particularly with the leftward turn, or "pink tide," there are numerous examples of nations' efforts to promote and deliver sustainable tourism in areas that recently shunned and were shunned by international travelers.

To offer just one example, an article appeared in the International section of the *New York Times* a month before Nicaragua's 2006 presidential election, announcing that this small Central American nation was introducing the winner of a competition for a newly invented cocktail to call its own, the *macuá*, named after a tropical bird in the region. This rum-based drink, it was hoped, would soon be as closely associated with Nicaragua as the margarita is with Mexico, the *mojito* with Cuba, and the *pisco* sour with Peru—all drinks that help "brand" the four countries discussed in this book. Nicaragua, the author wrote, "which many still associate with the guerrilla war that tore

1

the place apart in the 1980s, is eager to stand on its own two feet again." One of the judges in the contest was quoted as commenting that the invitation to Nicaraguans "to put their best drink forward" could serve as "a model for the politicians now vying for the presidency." He concluded that "it was a democratic competition, where the best drink wins" (Lacey 2006).[2]

Of Revolution and Resorts: The Allure of the Once Forbidden

Why examine societies that have experienced radical historical turns through the improbable lens of tourism? I address this question in *The Tourism Encounter,* based on my research in Cuba, Mexico, Nicaragua, and Peru—nations that in recent decades experienced political transitions that caused a decline in tourism and now, in spite of or in some cases because of that history, are once again becoming popular travel destinations. After writing about changing Latin American political economies in two earlier books, I turned my attention to tourism in postrevolutionary and postconflict nations as an agent not only for economic recovery and political stability but for the refashioning of cultural heritage and nationhood. Since 2000, I have made over a dozen research trips to my long-term sites of study in Latin America and the Caribbean to explore the new forms of cultural representation and historical understanding that accompany and contribute to the growth of tourism in these transitional societies. Through four comparative cases, I argue that tourism often takes up where social transformation leaves off and even benefits from the formerly off-limits status of nations that have undergone periods of conflict or rebellion. Moreover, tourism offers a window on shifting relations of culture and power as heritage, national identity, race, class, and gender are reconfigured. This work presents tourism as a major force in the remaking of transitional nations, with implications that extend beyond the Latin American region.

My research in Cuba and Nicaragua over the past two decades has shown that while these nations' tourism industries have sold travelers on scenic beauty and colonial charm, they have also capitalized on some travelers' desire for a brush with recent revolutionary history. Romantic notions of heroic struggles combine with consumerism to drive and sustain tourism, global capitalism's leading industry. In the process, selective histories are promoted and these nations are remade, marketed as exciting and sometimes challenging tourist destinations. In Cuba, monuments to the revolution are on proud display alongside the remaining big American cars of the 1950s, and Che Guevara's image appears on souvenirs for sale in exclusive hotels. As I will discuss in Chapter 1, the island is poised and waiting for the time when travel from the United States once more will be legal, opening the floodgates still wider to tourism. In Nicaragua, it is easier to learn of nineteenth-century conflicts than those of the last few decades, but travelers are seeking and finding traces of revolution in the remaining murals and on the T-shirts and postcards sold by street vendors. The return of Sandinista leadership following the 2006 Nicaraguan elections and the transfer of control to Raúl Castro in Cuba that same year have brought international attention once again to these nations and make this study particularly timely.

My research and travel in Peru and Mexico spanning three decades has benefited from revisits to the Andean region and Chiapas in the last several years. These areas, like Cuba and Nicaragua, have undergone recent political upheavals and have turned to tourism both as a development strategy and as a way to refashion nationhood in a time of neoliberalism and globalization. Well-established tourism industries were stalled in these areas for a decade by very different political movements—in Peru by ruthless forces of Shining Path and the military, and in southern Mexico by the antiglobalization Zapatista uprising. Tourism is thriving once again in both areas as conflict has subsided. Cultural and political tourism in highland Peru and Chiapas, Mexico, will provide significant contrasts to postrevolutionary tourism in Cuba and Nicaragua.

Tourism in postrevolutionary and postconflict sites may produce many of the same social dislocations as tourism elsewhere. In both past and present, tourism has had gendered and racialized consequences as constructions of the "exotic" are widely used to entice travelers and brand nations. Yet, as I juxtapose analysis of cultural heritage with critical attention to cultural difference in these sites of travel, I argue that the unequal effects of tourism may have particular salience in transitional societies that have sought to avoid capitalist excesses of tourism. Thus, Cuba and Nicaragua contend with sex tourism along with other forms of unregulated exchange, notwithstanding their expressed desire for "healthy" and sustainable tourism, and women of African descent are often the most marginalized workers in this sector. Cultural and community-based tourism in Andean Peru and Chiapas may introduce other gendered and racialized effects as travelers seek "authentic" experiences with indigenous women and men.

My work presents the stories of diverse individuals whose lives are closely linked to the growth of tourism, from government and industry officials, to informal-sector workers, to global (as well as domestic) travelers who come to consume forms of cultural expression and historical representation that have emerged in response to the tourist trade. In all four nations, my long-term research is based on a commitment to understanding contemporary processes as both constituted by and constitutive of cultural histories. My multisited research in these distinctly different transitional societies reveals how interpretations of the past and desires for the future coincide, and often collide, in the global marketplace of tourism.

Before I continue, a cautionary note on terminology is warranted since I do not always follow convention in my use of such terms as "postrevolutionary," "postconflict," and "transitional," all used in relation to the four nations I consider in this book. It is difficult to find words that do justice to the diverse histories and politics represented here. In the Latin American and Caribbean context, scholars are giving increasing attention to the aftermath of violence during civil wars and under military governments and to processes of democratic transition. Anthropologists have engaged in this important research into postwar (postconflict) periods when nations frequently experience continued violence despite efforts toward peace and reconciliation (Rojas Pérez 2008). Of the cases I consider, Peru best fits the description of a nation emerging from civil war and still struggling to put an end to conflict. Nicaragua following the Sandinista revolution and the Contra war might be another, though the present-day political climate makes notions of postrevolution and postconflict somewhat fraught in that case. Chiapas is harder to describe as "postconflict" since the Mexican state's harsh response to the Zapatista indigenous-identified social movement is ongoing, if quieter. And finally, my references to "postrevolutionary" Cuba should not be taken to engage in the contentious debates over whether there will be an inevitable transition toward a certain future in that nation. Rather, I wish to use this terminology despite its shortcomings in a processual way (not simply relating to *before* and *after* in an absolute sense) and as a shorthand for recent developments in societies undergoing significant, if often ambivalent, change.

Charting the Tourism Encounter

To describe a convergence of peoples or cultures as an "encounter" can sometimes be to divest a social interaction of its power and to render invisible the historical legacy of political or economic domination of one group by another. Recall the efforts to fashion the five hundred–year anniversary of the Spanish conquest of Latin America as an "encounter" (*encuentro*), suggesting that the European arrival in the Americas was a meeting ground for different though perhaps equal partners who would participate in a historic exchange of ideas, practices, and resources rather than an imperialist conquest of cultures and civilizations. The outspoken reaction of indigenous peoples of the Americas to that discursive move was a clear sign of the contentious politics of naming such a watershed moment in history. I do not mean to participate in any such revisionist project here, and indeed I utilize the notion of encounter that has been employed by critical theorists to examine earlier periods of global interchange that have resulted in world-historic upsets and contestations. I have in mind "the colonial encounter" of Talal Asad (1973) and "the development encounter" of Arturo Escobar (1995), anthropological formulations that opened highly productive lines of inquiry and debate regarding processes that are often taken as historical givens.[3] I also find inspiration in discussions of the Latin American region in relation to the United States that have been described as "close encounters of empire" (Joseph et al. 1998). Whether or not we elevate tourism to paradigmatic status, it may be possible to suggest that at a time when travel is on its way to becoming the world's largest industry, tourism's force in producing global encounters is unmatched and warrants closer examination.[4]

I employ the trope of encounter precisely because it foregrounds the intimate relationship of those coming together from different cultures and societies *and* it does not already assume the outcome of any given engagement, granting agency to players who may be historically disadvantaged on the global stage. Too often in tourism studies, Eurocentrism prevails and more attention is given to the active part of tourists from the global North than to the agency of host nations, communities, and individuals of the global South (noted by Chambers 2000; Stronza 2001). Thus, in my work on the tourism encounter I will not presume that visitors from the global North will always be privileged parties to tourism experiences in the global South, though this frequently may be the case (Nash 1989; Wilson 2008). The ability of southern nations, particularly those that have waged profound struggles, to set the terms of engagement in promoting tourism development will be seen in the chapters that follow. My emphasis is on the ways that actors at the local, regional, and national levels refashion areas for tourism and how visitors respond to such initiatives, an approach that allows us to discern more clearly the dynamics of these global encounters. We will see that although tourism development is rarely a purely revolutionary project, it does not always and inevitably require that nations buy in to global capitalism. I am a champion neither of the view that tourism will work wonders to salvage struggling economies of the global South nor of the alternative view that imperialist northern interests in the tourism exchange will ultimately triumph. Rather, I wish to illuminate the myriad ways in which transitional Latin American and Caribbean nations have looked to tourism as an industry that may further agendas for change, whether through economic advancement or political repositioning vis-à-vis other nations.

In his richly retrospective essays based on twenty years of ethnographic research on tourism, Edward Bruner (2005:17–18) comments on his use of notions of touristic border, or contact, zones. His interest in the narrative and performance of tourism leads him to comment that he wishes to avoid viewing locals as passive in the face of "touristic invaders" from outside. Instead, he sees locals and tourists engaged in "a coproduction." He departs from those who take a more critical view of tourism encounters as always inflected by relations of power. While I share Bruner's concern to make legible the active part of the toured, I nonetheless share with some of those he critiques a desire to recognize power and difference as inherent in the tourism encounter. This may be particularly salient in my work in postconflict and postrevolutionary societies.

As I became increasingly interested in tourism as both a phenomenon and a subject of study in these nations, I was intrigued to find in the work of pioneering tourism scholar Dean MacCannell brief invocations of revolution along with tourism as critical to understanding the modern condition. In his introduction to a more recent edition of his 1976 classic work, he self-reflected that "even the figure of the 'revolutionary' has a cameo role on the first pages of *The Tourist* and then, as if on cue, disappears" (1999:xvi). Of further significance to me, MacCannell noted that in retrospect, feminist theory might have contributed more significantly to his analysis of the unintended consequences of tourism (xxiv). I took inspiration from this acknowledgment of what remained to be examined in tourism research and brought my own preoccupation with these matters, revolution and difference, to the work I was carrying out in Latin America and the Caribbean.

Some of the most important research on tourism to date has examined how, in what I am calling the tourism encounter, cultural identity and difference have stirred the imagination of tourists seeking to discover exotic "others" (Bruner 2005; MacCannell 1999; Rojek and Urry 1997). The same concern is found in the work of scholars who have considered the ways in which national heritage is marketed on the tourist circuit in many regions (Chambers 2000; Coombes 2003; Graburn 1976; Hanna and Del Casino 2003; Scarpaci 2005; Van den Berghe 1994; Zorn 2004). Such questions of enduring significance—identity, cultural difference, and nation—have been viewed perceptively through the lens of travel and tourism (Clifford 1997). Yet there has been little scholarly attention to the prominent role that tourism is playing in the representation and reinvention of histories in postrevolutionary and postconflict societies. This is important both because nations and regions are marketing themselves for international tourism and because they are redefining themselves for their own citizens following periods of dramatic political change.

MacCannell (1999:85–87) gestured toward the relationship of travel and postrevolutionary societies in his passing observations about tourism in the socialist world. He commented that it might seem logical for socialist states to oppose tourism because of its association with market capitalism, yet it is sometimes close to the state "religion," with "commissars of tourism" using revolutionary heritage sites to draw admiring travelers and build nations. Several studies examine the development of tourism in postsocialist societies, though not in Latin America (Ghodsee 2005; Goldstone 2001; Teo et al. 2001). Another focuses on Havana's built environment, examining the makeover of the old city for tourism, but offers little on the interface of Cubans and tourists themselves (Scarpaci 2005). Two others take a historical view of tourism in nations included in my study (Berger 2006; Schwartz 1997) but without analyzing the uses of history in the contemporary period. Only a few examples of tourism research conducted in postconflict areas have given attention to the dramatic ways in which such nations are reinventing themselves as part of an effort to draw tourism (Little 2004).[5] Discussion of the contact zones in which cultural insiders and outsiders mix is found in the broadly conceptual work of Pratt (1992) and Prieto (2004), but the scarce writing to date on tourism in postrevolutionary and postconflict areas is often based on secondhand sources or textual material (Martín 2004).[6]

More attention to travel in such areas has come from popular writers than from academic ones. In a recent memoir, a young Chicana from South Texas documents her experiences over four years living in Moscow, Beijing, and Havana. During Stephanie Elizondo Griest's (2004) sojourn in the postcommunist world, she found in these cities both nostalgia for a more innocent past and impatience for what the growing market economy might usher in. She witnessed the tensions and contradictions as these societies underwent enormous changes in relatively short periods of time; the everyday ironies and the more serious dislocations (for example, sex trafficking) that she describes resonate with what I have seen in my research. She discovered, for example, that in Cuba in 2000, when 1.8 million tourists visited the revolutionary island, Fidel Castro "opened the doors to tourism with an ad campaign of *cubanas* in string bikinis that said 'Come and Be Seduced'" (318). When I read her account of a *jinetera* (sex worker or hustler) she met in an Old Havana bar (326–327), I was certain this was the same woman I describe as "Ana" in Chapter 1.

In recent decades, Cuba has doubtless received more attention from writers than any other postrevolutionary nation, and the island nation never ceases to surprise visitors. Historian Rosalie Schwartz (1997:147) offers a vivid account of the years leading up to the revolutionary victory in 1959 as an unfolding drama in which tourism played a leading role:

> As actors moved between the worlds of tourism and insurrection, the stage became a battleground. Fulgencio Batista, as tourism's producer, director, and stage manager, dealt with questions of money and scripts, always with an eye to the critics, at the same time fending off challenges to his authority. Then, in a plot twist, successful rebels took center stage. For a while they were the tourist attraction; they also were proprietors of hotels and business partners with gamblers. It was a play filled with dramatic irony.

Historical restoration under way in Old Havana

Years after the revolution took hold, C. Peter Ripley (1999:8) wrote a travel memoir based on a half-dozen trips during the 1990s, when tourism had returned following a long absence. In it he comments that "Castro had decreed that tourism would be Cuba's future," though this was "an unlikely front line for continuing Cuba's Revolution." He discovered a handmade billboard that read "To defend tourism is to defend the Revolution" (8) and concluded that "Castro needed tourism to revive the national economy and save the Revolution" (17). Ripley's observations during that time of crisis known as the Special Period are not surprising. My own work presents evidence of apparent contradictions in Cuba, but as in all the nations under consideration here, the improbable forms of tourism in postrevolutionary and postconflict societies are actually a calling card for many travelers.

Tourism's Contradictions in Transitional Societies

In conceptualizing my work, I have found inspiration well beyond the emerging field of tourism studies. The broad contours of north-south and east-west encounters led me back to the germinal writing of Edward Said (2003) on "orientalism" as a discourse of power that originated in colonialism. This foundational work has shaped the thinking of many who examine the politics of global interfaces, from colonial to post-postcolonial times. His commentaries on European travelers in the Orient and their appropriation of cultural difference, their exoticizing of non-Western societies, provide a powerful basis for critique of tourism as an imperialist practice. When desires for cultural difference are coupled with desires for travel to previously dangerous and forbidden lands, as in the areas considered here, the attraction may be formidable. Nevertheless, travelers' inclination to consume and subordinate other cultures as they consolidate their own greater power in the exchange is often tempered by their vulnerability as they are swept away by desire and as their hosts contrive to manage tourism in their own interests.

Mary Louise Pratt (1992) made penetrating observations regarding what she named "contact zones" and the process of "transculturation" to identify encounters and processes whereby representations from the global metropolis have been deployed by groups in the periphery. Even though contact zones involve two-way exchanges, they generally reference "the space of colonial encounters . . . usually involving conditions of coercion, radical inequality, and intractable conflict" (6). Her discussion of how travel writing "produced 'the rest of the world' for European readerships at particular points in Europe's expansionist trajectory" (5) meshes well with the notion of encounter that I wish to bring to tourism studies. Renato Rosaldo's (1989:68–87) exposition on "imperialist nostalgia" is also relevant here, as he describes the lament of Europeans that the cultures they have destroyed no longer have their earlier, characteristic charm. One might imagine that in the postrevolutionary and postconflict societies I consider we would not find the same lament. After all, such societies have for the most part undergone social transformations of their own making and have often fended off outside intervention and manipulation. Nostalgia for a more innocent past might therefore be absent.

However, we will see that in the four nations discussed, there can be multiple layers of history selectively evoked to produce nostalgia. In Cuba, some visitors yearn for the prerevolutionary days when Havana was a playground for international travelers, especially from the United States, while others miss the early days of the revolution before it was "tainted" by joint ventures and expensive tourist hotels. Similarly, in Nicaragua some travelers (like some locals) preserve memories of the elite pleasures under the Somoza regime while others recall the exuberant time following the Sandinista victory, when youthful travelers came to lend a hand to the revolutionary society. Recently, Chiapas, Mexico, has regained its privileged status among mainstream tourists attracted by the ageless beauty of its natural environment, colonial towns, and indigenous culture, but Zapatista tourism evokes memories of the recent past when an inspired social movement came on the scene and captured the imagination of activists on a global scale. In the case of Peru, the tourism industry seeks to eclipse the recent history of violent conflict between Sendero Luminoso (Shining Path) and the military, evoking safer, deeper memories of a rich heritage along with the present and more hospitable culture and environment.

On the subject of nostalgia in posttransition societies, Svetlana Boym's (2001) meditation on the postsocialist world of Eastern Europe shows that despite global media reports of the region's shedding of old ways and its embrace of new market economies, a profound nostalgia for the bygone era is in ample evidence.[7] I find her writing to be particularly evocative of the expressed longings of Cubans and of those visiting the island, longings for what was before and what may be in the future. This longing extends to such hybrid forms as Hemingway's Cuba and the pairing of John Lennon with Che Guevara, now features of Havana's tourism circuit. In Andean Peru and Chiapas, Mexico, we find present-day indigenous people standing in for a more "innocent" past before conflict and rebellion ushered in a crisis of modernity—even if indigenous men and women were centrally involved in those conflicts. I explore the place of collective memory and nostalgia in the studies presented here.

Beyond these potent interventions in cultural theory and analysis, another work has some resonance with mine. Naomi Klein's (2007) *The Shock Doctrine* has received wide attention for its claim that global capitalism seeks crisis conditions in order to restructure economies and societies to favor its own growth and dominance.[8] She presents ample evidence, ranging from the U.S. management of Hurricane Katrina, to the war on terrorism and the conflict in Iraq, to post–Tiananmen Square China. But how well does this apply to nations that have undergone radical transitions and that are looking to tourism for stability and growth? Are they servants of capitalism's open-market demands? Or are there exceptions to the argument, places that are charting alternative paths of development and change that might collaborate with capitalist interests, but on their own terms?

The comparative cases in the chapters that follow will offer different responses to these questions. Often, the evidence is contradictory and ambivalent. While it is possible to conclude that under conditions of globalization tourism must compete on the open market, we must be alert to alternative forms when and where they arise, whether at the community, regional, or national level. With the political sea change in Latin America and the Caribbean, tourism does not always conform to expected norms of capitalist development. And precisely after crises and transitions there may be movements for change that, to some degree, pose a challenge to the world capitalist order. In the final portion of her book, Klein (2007:447) acknowledges that resistance to neoliberalism and global capitalism never vanished altogether and that in recent years, "on the international stage, the staunchest opponents of neoliberal economies were winning election after election." She offers examples from Latin America's leftward turn in Venezuela, Ecuador, Bolivia, Chile, Brazil—and the list could go on. My work will foreground four more "exceptional" cases and contend that they may not be so exceptional after all as local, regional, and national actors develop new initiatives through the apparatus of tourism; as they do so, we may discover new narratives and practices of development in the remaking of these Latin American nations in transition.

The works I have cited devote less attention to gender in the tourism encounter than might be expected. In cultural analysis more broadly in recent decades, gender is understood along with race, class, and sexuality to be a critical social vector that, when examined closely, often necessitates a profound shift in perspective. From interventions such as Joan Scott's (1986) classic discourse on gender in historical analysis and Adrienne Rich's (1986) landmark writing on the gendered politics of location to Caren Kaplan's (1996) far-reaching feminist critique of postmodern narratives of travel and displacement, feminists have contributed significantly to our thinking about the contours and politics of travel. Regarding more focused studies of women's place in tourism development (Bolles 1997; Ghodsee 2005; Kinnaird and Hall 1994) and a more abundant body of work on sex tourism (Brennan 2004; Cabezas 2009; Padilla 2007), scholars have begun to bring needed attention to the gendered consequences of travel and of the tourism encounter. However, analyses have only begun to draw together feminist critique and broader questions of the cultural politics of tourism. My work attempts to bring feminist insights to the four cases that I examine as exemplary of nations in transition—nations that are hopeful that tourism will bring about what earlier social transformation did not. A section of this book is devoted to considering the gendered and racialized effects of tourism, but I would argue that feminism has its imprint throughout the text as

Tourists consulting a guidebook as they stroll in Lima

I question the ways that cultural difference, intimacy, and the "exotic" intersect with gender in these comparative cases.

Fashioning This Text

Until recently, I tended like most anthropologists to settle in one place at a time for a sustained period of research. My first two major projects, in Peru and Nicaragua, were decade-long explorations of areas I would revisit over many years. If a period of conflict had not kept me from continuing my research in Peru during the 1980s, I might not have had the impetus to begin a new research project in Central America. At the time, some friends thought that I was "out of the frying pan and into the fire," though my first trip to Nicaragua in 1989 was near the close of the Contra war conflict and my research there turned to the post-Sandinista decade of the 1990s. As I wrote my previous book, *After Revolution: Mapping Gender and Cultural Politics in Neoliberal Nicaragua*, I drew on my personal narrative of "arriving late for the revolution" to describe my research in Peru, Nicaragua, and also Cuba, where I had made several trips to examine questions related to my broader interests in Latin America and the Caribbean. The same late-arrival story might characterize my first trip to Chiapas, well after the emergence of the Zapatista movement.

My research interest in tourism grew as I made my way from areas where I had conducted long-term projects in the past to other areas that meshed well with the subject I undertook as a book-length comparative work. There is always some serendipity in research, and I did not originally set out to examine these four nations with the current project in mind. That said, my interests over three decades have led me to places that have grappled with processes of social and political change, making these transitional nations eminently suitable choices for this project. I hope that readers will indulge my desire to go beyond a single detailed ethnographic case study. My aim has been to take insights from several locations that may give us a broader picture of tourism's part in the remaking of nations in postconflict, and sometimes visionary, times. If I had the time and opportunity to include other nations in the region, for example, Guatemala in the postconflict period or Bolivia since the election of Evo Morales, this might enrich my analysis. I am all too well aware, however, of the pitfalls of extending myself too far, and I also know that other scholars are conducting research in those areas that will be of greater analytical depth than I could hope for; I look forward to the conversations we will have as tourism research advances in more Latin American nations.[9]

By the year 2000 I had grown intrigued by the way that Nicaragua and Cuba variously highlighted or erased signs of revolution in order to market tourism, and I made repeat visits to those countries to study the phenomenon (Nicaragua in 2000, 2002, 2003, 2004, 2008, and Cuba in 2001, 2003, 2005, 2008–2009). Moreover, I began to think comparatively about the other two nations I examine here, Peru and Mexico. These nations had experienced entirely different periods of conflict and uprising in which rebels and militaries clashed. After a nine-year absence, I returned to Peru during the summers of 2006 and 2007 to collect material relating to tourism in the postconflict, postviolence period. Although I had visited Mexico a number of times in the past, I made four research trips to Chiapas, in 2005, 2006–2007, 2008, and 2009, to consider the revival of tourism in the years following the 1994 Zapatista uprising.

My methods have been eclectic as I have tried to understand the changing currents of tourism in nations that are themselves undergoing substantial processes of change. In all four cases, I have observed tourism encounters at close range and interviewed diverse actors in those encounters, including tourism officials and operators and countless tourists, with whom I had conversations and gave out questionnaires. I have tracked mainstream tourism and given attention to solidarity tourism where it occurs, participating in tours catering to different interests. I have spent considerable time at heritage sites, museums, markets, national parks, and other tourism locations and visited libraries and documentation centers in tourism ministries, nongovernmental organizations, research institutes, and universities. I make use of travel writing, tourism literature and guides, advertising, Internet sites, and of course I benefit from and build on related research carried out by others. I consider ethnography to be at the heart of my work, but I call on other sources as "ethnographic partners" in this project.[10] My use of quantitative data on tourism may be scant by some standards, though I provide such material when it is useful to this work. I confess to having a preference for qualitative data, featuring narratives from my research, which will shed light on the questions addressed here.

My work responds to a critical need to develop sustained ethnographic and historical research on tourism in postconflict areas in a time of rapid globalization. Much is at stake, for if travelers' perceptions and practices serve to consolidate unequal power relations, then tourism has functioned like other global industries to widen the gap among nations. However, if travel enhances rather than diminishes opportunities for positive cultural exchange, then international tourism development and the tourism encounter may help lay the groundwork for a more just and democratic world.[11] In any event, it is certain that the new cultural and historical understandings that tourism promotes will be instrumental in shaping global encounters in the future.

Touring This Book

Here, I present tourism as a staging ground for national-heritage formation in societies undergoing abrupt political and economic transition. I suggest that actors are positioned based on differences of gender, race, and other vectors of power and argue that tourism encounters are both constituted by and constitutive of broader cultural histories. Furthermore, I set forth my argument that the nations under study have utilized tourism to continue processes that were begun as programs of social transformation. To be sure, market and other forces frequently compromise intentions and outcomes, and this work will consider the deep ambivalences that can accompany tourism development.

The chapters of this book are organized into three sections. In Part 1, I offer cases from nations that have advanced social revolutionary projects that galvanized populations over sustained periods of time, fully half a century in the case of Cuba and a decade in the case of Nicaragua. Chapter 1 shows that a successful amalgamation of seemingly contradictory tourist attractions in Cuba, from architectural history to revolutionary culture and politics, rests on ambivalent desires for times past, present, and future—expressed by both hosts and visitors. Chapter 2 argues that since the time of solidarity travel two decades ago, tourists coming to Nicaragua now find the country transformed as a safe and desirable travel destination, yet memories and desires for revolution appear to be making a notable comeback.

In Part 2, I present case studies from areas that offer significant contrasts given their recent histories of uprising and conflict. Chapter 3 traces the reversal of tourism's precipitous decline in Peru that began in the 1980s as a result of the conflict between Shining Path insurgents and the military. My findings show that cultural tourism draws tourists who often know little about the violence of the recent past and are seeking instead to engage with a "timeless" indigenous heritage. Chapter 4 discusses the gradual return of tourism to Chiapas, Mexico, since the Zapatista uprising in 1994. I suggest that the romantic appeal of an indigenous revolutionary movement along with enduring "traditional" culture helps to drive both solidarity and mainstream travel in the region.

Part 3 pairs the nations under study to offer a critical, comparative perspective that builds on the chapters in Parts 1 and 2. Chapter 5 shows that tourism in Cuba and Nicaragua has more often than not disadvantaged women and racial minorities. I argue that sex and romance tourism in these two transitional societies provides economic relief but that unequal power relations may be reinscribed in these intimate encounters. Chapter 6 examines areas that, although distinct, are both regions with large indigenous populations. In Andean Peru and Chiapas, Mexico, cultural tourism produces different yet substantially gendered and racialized exchanges. In these areas "native" women are turned into the repositories of national tradition, and their active participation in society may be overlooked. I examine the outcomes for women and men, both hosts and visitors, in the tourism encounter in the two regions.

In the Conclusion, I consider the broader implications of my study of postrevolutionary and postconflict tourism and the ways in which gender, cultural identity, and national heritage are being refashioned in these transitional societies. I discuss the analytical power of the lens of tourism in assessing the often contentious struggles among tourism industry elites, local tour operators, and tourists themselves over the terms of cultural and historical representation. I consider how recent developments in Cuba, Mexico, Nicaragua, and Peru support or challenge my argument that tourism has taken up where social transformation left off—and I ask how long the allure of these previously off-limits areas may last. Finally, I look toward the future as I consider how well tourism may serve, both as industry and as analytical lens, to shape and interpret the experience of these Latin American nations as they make their way through periods of dramatic change in a globalized world.

Postrevolutionary Tourism
in Cuba and Nicaragua

1 Che, Chevys, and Hemingway's Daiquiris

Cuban Tourism in Transition

IN HAVANA'S MUSEUM OF THE REVOLUTION, housed in a former presidential palace, a section is devoted to what the Cuban government termed the "special period in peacetime," a deeply difficult period of economic crisis after the fall of the Soviet Union.[1] A display case in this space quotes Fidel Castro in the early 1990s as he set forth three areas of development intended to resolve the nation's economic problems:

> [As] I have said on other occasions, our development efforts during the Special Period are based on three pillars: the food programme, which has to be among the first priorities, considering the difficulties that have to be overcome . . . the tourism programme, which is developing well . . . the biotechnology programme, which includes the pharmaceutical industry and high-tech medical equipment.[2]

Following this quotation are several images—cruise ship, hotel, and dancing girls—that appear to underscore the primary importance of the tourism component of Cuba's development plan. Indeed, in recent years tourism has become, along with nickel production, a leading industry in Cuba. Furthermore, Cuba has become a key competitor in Caribbean tourism, and despite a slight decline in 2006 and 2007, the number of foreign visitors to the island rose to 2.35 million in 2008.[3]

The return of tourism to this Caribbean island where it famously thrived as a tropical destination before the revolution has brought about a series of cataclysmic changes in Cuban society.[4] It has become de rigueur to describe the clash of socialist and market economies and desires on the island fostered by the growth of tourism and to ask whether tourism will bolster the enduring socialist economy or destabilize it and bring a full-fledged capitalist economy in its wake. Likewise, it is commonplace to ask if tourism can help build a democratic and open society or whether social conflict resulting from a two-tiered society divided into those with and without access to tourist dollars will carry the day.[5] I would suggest that we may view tourism as both "saving the revolution" from collapse and as a catalyst for further social and political change, as well as for engagement with the global market economy, in what one recent analysis refers to as Cuba's "hybrid transition" (Colantonio and Potter 2006:4–8).

Like others who have observed tourism's growth during the past two decades, I am struck by the ambivalence that Cubans reveal in response to the surge in the island's tourism, which has brought both economic recovery and social divisions precipitated by dollarization of the tourist economy (Espino 2000; Martin de Holan and Phillips 1997). At the same time, I have observed the fairly congenial way that diverse tourism niches have developed and offered relief to the suffering political economy. Thus, while my work agrees to some extent with that of analysts who emphasize the tensions and contradictions in Cuban tourism, I depart from them in some significant ways. I argue that just as socialist Cuba has moved toward a more mixed economy that allows for increased collaboration with capitalist nations while retaining centralized state control, the tourism sector has benefited from a similar development strategy. There is a decided advantage to state and society in allowing prerevolutionary capitalist attractions to coexist with socialist revolutionary ones, even as social and economic disparities become more apparent.[6]

My interest lies in examining how Cuba presents this diverse tourism package and turns ambivalent desires for both pre- and postrevolutionary times into a marketable commodity. Drawing on theoretical work coming out of anthropology and tourism studies, I call for attention to the tourism encounter between travelers seeking "exotic" new destinations and societies seeking to market their cultural and national heritage effectively to this clientele (see Bruner 2005; Hanna and Del Casino 2003; MacCannell 1999; Rojek and Urry 1997). I should be clear that the desires I refer to are expressed in different ways by Cubans on and off the island and by travelers making their way to Cuba— they manifest as desires for the familiar *or* unfamiliar landscape, people, music, food, and so on. Nostalgia for the way things were before as well as after the revolution (and even, perhaps, after an awaited "transition" in the future) has been a stock in trade in Cuba and represents the biggest calling card for tourism development. Even though nostalgia for the distant past would seem to be anathema to the revolutionary project, the government nonetheless participates in reimagining Cuba's history in such a way that the "bourgeois" prerevolutionary period may be viewed as the logical precursor to the triumph of the revolution.[7] Thus, there is less contradiction than first meets the eye in offering up historic Old Havana, Hemingway bars, Tropicana nightclub showgirls, and Buena Vista Social Club music along with revolutionary monuments for tourist consumption in present-day Cuba.[8]

During five research trips to Cuba between 1993 and 2009, I focused my attention on cultural politics and tourism as part of my broader comparative project in the Latin American region.[9] In my research in Nicaragua, I had observed the apparent erasure of the Sandinista revolution in that country and then the traces that still made an appearance on the developing tourism market. I was intrigued by what I describe in the next chapter as recycled notions of revolution in the midst of a commodified travel industry in the country. I judged that it would be instructive to examine similar questions in Cuba, where the revolution has held sway for half a century, albeit with substantial opening up of the market to local entrepreneurs and foreign investors. Staying in Old Havana or nearby Vedado, popular areas for tourists, I also traveled outside the capital to such tourist destinations as Varadero Beach, the model eco-community of Las Terrazas west of Havana, the Viñales valley in Pinar del Río, and the cities of Santa Clara and Trinidad. Twice I traveled with U.S. solidarity groups, and once I joined a Canadian group to "Discover Cuba."[10] I took city tours and day tours outside Havana to get a firsthand view of what guides emphasize and what tourists take away with them. When possible, I gave questionnaires to tourists to fill out on the spot with information on their expectations, experiences, and reasons for travel to Cuba. In addition, I interviewed tour operators in their off-hours and occasionally recorded them during tours.

Beginning with a consideration of diverse forms of tourism and their success in today's Cuba, I show that there are nonetheless social costs that are experienced differentially among the population. I go on to argue that the paradoxes and pleasures of prerevolutionary capitalist-identified tourism in one of the last bastions of socialism are precisely what make Cuba a desired travel destination. With Havana as my principal site for ethnographic research, I describe the packaged "City Tour" as a microcosm of how the capital presents itself to visitors: as an amalgam of colonial architecture and traditional life; prerevolutionary

Che T-shirts for sale in a Havana market

extravagance and nightlife; and socialist modernity and revolutionary culture. In the concluding section of the chapter, I show how these elements come together to offer up a city and nation that is ready for foreign consumption. As José Quiroga so aptly describes, the "ideological memory project [of producing a past based on] what needed to be saved from the period before the revolution" is then put up for sale on the global capitalist market (2005:103).

Tourism in a Mixed Economy

The Cuban government's call for a Special Period in late 1990 was a way of introducing a series of austerity measures and other initiatives to overcome the country's deepening economic crisis. In one assessment of this emergency period following the dismantling of the Soviet Union and its trade with Cuba, sociologist Susan Eckstein (2003) showed that Fidel Castro looked not only to socialist strategies but also to capitalist and indeed precapitalist ones in order to rescue the economy. For example, to maintain the food program, the government allowed socialist principles of collectivist development to remain in place but also permitted *agromercados* (free markets) and encouraged urban subsistence gardens as a sort of precapitalist alternative for surviving the economic crisis. As necessity became a virtue, saving energy and foraging for needed resources became desirable. Cuban lives were dramatically affected as the nation experienced gasoline and cooking oil shortages and tried to become self-sufficient in food production. The socialist program of agricultural diversification and reduced energy consumption was coupled with a precapitalist reliance on bicycles and horse-drawn carriages for transport as well as production of homemade soaps, herbal medicines, and other goods to meet household needs.[11] At the same time, ironically, new capitalist relations of globalization were introduced to rescue the revolution, as Castro courted foreign investment and encouraged the development of internationally competitive manufacturing and marketing.[12]

Just as Eckstein has noted the multiple strategies of the Cuban state and society for confronting the Cuban economic crisis, I have found such diverse approaches in the area of tourism development. Visitors often note the contradictions of tourism on the island: on the one hand, offering the pleasures of high-end beach resorts and nightlife, luxury hotels in the capital city, and rich architectural history; and on the other hand, promising to show travelers a model of long-lasting revolutionary politics and culture. The nostalgia we find for both the idealized revolutionary past (before the Special Period) and the hedonistic capitalist prerevolutionary past in Cuba is evident on the tourist circuit. The peculiar amalgamation of tourist attractions is precisely what accounts for Cuba's global appeal and its economic advantage. Travelers who pay homage to Che Guevara at the Museum of the Revolution later flock to the famed "Hemingway bars" in Old Havana, the Floridita and the Bodeguita del Medio, followed by an evening out at the Tropicana nightclub to watch racy and extravagant shows.[13]

As tourism has been reestablished as a mainstay of the economy and a key component of the strategy to make gains in the global market, it has also become a window on the many ironies and contradictions in Cuba. Thus, we are struck by the inconsistencies with socialist goals, such as the evident sex tourism and the socioeconomic inequalities in the form of tourism "apartheid," whereby Cubans lack access to tourist venues and revenues unless they work and receive tips in the industry.[14] It is true that with the transition of leadership from Fidel Castro to his brother Raúl there has been an official easing of restrictions on places Cubans can patronize, yet the majority of Cubans still do not have the resources to visit tourist hotels and restaurants. Although the government has sought to showcase its enduring nationalist ideology to visitors, sharp distinctions remain within the Cuban population.

While analysts generally agree upon Cuba's accomplishments in education, health care, social welfare, sports, and the arts, they also point to the differential consequences of the Special Period for Cuban citizens depending on their gender, race, and socioeconomic level, as well as their location, whether in Havana or the rest of the island (Holgado Fernández 2000; Safa 1995:166). The Cuban government has suggested that tourism development per se has not entailed a compromise of revolutionary principles and that any problems that have arisen are due to "antisocial" elements in the society. That is, hustlers and sex workers, jineteros, are said to be seeking personal gains at the expense of the revolution rather than responding to a difficult economic climate (Berg 2004b). Like other scholars, I am intrigued by the various aspects of tourism that seem to both undermine and support this socialist nation. However, in my view the resulting tensions are part of the powerful attraction of tourism to what one visitor described to me as "the last Marxist resort."[15]

Tourism's Return in a Transnational Era

Tourism in Cuba has a long history from the late nineteenth century and extending through its mid-twentieth-century heyday, when the United States supplied the majority of visitors to the country. During that time, Havana was called the "Paris of the Antilles" and drew pleasure seekers to the glamorous, tropical destination known for its abundant nightlife. The city became the playground of U.S. mobsters, media celebrities, and the middle class (Pérez 1999; Schwartz 1997). The American influence through tourism allowed for peaceful political and economic control. However, with the revolution in 1959 and the U.S. embargo on trade and travel to Cuba in 1962, the Cuban government halted tourism development as a vestige of the bourgeois past. Hotels were nationalized, clubs were closed, and prostitutes were "reeducated" to become seamstresses and other morally correct citizen-workers of the new society. Ordinary Cubans were offered the chance to enjoy the pleasures of the island that were formerly the exclusive province of the elite and foreign visitors (Cabezas 2009).

In the period following the revolution, travelers to the country were most often activists like those in the Venceremos Brigades coming to cut sugarcane in solidarity with the young revolution. In 1977, the Antonio Maceo Brigades opened up the possibility for Cuban exiles living in the United States to travel to Cuba, which they began to do in large numbers in 1978.[16] However, it took the Special Period to bring mainstream tourism back, and its level has surpassed that of the earlier heyday. When I made my first trip to Cuba in 1993, the country was experiencing the severe effects of economic crisis, with residents eating meager meals and sometimes malnourished, facing power outages, and walking or riding bikes to work. I heard many stories of women bearing the burden of feeding families, finding alternatives to such everyday needs as soap and shampoo (often mentioning the use of leaves and other natural materials), and using their ingenuity to acquire scarce goods on the market. Tourists were treated to the best of what the island had to offer, including luxury accommodations and lavish culinary displays, but Cubans were unable to partake in the pleasures of the new tourist economy.

While much scholarly research has been directed to official Cuban policies and formal structures set in place to bolster the state-led economy, less has been directed to the multitude of informal ways in which ordinary Cubans managed to cope with hardships of that time. The period was characterized by what Damián Fernández (2000) so aptly terms Cubans' "passionate politics"—both supportive and critical of government handling of the crisis—and by the intimate and affectionate forms of help that Cubans offered to one another when the state failed to provide its customary (if limited) assistance. Women along with men carried out what was necessary to get by despite crushing conditions, enabling the Cuban state to survive the enormous blow that had struck its foundation.

As the economy began its recovery and cultivated foreign investment, new hotels were built and old ones were renovated. Old Havana received a makeover so that the historic colonial district—designated a UNESCO World Heritage Site in 1982—would attract more international visitors.[17] By the mid-1990s, restoration was well under way, particularly in the principal plazas and those streets surrounding them. After forced relocation of some of the local population, the historic area became increasingly a space for international visitors to pass through, enjoy hotels and restaurants, and occasionally make their home. One compelling view is that in restoring the colonial heritage of Old Havana, Cuba has been able to present to its visitors a very selective past that includes previous centuries of settlement and mid-twentieth-century haunts of a celebrated American writer and, in so doing, largely overlooks the later revolution; thus, a new narrative of Cubanness is constructed, largely excluding nonwhite Cubans and ignoring the second half of the twentieth century (Berg 2005). Although this narrower account is part of the larger story made available to tourists, it is also important to consider the degree to which the efforts to restore this leading travel destination were what allowed the socialist government to persevere, with all its flaws. As Matthew Hill (2007:71) describes, reclaiming the

distinctive colonial past meant continuing erasures of other pasts, yet success-
fully "further[ed] the socialist project in a post-socialist world."

Since the United States imposed its long-lasting embargo on trade and travel
to Cuba, the majority of tourists have come from Canada, Europe, and Latin
America, but Cuban officials predict that when the embargo ends, the floodgates will open and U.S. tourism to the island will soar. Although Cuba's near
neighbor contributes little to its tourism,[18] the Caribbean nation nonetheless
has captured a large global market. The economy's diversification is reflected in
tourism, which targets a number of specialized niches: for example, sun, sand,
and sea tourism and eco-, educational, heritage, cultural, and health tourism.
Until the U.S. government canceled people-to-people exchanges at the end of
2003, groups like Global Exchange based in San Francisco gave those who were
sympathetic with the Cuban revolutionary project the opportunity to travel
through educational and cultural tours.[19] Still, many other international travelers are attracted to see one of the "last bastions of communism"—if only because
its ideological stance has protected the island against overdevelopment—even
as they enjoy beaches, nightclubs, and the music scene.

Tourism's return to Cuba must be seen against the backdrop of transnational
flows of people and their evident desires, both to and from the island, resulting in global travel and consumption practices. Although Cuba is often viewed
from the United States as an isolate, a place cut off from the rest of the world,
it is far from remote and hardly out of touch with political and cultural currents beyond its shores. Contributors to Fernández's (2005) *Cuba Transnational*
examined the migration flow of Cubans from the island and the sizable Cuban
population living in the United States and elsewhere; they bring attention to
the significant ties maintained between diasporic Cubans and family back
home (through visits, remittances, and phone calls), creating a two-way stream
of travel that connects Cuba to other nations. Duany (2005:3) shows that Cuba
shares with other Caribbean nations an active migration process and an emergent transnational identity associated with being Cuban, or *cubanidad*. And
Lima (2005:85) finds that "yearning" characterizes Cubans both on and outside
the island, who may yearn to leave or yearn to return: Miami's so-called Yucas
(young, urban Cuban Americans) born in the United States "traffic in their
parents' nostalgia and the memory of loss with Cohiba Cigar T-shirts; food and
dance music inflected with the memory of displacement; and plastic busts of
San Lázaro . . . all safely marketed and consumed in the cultural spaces of Metro
Dade and SoBe [South Beach]" (2006:86).[20]

Prospective tourists may express yearning for the Other, nostalgia for a place they have heard much about but have yet to discover. The hipness of cubanidad in South Florida joins with a wider appreciation of things Cuban—what anthropologist Ruth Behar (2002) has called the "Buena Vista Socialization" of Cuba, referring to the global impact of the 1999 documentary tribute by Wim Wenders to the lives and music of a group of musicians in Havana. Others are drawn to the edgy quality of more contemporary music popular among youth in Cuba and the diaspora, music that is played in Havana's dance clubs, attracting tourism and sexual license—the music's suggestive lyrics produce disapproval and even scandal in Cuba (Perna 2005). Whereas some older travelers are more apt to be attracted by a desire to see the "authentic" Cuba or to express solidarity with the revolution, younger generations are often drawn by the perceived romance, adventure, and cultural expression found there.[21]

Tourism's Ambivalent Mix

In the Hotel Habana Libre, built just a year before the revolutionary victory as the Havana Hilton, desks in the lobby are staffed to sell tour packages.[22] Employees of the state-run tourism companies Havanatur, Cubatur, and Gaviota offer tours to the same destinations, with nearly identical itineraries and rates.[23] Thus, a day at Varadero Beach will cost approximately fifty dollars for transportation and use of facilities at an all-inclusive resort, and a three-hour bus tour of Havana will cost a more modest fifteen dollars.[24] I found no single tour that specifically highlighted revolutionary monuments and history, but these locales are incorporated in the popular city tour—and one state tourism office, Amistur, located in the Instituto de Amistad con los Pueblos, organizes international solidarity group travel to various sites of historical importance to the Cuban revolution.

In numerous conversations with tour operators and those connected to the industry, few mentioned the appeal of the Cuban revolution when I asked what sort of tourism they are promoting. Perhaps the reason is that Cuba seeks to compete with other Caribbean nations for tourists with more mainstream interests or that most tourism is synonymous with leisure activity. Yet a frequently visited site in Havana is the three-story palace that is now the Museum of the Revolution, and outside it the glass-encased *Granma*, the vessel made famous when Fidel Castro and Che Guevara, along with other rebels, sailed from Mexico to Cuba in 1956. Another major monument to the revolution is the vast paved space of Revolution Square with its museum honoring José Martí and with Che's portrait in bold neon silhouette. Tour buses line up so that visitors may pay homage to or at least marvel at this leading attraction, as they stop briefly to take pictures.

As we turn to consider some ambivalent aspects of tourism in Cuba that mirror the nation's rather hybrid dependence on precapitalist, capitalist, and socialist economic forms, it is clear that tourism at once highlights the vibrant natural environment, recognizes colonial history and architecture, memorializes prerevolutionary extravagance, and honors the revolution. Tourists become entranced by enduring and now exoticized cultural forms like the Afro-Cuban religious practice of Santería,[25] as well as contemporary forms such as Cuban hip-hop, cinema, and conceptual art.[26] Often, these cultural forms and tourist attractions are closely intertwined, although they may appear to be in conflict with one another. Any Cuban travel guide will direct visitors to historic Old Havana, with its museum-like quality since restoration began in a serious way a decade ago, and many will direct travelers to the monuments of the revolution that are found in abundance in the capital city and elsewhere.

A starting point for many is the Museum of the Revolution, whose extensive, triumphalist displays trace the early history of Cuba and the war of independence through the Batista dictatorship, the post-1959 revolution, the building of socialism, and finally, the Special Period. The celebration of things Cuban continues in the museum shop, where one finds T-shirts featuring Che's ubiquitous portrait and other revolutionary themes, as well as images of Havana Club rum and classic American cars. Some travelers make their way to the Comandancia Che Guevara, a small museum located at the historic Fortaleza de San Carlos de la Cabaña; the Literacy Museum, which features the gains made by literacy brigades during the revolutionary era; or the José Martí monument and museum in Revolution Square. Those venturing into the provinces may travel to see the José Martí monument in Cienfuegos or Che's mausoleum in Santa Clara, where they can also visit the site where the rebels derailed Batista's train in 1958.

Even while seeking out such colonial and revolutionary heritage sites, one continually comes across another current strain of Cuban tourism, that of the alluring prerevolutionary period, with its celebration of another sort—favoring old American cars, Hemingway haunts, music now associated with the Buena Vista Social Club, and Havana's sexually edgy nightclubs and street scene. The American cars are everywhere, many serving as ramshackle taxis for Cubans paying in pesos, while tourists generally take the newer taxis built in the Soviet Bloc, paying higher prices in dollars (now convertible pesos).[27] For still higher fares, tourists may ride in one of the rare old American cars that have been kept in mint condition; a state-owned company, Gran Car, offers vintage rentals accompanied by well-attired drivers. The most popular souvenir selected by tourists in craft markets and shops may be the ubiquitous painting of a looming American car parked outside the Bodeguita del Medio, one of the famed Hemingway bars.

The Bodeguita is one of a number of places now celebrated in Havana for having housed or been frequented by the renowned American writer, who made his home in Cuba for almost twenty years. Tourists rush to the Bodeguita, where he enjoyed mojitos, as well as to another bar, the Floridita, where he drank daiquiris. The latter boasts a life-size figure of Hemingway seated at the bar, a perfect photo opportunity for patrons, and his commodified image is available in a number of items for sale. The room where he lived and wrote in the Hotel Ambos Mundos has been kept as he left it, with typewriter and manuscript pages, and can be visited for a modest fee. His country home, Finca Vigia, is now a museum site, and those who are curious, accompanied by a tour guide, can peer through its windows for the price of a ticket. Tourists make pilgrimages to the fishing village Cojímar, the setting for *The Old Man and the*

Bodeguita del Medio, a Hemingway haunt in Old Havana that is popular among tourists (photo of Ernest Hemingway and Fidel Castro above the bar)

Sea, and to the local restaurant he frequented, which now attracts tour buses. Although the majority who visit these sites are tourists, Cubans themselves still share fond memories of the writer they admired, and as Schwartz (1997:208) writes, "Hemingway's and Cuba's years-long mutual affection anchors part of Castro's tourist effort."[28] All these sites honoring Hemingway in Cuba can serve to validate prerevolutionary life *and* the "normality" of the revolution.[29]

To these iconic (and American) prerevolutionary tourist attractions we must include the return of the sexualized culture of the 1950s, a time remembered for its great licentiousness and excess. The Tropicana nightclub has been in operation since 1939 and offers to patrons with about a hundred dollars to spend an extravagant evening of showgirls (generally darker-skinned and fine-featured *mulatas*, women of mixed race) in lavish costumes on an outdoor stage. For others there are less expensive venues, or if desired, purchase of direct sexual services. Sex and romance tourism, discussed in Chapter 5, forms a continuum from prostitution to intimate relationships that range from the one-night stand to the duration of a vacation or longer. For the Cubans involved, the hope is to receive gifts and cash remittances into the future, or even marriage and a ticket to leave Cuba. The Cuban government has made weak attempts to curtail *jineterismo* (hustling), as it signals the failings of the socialist nation. Yet it is thriving in the streets and clubs of Havana, particularly in parts of Old Havana, Vedado, and Miramar (an upscale area of the city with large hotels and convention centers). Later, I will consider how this form of tourism in Cuba (and to a lesser extent in Nicaragua), like other forms, plays on nostalgia as well as desires for intimate contact with and consumption of the exotic.[30]

Un mal necesario

The ambivalent aspects of Cuban tourism that I have described here, most notably revolutionary heritage tourism on the one side and tourism that is nostalgic for prerevolutionary extravagance verging on decadence on the other, mirror the two faces of Havana as Antillean metropolis (Scarpaci et al. 2002; Sanchez and Adams 2008). These two faces of tourism are not always separable, however, and I would suggest that they are really two versions of the same nostalgia. As noted earlier, many tourists pass unselfconsciously from the world of revolutionary monuments honoring Che or Martí to the world of the Tropicana nightclub, all in the course of a day discovering Havana. The improbable interlinkage of yearnings for both socialist and capitalist (prerevolutionary) Cuba has been manifest for some time on the island.

Historically, the same revolutionaries who toppled the U.S.-supported Batista regime also adored their American cars: Che his Chevy and Fidel his Oldsmobile. The author of a "car-centered history of life on the island," Richard Schweid, comments that "numerous North American heroes of the Cuban Revolution . . . remain unsung, and they *do* have brand names—names like Chevrolet, Ford, Studebaker, Chrysler, Rambler, Cadillac, Plymouth, Dodge, and Buick" (2004:5). He remembers his disconcerted reaction upon seeing the National Capitol in Havana, which was built in 1929 as a replica of the U.S. Capitol, with long lines of pre-1959 American cars parked outside. Indeed, he writes, "A photo of a 1957 Chevrolet Bel Air in front of an arched colonnade means Havana and Cuba all over the world, much as does Che's image on scores of products from T-shirts to postcards. Detroit's cars have been absorbed into the extensive iconography of Cuban history" (6).

Visitors to Cuba's internationally acclaimed Varadero Beach may find it surprising that their tropical paradise, a couple of hours out of Havana and seemingly on another planet, flaunts billboards in praise of the revolution.[31] In a country where advertising is prohibited, bold signage proclaiming "Varadero: Revolución es para construir" (Varadero: Revolution is for building) or Che's image with the well-known slogan "Hasta la victoria siempre" (Toward victory always) may appear rather quaint to those Canadian and European tourists who come directly to all-inclusive resorts and see little more of Cuba. Attending a baseball game in Havana, I noted the neon sign above the stands exhorting all Cubans to become involved in sport: "El deporte es para todos" (Sport is for everyone), it proclaimed. Thus, Cuba's love affair with American cars, beaches, and baseball presents opportunities for prominent displays of socialist propaganda, taken for granted by Cubans but, for at least some visitors, adding to the cachet of tourism in a "communist land."[32] Some visitors worry, however, that tourism may destroy this aspect of Cuba; as one British visitor noted to me, "I understand the ethic but can't help but feel that tourism will upset the balance of a communist state."

Many Cubans would agree with Fidel Castro's pronouncement that allowances to a globalizing capitalist market economy—tourism, private enterprise, and creeping inequalities—are a *mal necesario* (necessary evil). Since the Special Period, Cubans have been ingenious as they discover ways of getting by, gaining access to tourist dollars through the legal practice of renting rooms to tourists and setting up *paladares* (small private restaurants) or trading on the black market. Indeed, two expressions that one hears frequently are "inventar" (the act of inventing, or coping) and "no es fácil" (it's not easy) (Barbassa 2005). A researcher I spoke with at the University of Havana echoed the point when she called tourism "un mal necesario"—needed for the economic relief it offers the nation but bringing with it a host of undesirable effects from jineterismo and especially sex tourism, to cultural commodification more generally, as the tourist industry drives development across the island. Yet, ironically, as I argue here, it is just this mix of revolutionary and capitalist culture—accompanied of course by lovely beaches, splendid cities, and rich history—that lures increasing numbers of tourists to its shores. To illustrate the seduction of Cuban tourism as it responds to both sorts of yearnings, I turn now to a description of an afternoon tour I took with a group of tourists in Havana.

The City Tour

In December 2003, I planned to take a city tour of Havana to see how the guide's scripted narration and the places visited would portray life in the Cuban capital. When I was beckoned one afternoon in the Hotel Habana Libre by a Cubatur guide rounding up tourists for a three-hour tour by minivan, I seized the opportunity. If tourism is a performance of cultural authenticity (MacCannell 1999), then I reasoned that this tour could shed light on the way that Cuba is performing "the island nation" and its capital for the benefit of foreign visitors. More broadly, it could offer a view of how Cuba is refashioning itself for tourism development—and, as a consequence, for its own citizens.[33] All that was on my mind as I settled comfortably into the van with about fifteen fellow travelers from Belgium, Malta, and Mexico (no others were from the United States). The guide told us that he would use English and Spanish, although English was the common currency of the group and was the language he continued to speak. He promised to take us to Revolution Square, the Capitol building, and "Colonial Town" (i.e., Old Havana). Since it was raining, we actually covered much more of the city, infrequently leaving the van, while he kept up a steady monologue.

As we departed from the Habana Libre, our guide, whom I'll call Francisco, noted the symbolic as well as political importance when the revolutionary government nationalized the Havana Hilton and gave it a new name, meaning Free (or Liberated) Havana. Driving down well-known La Rampa, a busy street frequented by many tourists, he told us we would first see the more modern Havana. On our way along the Malecón, the city's emblematic seaside drive, he pointed out the Hotel Nacional and the U.S. Interests Section as two more emblems—the stately Cuban landmark and the hostile North American presence. Cracking jokes in the manner typical of tour guides everywhere, he teased about letting us out of the van to get wet in the waves that were slapping the Malecón. Later in the tour, the jokes would become more politically risky, though they may have been carefully scripted.[34]

We drove to the exclusive district of Miramar, the more recently built suburban area known for its many embassies, large hotels, and aspirations to become Cuba's equivalent of the Riviera. We were given the "inside story" on a hotel built by drug money and told that the broad and opulent Fifth Avenue in this part of the city was built by an elite who wanted an area like the street of the same name in New York City. Francisco pointed out a number of embassies and joked that he was a neighbor of the Belgian ambassador. He playfully alluded to social class differences, keeping us guessing about his own. This subtext of references to inequality and social difference, without giving the issues too much importance, was present through much of the tour. There was an unspoken acknowledgment of visitors' curiosity about how far Cuba had held to socialist principles and how far it had allowed inequalities to develop in recent years.

Passing La Concha Beach Club, the Havana Yacht Club, and Marina Hemingway along with the tourist complex named Papa's (after the Lost Generation writer), Francisco related that there are separate marinas for Cubans and foreigners (an allusion to tourism "apartheid") and added that in any case they were about the same. He called our attention as we passed the Chan Chan Nightclub, boasting the "rhythm of Compay Segundo," assuming universal knowledge of the Buena Vista Social Club. We noticed a school for learning Marxist-Leninist theory, and Francisco quipped that they practice this theory at the marina. Telling us that Fidel was a personal friend of his and that they visit one another all the time, he said with a wink that tourists were not invited. His playful ambivalence about the presence of tourists in Cuba may have mirrored the government's deeper ambivalence, despite its heavy reliance on tourism.

Francisco talked about the old American cars used as taxis in Havana. Then he smiled as he said that "poor" people in this part of Havana can't take the common bus and must drive Mercedes. As for us, he said, we would all be required to take one of the *camellos* ("camel" buses), truck-pulled train cars so-named for their distinctive shape and the workhorses on Havana's streets. Although he did not wish to be called a "dictator," he wanted each of us to choose to ride a pink, blue, or red one—adding that red ones were for communists. "Who wants to ride a red one?" he asked coyly, and a man in the front of the van said quickly that he did not care to do so. I was struck both by the class-conscious remarks of our Cuban guide and by the tourists' subtle tone of nervous disapproval of Cuba—or at least a performance of disapproval—even as they eagerly consumed what its famous capital city had to offer. Here, it appeared that socialism offered a backdrop and local color to be contemplated for its aesthetics, from a safe distance.

When we passed a row of distinctly impoverished shacks, Francisco informed us that these were the homes of "other ambassadors." Was he reflecting a socialist principle of egalitarian self-worth, calling attention to the presence of poverty despite official reports of its absence, or mocking the residents? Or perhaps smoothing over the evident disparities in wealth? From there, we drove to Revolution Square and got out to admire and take photos of the tall obelisk of Cuban marble, the Martí statue and tribunal where (until recently) Fidel Castro made his speeches, the Communist Party headquarters, and the likeness of Che. Our guide joked again that as he approached the age of eighty, "Fidel" was not receiving tourists. He pointed to two buildings on the plaza, a somewhat smaller one that houses the national library and a larger one housing the defense department, smiling as he said that he would switch the two when he is elected president. His intimate tone, allowing us to share in his affectionate, if occasionally cynical, view of the city, had the effect of drawing in our group and conveying a sense that we were getting an inside story.

In Central Havana, we stopped at the Capitol building, which now houses museums and an Internet café, and some of us got out to take pictures of the historic site. We found photographers with apparently ancient cameras on tripods ready to snap pictures of tourists on the Capitol steps; the poor-quality instant photos they take evoke the nostalgic illusion of a time gone by.[35] We were approached by an aggressive cluster of men selling Che coins and the official newspaper *Granma*, as well as by vendors of popular hand-wrapped paper cones of peanuts. Then on we went, looking out from the van on Central Park, the Floridita bar and restaurant, the old Bacardí building, the Museum of Fine Arts, and the Museum of the Revolution, as well as remnants of the old city wall.

We drove to Havana's Bay and Old Havana, leaving the minivan to walk around the Plaza de Armas. Francisco provided a short history of the city, founded in 1519, and its oldest fortress, which carries the symbol (La Giraldilla) now found on the label of Havana Club rum. This provided a useful segue as we were ushered into the Café de Cuba, an espresso café and shop selling Cuban rum, cigars, and coffee. He introduced us to the classes of cigars, noting that Arnold Schwarzenegger, like Fidel, bought the best ones, Cohibas—clearly, men of good taste, whether capitalists or socialists, could agree on quality Cuban cigars. We were assured that the prices were the same throughout the island and then left to consider making purchases. While a couple of us ordered espresso and others waited around, Francisco admonished us for being poor consumers. He seemed motivated to encourage sales, whether or not he benefited directly from what was sold in the shop. By this time, it was clear even to those less familiar with the seduction of the tourist dollar that shopping and leaving tips for the guide were expected, if not required.

As we walked through the most historic parts of the city, Francisco asked us to admire the Plaza de la Catedral as well as the newly refurbished hotels, restaurants, and Hemingway sites, including the bars and the Hotel Ambos Mundos, where I happened to be staying. What we did not hear about was what urban geographer Joseph Scarpaci describes as the removal of many local residents to marginal areas of the city in order to turn Old Havana into a space for an uncluttered tourist gaze. Ironically, this runs counter to the government's stated policy of favoring the grassroots over urban elite culture. In pursuing its heritage tourism objectives, "socialist planning in the old city has gone from an anti-urban bias, rejecting a capitalist past, to one seemingly unable to commodify the colonial city quickly enough. In so doing, it runs the risk of becoming another Caribbean port" (Scarpaci 2005:205).

As the rest of the group headed over to complete the tour at the Palacio de Artesanía, another shopping venue, I offered my tip and said my good-byes. Thus ended, for me, an excursion into today's Havana as packaged for tourism: a gateway to Cuba, constructed as an "authentic," safe, and vibrant place that is at once proud of its history and culture and good-humored about its apparent social contradictions. Tensions are minimized to set travelers at ease and to encourage them to spend their dollars or, now, convertible pesos, on the pleasures of the island. The ambivalence about the present is evident, but any cynicism stays within bounds—"communism" is thus made safe for touristic consumption by means of a calculated strategy for enhancing economic development and refashioning the capital city and nation.

Tourism and Nostalgia

In one of the few Cuban works to offer a critical appraisal of outsiders' views of the island, Alfredo Prieto (2004:7) reflects on a widely circulated U.S.-produced poster from the 1940s promoting tourism to Cuba, now recycled as kitsch:[36] a smiling mulata with stereotypical hat and maracas is seen leaping in the air as she energetically dances the rumba. Beneath the image the text reads, "Visit Cuba. So Near and Yet So Foreign, 90 Minutes from Key West."[37] The nostalgia that makes this image popular today is a significant force driving contemporary tourism. Prieto points to a number of other iconic symbols of Cuba that I have discussed in this chapter: antique American cars, streets of Old Havana, Hemingway bars, and so on.

The Cuban revolution introduced new enticements to some to visit the island, drawing volunteer work brigades and solidarity travel that would promote and advance the process of social transformation. In contrast, the Special Period brought back mainstream tourism alongside the more politicized tourism of intervening years, but still with the objective of supporting the revolutionary project.[38] Whether tourists wish to spend time relaxing at the beach, hanging out at local jazz clubs, learning to dance the rumba, or exploring monuments to the revolution in the historic cities, they are attracted to Cuba precisely because it is not Miami Beach, because it holds the cachet of offering tourist comforts without the onslaught of McDonald's golden arches and crowded beachfront properties.[39] An episode of the popular HBO series *Sex and the City* illustrates this point well: at a party, the character Charlotte is approached by a man who flirts with her, saying, "You've got to go to Cuba now; another year and it will be too late." He assures her that it is possible to get there via Canada and offers to show her his travel photos. Cuba is quite clearly seductive, even when used as a conversational gambit on the dating scene.

Whether Cuba is resistant to or eager for change, the trope of the nation's waiting for change (however uncertain) is a singular one expressed on both U.S. and Cuban shores. The grand-prize winner in the 2003 Cuban Film Festival was Cuba's *Suite Habana* (Pérez 2003), a melancholy and affectionate look at the everyday lives of ten city dwellers. The languid pace and sad overtones in the film convey without dialogue a sense of dreams deferred. A couple of years later, the *New York Times* Travel section ran a feature article entitled "Waiting for Havana," presumably referring to a desired opening up of U.S. travel to Cuba and to Castro's passing (Lopez Torregrosa 2005). While cautioning readers that few U.S. citizens can travel legally at present to Cuba, the author offers suggestions to the "intrepid" traveler and predicts, based on widespread views in Cuba and the United States, that when the travel embargo is lifted, the sleeping giant will reawaken and mass tourism will hit the island. He writes that "plenty of hoteliers, resort companies and cruise lines are already planning for the day when this off-limits country once again becomes a Caribbean playground for United States citizens" (1). Many travelers, including a good number from the United States, see little reason to wait and every reason to go to Cuba before any post-Castro transition, as expressed in the TV flirtation ploy noted previously.

In 2005, travelers from many countries, including the United States, repeatedly told me that they had wished to visit Cuba "before the embargo is lifted" or "before Fidel dies." These individuals were certain that a transition was near and that, like it or not, the Cuba of today would soon be a fond memory (the change of leadership to Raúl Castro that took place not long after my visit is discussed in the Conclusion). An older Puerto Rican woman told me she had always wanted to visit Cuba, and on reaching the island it was perhaps already a memory; she wrote in a questionnaire, "My expectations were met and it was with great awe that I saw the exuberance of an era long gone." A young Canadian woman wrote, "I really didn't expect much, but to have a feeling of going back in time. With the people, the cars, the architecture, the music, etc., time did go back."

Younger travelers did not share the long view of the revolutionary past recalled by their parents' generation, much less their grandparents' prerevolutionary memories, yet they too described Cuba as a romantic and distinctly different destination. In filling out my questionnaire, a sixteen-year-old from the United States who was traveling with a choir emphasized the contrasts in Cuba; she noted that what surprised her most was "the mix between old and new. To, for one moment, be in what seems like the heart of a ghetto, and then be surrounded by a building built last year, or some beautiful park. It's very Twilight-Zone-esque." A twenty-year-old woman from the U.K. wrote in a questionnaire, "I have always wanted to visit Cuba. It has been one of my top ten destinations of the world to visit because of its amazing culture, history, and of course, romantic ambiance." Among younger visitors, it may have been the not-at-all-memorable *Dirty Dancing: Havana Nights* (actually filmed in San Juan, Puerto Rico) or the acclaimed *Motorcycle Diaries* (relating to Che's early experiences in South America) that has made Cuba a desired place to travel. Across the generations in the United States, travelers are often tempted by the "forbidden" nature of tourism in Cuba. Whether they come legally or not, many might agree with one young man who told me he wanted to come "because the government says I can't."

The nostalgia and ambivalent desire that characterize Cubans on the island and in the United States, and that draw tourism to Cuba as a place where there

A vintage American car for hire outside the Hotel
Nacional in Havana

is "a feeling of going back in time," may help stabilize the nation's political economy. Besides tourism's success as a leading industry on the island, its distinct
allure lends legitimacy to apparently contradictory tendencies toward both enduring socialism and an advancing market economy. On the other hand, the
tendency for tourism to introduce more social differences, to the point that
Cubans complain of apartheid-like practices, can serve to undermine the revolution's claims to promoting social equality. Here I have argued that the irony
is that, for better or worse, the Cuban approach to tourism development with
all of its improbable features seems to be working. Providing vital support for a
struggling economy and raising its international profile, Cuba's encounter with
tourism has to a considerable degree enabled the nation to continue the process
that began with the revolution.

At the historic Hotel Sevilla in Central Havana, tourists can pay $3.50 in convertible pesos for a quick class to learn the secret of preparing mojitos. The sign announcing this opportunity reads "Es vivir una fantasía" (It's to live a fantasy). This repeats the offer made to those hiring a classic American car and Cuban driver that they can "Rentar una fantasía" (Rent a fantasy). Not coincidentally, we find a life-size sculpture of John Lennon seated on a park bench in Havana and his image appearing side by side with Che's on the tourist art market, idolizing the two as realists and dreamers. This broad appeal of experiencing and consuming a dream—whether that dream is of the early, idealistic years of the revolution or the more distant past of life writ large in a tropical paradise—sustains tourism in Cuba. When I met an older man from Spain wearing a Che T-shirt in my hotel, he told me simply, "I'm in love with the Cuban revolution." As the country sets another goal of welcoming a record number of tourists, many will be seeking their nostalgic dream of Cuba. Still others, like a young Cuban American boy I overheard on my charter flight back from Havana to Miami, will be glad to return home to the pleasure of Kentucky Fried Chicken, which has yet to make its way to Cuba's shores.

2 Recycled *Sandalistas*

From Revolution to Resorts in the New Nicaragua

And why must we develop tourism in this God-forsaken country?
Because It's the path to salvation for the national economy.
                                        —Comandante Tomás Borge[1]

SEVERAL YEARS AGO, I came across an advertisement in the *New York Times* for sandals from the Madison Avenue store Barneys with a single word that caught my eye: *Sandalista* (2002:7). It was not only the word but also the bold font used that clearly invested the word with political meaning. Surely, I thought, there are few readers of the *Times* who will realize that this was a term used in Nicaragua during the 1980s to refer to international supporters of the revolutionary *Sandinista* government then in power. Certainly, most of those attracted to the photograph of a single shoe, a sort of upscale version of the rubber tire–soled sandals worn by the rural poor in Latin America, here selling for $165, would make no such connection. But when I was in Nicaragua over the summer and showed the ad to several U.S. citizens living in the Central American country, they reacted as I had. Seeing the ad took their breath away.

I found another invocation of the word *sandalista* around that time in an issue of *Condé Nast Traveler* (Wilson 2002:98–112), the glossy travel magazine, which featured a lengthy article on travel in the "new" Nicaragua. There, however, the term had acquired a new meaning. The author gushed, "Here come the foreigners: 'sandalistas' with backpacks, businessmen in short-sleeved shirts trying to look tropical casual, church missionaries sweating under straw hats, and me" (100). He went on to confess that although he was a journalist, on that day he was doing what many other U.S. tourists have been doing in Nicaragua: "scouting property" (100). In fact, many of the 360 small islands in Lake Nicaragua are up for sale and are being purchased "for a song" by U.S. residents looking for a bargain. Although the article describes Nicaragua as "a little rough around the edges" (99), readers are assured that a trip is well worth it, because the country has had a real makeover since the revolutionary period (1979–1990).

During the last two decades, I have observed the quickening pace of change in Nicaragua[2]—or at least the appearance of substantial change, even if the country undertook a rather grim program of neoliberal free-market development after the Sandinistas lost the 1990 election. The measures mandated by the International Monetary Fund and administered by the U.S. Agency for International Development produced a turn toward economic privatization and the shrinking of state-led social development. This meant rising unemployment, ill health, and growing illiteracy for a majority, with only a small elite benefiting from new products on the market, new restaurants and clubs, and a new look to the capital city of Managua, where a third of the nation's population lives (Babb 1999a). Other parts of the country, notably the colonial city of Granada and the Pacific coast, have also seen a host of renovation and construction projects designed to attract moneyed interests and tourism. Examining these localities in a time of transition can tell us much, beyond the Nicaraguan case, about the politics of tourism in the Latin American region.[3]

Twenty-five years ago, Nicaragua was the destination of "tourists of revolution," in the wry words of poet Lawrence Ferlinghetti (1984). Now it is being refashioned as the destination of another category of tourists, some adventurous and environmentally conscious and others simply eager to find an untraveled spot in the tropics. In this chapter I consider the remaking of the country, from within and without, as Nicaragua struggles to make tourism its leading industry (surpassing coffee production) and as an international clientele discovers a new region to call its own. Until recently, the revolutionary nation was considered off limits to uninformed travelers, and its inconveniences made even adventurous backpackers uneasy. Today, in contrast, the nation attracts these travelers and others desiring more luxurious accommodations. While postrevolutionary Nicaragua remains one of the poorest countries in the hemisphere, it is now getting the attention of those who shunned it not long ago. Nicaraguans themselves are divided between cynicism and a desire to bring needed revenue to their impoverished economy through tourism. We will discern how these developments are being experienced locally and globally as the Nicaraguan nation is reconstructed as a safe and desirable location that offers both the "traditional" and the "modern" (pre- and postrevolutionary) for foreign consumption.

As we saw in the case of Cuba, some places appeal to travelers who are seeking more than a comfortable holiday at the beach or a visit to colonial towns.

Recently, we hear of not only "political" tourism but also "danger" tourism; not only religious pilgrimages but also "red" pilgrimages to postsocialist countries; not only "socially responsible" tourism but also tours to the world's "trouble spots." *Newsweek International* reports on organizations like San Francisco–based Global Exchange, which has taken groups to such destinations as Kabul to "vacation in the remains of the Afghan capital" (Eviatar 2003). Other groups visit "areas under siege" in Israel and the Palestinian territories or learn about "social struggles" in Chiapas, Mexico, and the "legacies of war" in Vietnam. Having traveled with this organization to Cuba and Chiapas during the past decade, I became aware that some group members particularly relish going to areas designated as illegal or risky for U.S. tourists or requiring special licenses for entry. I will suggest that Nicaragua holds the same allure for travelers who desire to see for themselves "the land of Sandino," even years after the victory of the revolution. I reflect later on the rather cynical return of Sandinista leader Daniel Ortega to the office of president in 2006 and offer comparisons between tourism in Nicaragua, Cuba, and the other regions discussed in this book.

Dean MacCannell's seminal work *The Tourist* delved beneath surface appearances to advance the argument that tourism offers "staged authenticity," inviting visitors to "make incursions into the life of the society" (1999:97). More recently, writers have emphasized that representations and readings of tourist sites are always contested, so the sites and their meanings are subject to interpretation (Hanna and Del Casino 2003; Rojek and Urry 1997). My work follows this line of research insofar as I view tourism as a set of cultural practices that are under constant negotiation and that may illuminate broader social and historical processes. We will see a connection to tourism in past and present "danger zones," in this case a revolutionary nation that experienced prolonged instability and civil war and, since 1990, has undertaken new ideological projects that are still under construction (Gold and Gold 2003; Little 2004; Rojek 1997).

This chapter uses textual and ethnographic analysis to consider travel in the prerevolutionary era and later "solidarity" travel to the country. Then, based on my travel to tourism sites and interviews with tour operators, government officials, and tourists themselves, I examine the way in which Nicaragua has undergone a transition from being a revolutionary destination to one of interest to mainstream travelers. Finally, I present evidence from recent research that, contrary to my earlier expectations, indicates that the revolution, even during the neoliberal era, has made a reappearance on the tourist circuit. By considering the Nicaraguan case, I illustrate what may also be observed in other postrevolutionary societies such as Cuba, China, and Vietnam, as the past figures in the remaking of these nations for tourism in the present era of globalization.

Nicaraguan Travel, Past and Present

Long before Nicaragua was remade as a tourist destination, the country captured the interest of foreigners. In earlier times, the country attracted some adventurous travelers who were making their way by sea from one coast to the other in the United States or who were going on to Europe via the Central American Isthmus. No less celebrated a traveler than Mark Twain ventured there with a companion by ship from San Francisco during a transatlantic voyage in 1866–1867. This was only a decade after William Walker, the U.S. expansionist, defeated warring factions in the country and made himself president, ruling for a year before he was routed. Writing *Travels with Mr. Brown* for the San Francisco *Alta California*, Twain described the passengers' arrival at the Nicaraguan port town of San Juan del Sur during an outbreak of cholera. He and his companion found "a few tumble-down frame shanties—they call them hotels—nestling among green verdure . . . and half-clad yellow natives, with bowie-knives two feet long," the citizens of the town (Walker and Dane 1940:39). Some four hundred passengers endured twelve miles of land travel by horse, mule, and vehicle to Lake Nicaragua in order to cross the isthmus. This gave the two men a chance to appreciate the passing scene, about which Twain commented, "Our interest finally moderated somewhat in the native women . . . but never did the party cease to consider the wild monkey a charming novelty and a joy forever" (Walker and Dane 1940:42).

In the 1880s, a member of the East Coast elite, Dora Hort, made the trip from New York by steamer along with her sister, a gentleman companion, four nephews and nieces, and a male servant, crossing the Central American Isthmus before taking a boat bound for San Francisco. This Victorian lady traveler's fascination with Nicaragua and its people is revealed in her memoir, *Via Nicaragua*, published in 1887. Hort describes the arduous trek through jungle with brilliant birds and an "imbecile" guide who led them across to the "uninteresting, desolate hamlet of San Juan del Sur" (Agosín and Levison 1999:223)—a town that has become a popular seaside resort in recent years. Early travel writers like Hort exemplify what Pratt has aptly described as "imperial eyes" producing "the rest of the world" (1992:5).

During four decades prior to the Nicaraguan revolution, the Somoza family dictatorship held sway and imposed harsh conditions for the majority of

citizens of the country. Nevertheless, the Somoza period held certain pleasures for the national and international elite. The widely traveled British writer
Maureen Tweedy wrote a memoir entitled *This Is Nicaragua* (1953), in which she
compared the country favorably with her own. She paid Nicaragua her highest
compliment when she wrote, "The placid river flowing so gently through the
cattle sprinkled meadows beyond Nandaime reminds me of the upper reaches
of the Thames" (60). She admired the people as well for their simple, friendly
manner, writing, "In the springtime, in preparation for Holy Week, the thrifty
peasants build huts and shelters of pineapple leaves, palms and bamboos, to
rent to the picnickers and bathers who throng the beaches" (61). The book concluded with Indian legends as well as advertisements for Coffee Planter and
Exporters based in Managua, and for the capital city's Gran Hotel and Lido
Palace Hotel, which offered amenities to foreign guests. Folkloric and modern
images of the country thus shared the same textual space in this travel memoir.

The Sandinista victory in 1979 drew another class of travelers to Nicaragua.
Journalists, artists and writers, engineers, and activists of many backgrounds
made their way to the country, often in delegations, from the United States
and elsewhere. Some stayed for a time and wrote books based on interviews
with militants and celebrated figures, for example, Margaret Randall's *Sandino's
Daughters* (1981), or memoirs, notably Lawrence Ferlinghetti's *Seven Days in
Nicaragua Libre* (1984) and Salman Rushdie's *The Jaguar Smile* (1987).[4] Some
visitors came simply to see the revolutionary society for themselves, and others
determined to stay a year or longer in order to contribute to what many of them
viewed as the most significant process of social transformation in the Americas
since the Cuban revolution. A cottage industry in guidebooks for *internacio-
nalistas* (international activists) grew out of the solidarity movement influx to
Nicaragua during the 1980s.

The new travel guides were an amalgamation of brief historical and cultural
background, emphasizing the profound changes recently brought about, along
with practical information about where to find cheap lodging and meals, survive the tropical heat, and link up with other solidarity workers. One, entitled
(like Tweedy's book) *This Is Nicaragua* (1988), was made available in several
languages by the Nicaraguan Institute of Tourism and could be purchased on
arrival in Managua. It mimicked standard travel books in its attention to the
natural environment and the everyday concerns of getting around a new place,
but with one major difference: the guide begins by celebrating the "General of
Free Men," national hero Augusto César Sandino, who was killed by Somoza's

National Guard in 1934, and by heralding "a new geography for a new nation" (xi–xiii). Indeed, the Sandinista government redivided the country into political and geographic regions and gave revolutionary names to the streets and neighborhoods of the capital city. The new political culture was imprinted on the national landscape, not only through rezoning and renaming but also through the widespread painting of murals and construction of monuments to the people's history of struggle (Kunzle 1995; Sheesley 1991; Whisnant 1995).

Some guidebooks were clearly directed to the new breed of visitors to the country. *Not Just Another Nicaragua Travel Guide* (Hulme et al. 1990) proclaimed its intention loudly, and ads in its front matter included not just hotels and car rental agencies but also language and culture schools, fair-trade coffee outlets, and the Bikes Not Bombs recycling outfit in Managua. Readers were congratulated for choosing to travel to a place "poised on the cutting edge of history," serving as a "perfect vantage point to study the world" (9). The country was summed up in a few words: "Revolution. Empty beaches. Lifelong friends and cheap rum. Priests, poets and rocking chairs" (9). Many young people from the United States used the book to find their way to Managua's centrally located Barrio Martha Quesada, named for an urban combatant who was shot in the neighborhood by the National Guard in 1978. The barrio is sometimes referred to as "Gringolandia," since so many U.S. and European travelers have made its inexpensive hostels their base camp. Buses arrive and depart frequently in this barrio for neighboring Honduras and Costa Rica, so there is a steady flow of budget and activist travelers making their way through Central America, along with others who stay much longer in Nicaragua. From the barrio, travelers may walk to the shore of Lake Managua and pay respects nearby in Plaza de la Revolución (renamed Plaza de la República after the Sandinista electoral loss in 1990); there they can visit the National Palace (now the National Museum), which was famously taken during the insurrection by Sandinista Comandantes Eden Pastora and Dora María Téllez, and the tomb of the celebrated martyr Carlos Fonseca.

After the Sandinista electoral loss to opposition candidate Violeta Barrios de Chamorro, some loyal solidarity workers remained in the country and some curious travelers continued to arrive looking for traces of revolution. Their number was much reduced, but they could be recognized by their oversized backpacks and copies of such "alternative" resources as the Ulysses travel guide to Nicaragua. In its second edition, author Carol Wood's (1999) tone was still sympathetic to the Sandinista government and what it accomplished, but she

Artesanía and T-shirts with images of Sandino and Che
on sale in Nicaragua's international airport

acknowledges that Nicaraguans became weary of the U.S. opposition that produced the Contra war and the economic embargo. There is more attention to
the natural wonders of the country than to its politics, and, indeed, the guide
even urges visitors not to miss touring the Isletas, the small islands in Lake Nicaragua, noting that "it's a great spot to dream about living on your own little
tropical paradise" (162). This casual remark presages the rapid sales of islands to
foreigners that was trumpeted a few years later in *Condé Nast Traveler*.

From Revolution to Resorts

The Chamorro government did not bring about the economic recovery that
had been promised during the national election, but political stability was
gradually achieved with the cooperation of the Sandinista Party. When the

United States failed to offer assistance at the level expected and international coffee prices plummeted, Nicaragua sought to further develop tourism. By the mid-1990s, the Nicaraguan Institute of Tourism (INTUR), in collaboration with the national universities, promoted tourism as a key area for professional training. Reports of increasing levels of tourism showed that although the largest influx of visitors still came from the Central American region, a new class of tourists was arriving from the United States and Europe. Efforts were made to capture more of this market through improvements in infrastructure catering to tourists and more effective means of marketing the country as a tourist destination (Ministerio de Turismo 1995). By the year 2000, the annual number of visitors to Nicaragua approached five hundred thousand, significant in a country with a population of four million—although as many as half came for business rather than pleasure.[5] The goal became to entice visitors to stay longer and spend more money and to provide more facilities for them to enjoy during their stay (Instituto Nicaragüense de Turismo 2001:5).

To that end, a number of sites were enhanced and promoted for tourism. The premier Pacific coast beach destination Montelimar, which formerly was owned by the Somoza family and then nationalized under the Sandinistas, was sold to the Spanish interest Barceló and turned into a five-star, all-inclusive resort. San Juan del Sur worked hard to attract cruise ships to its sleepy fishing village and to appeal to a younger and environmentally conscious clientele to come to newly constructed guesthouses and hotels. Selva Negra, in the mountainous north, also sought to capitalize on a more robust tourist industry to draw visitors to its German-style cottages and restaurant, where guests could visit a local coffee plantation and walk through tropical forest to spot howler monkeys and exotic birds. The colonial city of Granada was privileged to have a more complete makeover as a charming destination or stopping-over place for those traveling through the country. Already an architectural marvel and historical draw, the city received international support to renovate and restore its cathedral, convent, central plaza, cultural institute, and oldest hotel, making it attractive to international visitors. By adding canopy tours of the nearby forest and boat trips to the Isletas, the city has catered to the diverse interests of travelers in recent years.

Research over the last two decades in Nicaragua has allowed me to observe the refashioning of Managua, Granada, Montelimar, and other well-traveled areas throughout the country, as part of the national effort to attract tourist dollars (Babb 2001a, 2001b). On arrival at Managua's international airport, recently spruced up with five million dollars in U.S. support, visitors are greeted by signs for high-end hotels and the Hard Rock Café, in addition to the old signs for Victoria Beer and Flor de Caña rum. Since 2000, I have gone where tourists travel in order to consider how postrevolutionary Nicaragua has readied itself for an influx of newcomers who may know and care little about the country's history and recent political upheaval and who expect to find a well-established tourist industry in place.

Before making my way to INTUR in Managua in 2002, I had been interested to discover its colorful, attractive Web site.[6] The site offers a brief introduction to the country, a friendly appeal to tourists, and advice to those investing in the tourist industry or buying private property. The INTUR office itself, tucked away just a few blocks from the landmark InterContinental Hotel (now the Crowne Plaza Hotel), was not as impressive. A woman at a desk in the small reception area welcomed me and offered several brochures featuring the usual half-dozen attractions, all outside Managua: Masaya and its volcano, Granada, León, San Juan del Sur, Montelimar, and the Río San Juan (serious travelers would also be told about Selva Negra and the Atlantic coast). She told me that on a typical day only about three visitors come to their office. Across the street, there was more activity in INTUR's documentation center, as secondary school and university students crowded around the few tables there. The woman heading the center confirmed that they were students of tourism, which has replaced computer school as young people's best hope for future employment. The walls of the room were decorated with framed pictures of the country's natural beauty and folklore; a portrait of a woman entitled *India Bonita* was emblematic of both aspects that INTUR hoped would enhance tourism.

Although Managua now has improved roads, a new city center, hotels, casinos, and shopping malls in the area left devastated by an earthquake in 1972, Stephen Kinzer, writing in the *New York Times*, described it as "still among the ugliest capital cities in the hemisphere" (2002:10–12). Visitors to the city are often there on professional business, as I learned during forays into the Princess Hotel, Holiday Inn, and Hotel Legends. Employees at the hotels offer suggestions about night spots and a few places worth visiting in the city, but in general Managua is regarded as uninviting to international visitors who would rather venture out to other parts of the country. Tour operators often recommend just a half day in the city to see the ancient footsteps of Acahualinca (evidence of early human presence), the National Museum and the National Theatre, and the view from Sandino Park. Those who stay longer might visit the artisan market known as Huembes, the *malecón* (waterfront promenade) alongside Lake Managua, or the volcanic Lake Xiloa just outside the city—but they find a better market for shopping in nearby Masaya and a lovelier lake in Catarina just forty minutes away.

Indeed, many bypass the sprawling capital altogether by going directly from the international airport to Montelimar about an hour away on the coast or traveling in tour groups through Central America and stopping only in the more historic cities of León and Granada before heading on to San José, Costa Rica. The ruins of Old León have a unique distinction in Nicaragua as a designated UNESCO World Heritage Site (Patrimonio Mundial). The colonial city of León may emerge in the future as the most popular destination in the country for tourism (as some operators predict), but for now Granada draws the greatest number of international visitors, as well as a growing expatriate community of retirees from the United States.

Visits to Granada, which claims to be the oldest city in the hemisphere (much of it destroyed in a fire ordered by the failed dictator William Walker in 1856), provided opportunities to observe and query travelers and residents. The visitors are a diverse group, ranging from the so-called relax category of international travelers and longtime residents in Managua wishing to get away from the "big city," to day-trippers traveling in from cruise ships on the Pacific coast, to backpackers pleased to find cheap accommodations in a place modern enough to have Internet cafés and a laid-back attitude. Well-heeled travelers stay at the landmark Hotel Alhambra with its arcade looking out on the central plaza or at newer and more expensive places like the Hotel Colonial. Several restaurants cater to this clientele, who are sought after by guides clamoring to provide package tours for fees that are very high by local standards.

European and U.S. travelers on limited budgets stay at the Hospedaje Central (Central Hostel) or other inexpensive lodging a few blocks from the plaza. The popular Bearded Monkey, a hostel operated by a young couple from England and the United States, is reminiscent of the hippie generation. Guests at this hostel listen to mellow music from places distant from Nicaragua's shores as they relax in hammocks, eat natural foods at the small restaurant, borrow books and videos from a lending library, and contemplate their travels. Access to the Internet and to phones for making international calls—as well as arrangements for getting a massage or even a tattoo—add to the hostel's "hip" appeal. Speaking with travelers at several of these venues in Granada, I found that only a few knew much about Nicaragua's recent political history that went beyond what could be read in the Lonely Planet guidebook.[7] Nonetheless, some of these travelers on a shoestring stayed long enough in the country to learn more Spanish, make local friends, and absorb more knowledge of culture and history.

At the other end of the spectrum are the retired residents who have come to live in Granada in recent years. Some have turned to Nicaragua rather than Costa Rica (a neighboring competitor for tourism and property ownership) because they find it to be less expensive and to suffer less from the overdevelopment of tourism. One tour operator credited the revolution and past conflict for having held off tourism development long enough that the city could now thrive—a point I make for all four cases I examine in this book. Capitalizing on Nicaraguans' willingness to sell off property at locally high prices (only to see the value soar quickly in the hands of foreign investors and property owners), Granada's historic center is fast becoming Americanized both in terms of ownership and cultural identity. All five real estate offices in the city are owned by U.S. citizens, men who see an opportunity to get rich quick. In interviews with two of them, I discovered that they fit the local pattern of

A tourist walkway in historic Granada that is undergoing revitalization with support from Spain

older "gringo" males linking up with local "Nica" girlfriends or wives who were young enough to be their granddaughters—trophies and service providers in their homes and businesses.

An Austrian historian living in Granada, Dieter Stadtler, has been central to the restoration project in the city. He qualified the enthusiastic reports of tourism in Granada when he told me that at the time of our conversation there were only about 450 beds in first- to third-class hotels in the city of some one hundred thousand residents. Most people who travel there are either backpackers, who spend little money, or Nicaraguans coming back to visit relatives over the holidays, who spend even less (but who may bring gifts and monetary remittances). Thus, despite heavy reliance on financial support from Spain, Sweden, and other nations to restore the city to its former grandeur, the present potential for tourism is limited (Stadtler, interview, June 22, 2002).

Nevertheless, tourism was touted in a two-page article from the *New York Times* (Rohter 1997:sec. 5:10) that was still displayed prominently five years after publication on a stand adjacent to the Alhambra's registration desk. Entitled "Nicaragua on the Mend," the article commented:

> Seven years after its brutal civil war, the country is at peace and putting out the welcome mat. . . . For more than a decade, the only foreigners likely to visit Nicaragua in any numbers were "internationalists," sympathizers of the Sandinista revolution inspired by the idea of sharing the hardships and dangers of a country under siege. . . . Ordinary visitors were encouraged to stay away. (10)

But, the author asserted, "Nicaragua has changed enormously," and then he quoted Nicaragua's Minister of Tourism Pedro Joaquín Chamorro: "We are on the brink of an awakening to tourism. . . . We want to make tourism the main product of Nicaragua, and we plan to do that by promoting our country as an exotic destination at a reasonable price" (ibid.).

Nicaragua is represented in various ways to different potential travel clienteles. To Nicaraguans themselves, notably the elite, there are efforts to eclipse the revolutionary past and show continuity from the Somoza family regime through the present, excising the Sandinista decade in a new revisionist history. A video produced a few years ago by the government's Institute of Culture, *Managua en mi corazón* (Managua in My Heart, 1997), shows the capital city in ruins after the earthquake and, as if immediately after, the rebuilding of the 1990s, with no indication of the social transformation that occurred a decade before—and no irony as the spectacle of movie marquees and huge traffic circles are deployed as hallmarks of modernity. Another video, *Tierra mía, Nicaragua* (My Land, Nicaragua, 2001), is directed to Nicaraguans living outside the country, especially in the United States, luring them back with the promise that "when you return to Nicaragua, it will all be as you remember." Nostalgic images in both videos serve up a shared history and cultural identity that scarcely existed in the class-divided dictatorship, in order to endorse the present national project of neoliberalism.

The shared cultural identity that is frequently held out to both Nicaraguans and international visitors generally relies more on memories of the natural beauty of the land, its people, and ceremonial traditions than it does on any moments in the nation's history. Localities like the Pacific coast beaches, the mountainous north with its exotic birds and monkeys, and the Río San Juan bordering Costa Rica produce longings in those whose origins are in the country, as well as in those who know these places only through INTUR's Web site or the available guidebooks. Music, dance, performances, and masks worn in traditional fiestas serve to conjure idealized and timeless sentiments of belonging for insiders and exoticism for newcomers. Urban attractions like the central plazas of León and Granada, with their colonial-era cathedrals, arcades, and monuments, evoke the nation's often conflicted past when Liberal and Conservative parties in the two cities vied for control; the political turmoil of the nineteenth and early twentieth centuries is sufficiently distant that it may safely be remembered in travel promotion literature and city tours.

In contrast to other parts of Latin America where indigenous culture and identity are utilized to encourage tourism, in Nicaragua's Pacific region (where most travelers venture) only the area of Masaya is known for its indigenous artisans and uses this association to draw domestic and foreign visitors (Scruggs 1999). The Nicaraguan notion of *mestizaje* (mixed racial identity) powerfully erases cultural difference so that one finds only passing references to enduring indigenous peoples and places. The recently constructed Güegüense Plaza in central Managua is a singular landmark celebrating the foundational narrative of mestiza Nicaragua as a land where the indigenous and the European long ago fused into one shared identity.[8] Only the rare tourist who travels to the less accessible Atlantic coast area is likely to become aware of that region's diverse indigenous and Afro-Nicaraguan population.

Related to this homogenized depiction of Nicaraguan culture, there is little marketing of crafts and other products unique to regions in Nicaragua such as one finds in Guatemala, Ecuador, or Peru. Travelers may take home handmade hammocks, rocking chairs, wall hangings, black coral jewelry, leather belts, carved wooden birds, CDs of traditional music, and even shellacked frogs playing marimbas; but taken together, this does not provide a great deal of revenue in the country. Some effort is being directed toward producing higher-quality items for tourist consumption as part of a national initiative to support small industries and microenterprises.[9] However, tourists I have interviewed complain that the country's *artesanía* (handicraft) "all looks the same," as if mass-marketed, and more foreign currency is spent on ephemeral pleasures such as lodging, dining, and sightseeing. An emphasis on adventure tourism has expanded the offerings to include not only fishing, hunting, boating, and swimming but also surfing, kayaking, forest canopy tours, hot-air balloon rides, and biking down the sides of still-active volcanoes.[10]

Whether sex tourism will be added to the list (unofficially) as a significant aspect of international travel to Nicaragua remains to be seen, though there is already increased prostitution, sometimes associated with nightclubs and casinos in urban areas and no doubt growing as a result of high unemployment and economic need. This question will be taken up in more detail in Chapter 5, but here it may be noted that young girls awaiting clients along the road to the international airport and in Granada's central plaza, and sex workers—including transvestites—in certain locations around Managua are now commonplace. Massages and lap dancing are advertised in urban centers, and sexual satisfaction is often an assumed part of the arrangement. Men from the United States, traveling or living in Nicaragua, have told me of their surprise in being approached by young women and girls—and, sometimes, young men and boys—offering sexual services for payment. There is a gendered politics of tourism as women and girls cater to male desires, whether for sexual or other services. Although women travelers may also expect and enjoy the services of male providers in the tourist industry, from what I have observed, these are far less often sexual in nature.[11]

Revolution Rehabilitated

One may ask which Nicaragua will be promoted and consumed in the future: popular or elite, traditional or modern, environmentally conscious or exotic and culturally different? How will the revolutionary past figure, if at all, in the imaginations of travelers to the country? I will consider the last several decades of tourism in the country and then turn to the evidence that the revolution has made a comeback on the tourist circuit—even before the Sandinistas themselves returned to power in 2006.

Although there are few published sources that address tourism during the Sandinista period, one analysis takes a harshly critical stance on "political hospitality and tourism" of that time. In a report published by the right-wing Cuban American National Foundation, sociologist Paul Hollander (1986) contends that the Nicaraguan wave of "political tourism" followed the Cuban model in cultivating global support for the revolutionary government in the 1980s. He notes that visitors in solidarity tours were treated to devoted service and generally close monitoring, resulting in a selective view of the country. Hollander singles out the Sandinista minister of the interior at that time, Tomás Borge, for his generous hospitality to international visitors, particularly those of high social or political stature. While the report's excessively negative view of the revolutionary government and political tourists should be questioned, the account is nonetheless revealing of certain aspects of the period. Hollander is correct in suggesting that some travelers were so enamored of Nicaragua that they wrote reverential travelogues based on their experiences.[12] Staging tours to appeal to visitors and leave them with a favorable impression of the country is hardly unique to Nicaragua or Cuba, but these nations' revolutionary governments have been highly motivated to counter mainstream U.S. views through carefully constructed tourism. The one hundred thousand U.S. visitors to Nicaragua between 1979 and the time of Hollander's writing did indeed play a part in undercutting the effectiveness of Reagan's Central America policy when they returned home to earnestly spread the word about the social transformation that was under way.

One man's memories of the tourism industry before and after the revolution is instructive. In an interview, the head of the domestic travel division of Nicaraguan-owned Munditur spoke about the company's early years, dating from when it opened for business in 1966.[13] Adán Gaitán was just eleven years old when his family, after living some years in the United States and Argentina, returned to Nicaragua to launch Munditur, one of the earliest travel and tourism agencies in the country (Gaitán, interview, July 1, 2003). While attending the American Nicaraguan school, he earned a few dollars by taking tourists to Masaya or Granada or on an afternoon tour of Managua—the tourist options still offered today by a majority of tour operators in the country. After graduating from the school, he worked in the family's travel agency and tourism office before going on to study law. In 1976, he founded the National Chamber of Tourism (CANATUR), and he has continued to play a leadership role in tourism development and in promoting what he calls "a tourist culture."

In the mid-1980s, when the Sandinistas were in power, the business was "confiscated" and, according to Gaitán, Herty Lewites, a Sandinista who later became the mayor of Managua, was responsible for the seizure of their tour vehicles and imprisonment of several family members. After the 1990 election of Chamorro, the business started up again, but the family's experience during the Sandinista period colors Gaitán's political outlook today. He remembers the Sandinistas' tourism division, Turnica, and the consequences of state control of travel in the country. He offered the example of the InterContinental Hotel in Managua, one of the few notable structures that remained after a devastating earthquake in 1972, commenting that under the Sandinistas the hotel made no profit because income went into state coffers. Like other tour operators, he resents the period of Sandinista government expropriation of private businesses and the legal decision made in the 1980s to keep international travel agencies and domestic tourism companies separate, so that even today their business carries an extra tax burden.

When archaeologists began excavating the ruins of Old León in the late 1960s, Munditur was the first to offer tours to the first Spanish settlement in Nicaragua, and they have continued to offer city tours in Granada, Masaya, and Managua. However, they have become best known for their dove- and duck-hunting trips in the San Juan River area, their "jungle safaris," and sport fishing. Gaitán is proud to play host to well-known business, media, and sports figures from the United States—for example, people from Exxon, ESPN, Hollywood, and the Texas Rangers—and to offer high-end tourism with great attention to detail. The kind of sport and adventure tourism that Munditur promotes relies on careful advance planning and a quality "product" (i.e., tour package), and their clients have little need to come versed in Nicaraguan history and culture or to know how to maneuver around the country independently. Gaitán would like to see Nicaragua shed its old image and attract more travelers like his discerning customers; as he put it, "The image of Nicaragua is like a lady that has not washed off her old makeup to put on her new makeup."[14]

For the majority of tourists who do not have a thousand dollars per day to spend on the sort of travel described by Gaitán, guidebooks are all important in preparing them to make their way around the country. Several that were in use during my period of research, *Let's Go Central America* (Gardner 2000), *Footprint Nicaragua Handbook* (Leonardi 2001), *Moon Handbook* (Berman and Wood 2002), and Lonely Planet guide *Nicaragua and El Salvador* (Penland et al. 2006) offer brief historical background.[15] Perhaps, like returning Nicaraguans, these visitors will forget the revolution they never knew and seek fulfillment of the sort described in Irving Berlin's popular song lyrics of the forties featuring

Managua, Nicaragua: the satisfaction of enjoying, or even purchasing, a place in the tropical sun.

The tourism office, INTUR, would clearly like visitors to shed the notion of Nicaragua as a place of political conflict and danger and to discover a land of beautiful landscapes and friendly people. Both the director of promotion and marketing, Raúl Calvet, and the head of the image and international relations section of INTUR, Regina Hurtado, expressed this sentiment (interview, June 27, 2003). Hurtado emphasized the "image problem" in Nicaragua, which since the 1980s and 1990s has been viewed as "dangerous." She confronts the problem by seeking to give a positive impression to the international press on whom they depend to build a market. To that end, they work with mayors throughout the country and seek guidance from international tourism organizations. In addition, their institute conducted a survey at the international airport and found that, in fact, many tourists were coming to Nicaragua with vague notions of a country that had been at war but left with admiration for the welcoming people they met there.

INTUR has promoted tourism development through an incentive law, which benefits hotels, restaurants, and other highly capitalized venues that require large investments—not the small-scale artisans whom tourists often desire to meet and from whom they wish to buy souvenirs. Nicaragua has participated with its neighboring countries in a campaign to draw tourism to the region, targeting Europe in particular with the slogan "Central America: So small . . . so big . . ." Yet Nicaragua also competes with Guatemala and Costa Rica for tourist revenue, and in those countries "the tourist product has been more clearly identified" (Hurtado, interview, June 27, 2003). Most who choose to spend time in Nicaragua fit the category of "adventure tourists" (the backpackers) and do not expect a high level of comfort or sophisticated service infrastructure—though INTUR would like to "sell Nicaragua" to tourists with more money to spend.

The wealthiest tourists may be those who stop briefly on cruises handled by Careli Tours, a Swiss-owned company with a Central American office in Costa Rica. However, those passengers landing at San Juan del Sur and traveling for a half day to Granada or Montelimar are not filling hotel rooms or leaving significant revenue behind. More potential lies in those travelers visiting and occasionally remaining to buy property in the colonial city of Granada. If there is concern about the cultural impact on the local population, it manifests only in the city's requirement for historic preservation (which also has market value); foreign investors and retirees in general are better able than Nicaraguans to maintain the colonial heritage, making them desirable property owners, at least in the short term. INTUR officials used the language of marketing, telling me that in order to attract such individuals, they need a "national brand"—something to capture buyers' attention. Added to this, they seek to develop a "comeback package" to appeal to the many Nicaraguans who left the country during the Sandinista period and need to be coaxed back with nostalgic and sanitized images of the country of their childhood and early adulthood. The video *Tierra mía, Nicaragua*, mentioned earlier, is marketed to this target group, complete with discount coupons to use on their return. For this clientele, references to the recent revolutionary past are to be avoided at any cost (Hurtado, interview).

However, for some travelers there is a certain cachet in referencing the revolutionary society that has left only traces. Several young backpackers indicated to me that they had selected Nicaragua just because of its "different" and more "radical" image. One man from the United States told me that his mother had been to Costa Rica, but for him Nicaragua held more hope of adventure: whereas Costa Rica represented comfortable middle age, Nicaragua had a more youthful image. A young Russian woman traveling with him came because she was intrigued by the country's revolutionary past, and she made some comparisons from her own experience living in a postsocialist society (field notes, June 30, 2003). Some lingering "humanitarian" groups coming to the country for shorter or longer periods are more aware of the revolutionary past and, depending on their politics, wish to revive its cooperative spirit or replace it with the sort of individualist entrepreneurial outlook associated with neoliberalism.[16]

I want to suggest that in due time, and perhaps sooner rather than later, the Sandinista revolution will be restored to history, even if rehabilitated to suit specific political desires. Kinzer, in his travel article on Granada, reflects on the distant past of a city torn apart by rival political factions and ravaged by William Walker in the nineteenth century but only notes in passing "the civil war that tore the country apart during the 1980s" (2002:12). Some years from now, I anticipate that tourists visiting Nicaragua may hear idealized references to the Sandinistas and their struggle in much the same way that they now hear about the warring Conservatives and Liberals of the distant past.

At INTUR, Raúl Calvet spoke with me about the tendency, not only in Nicaragua but elsewhere in Latin America, to reference the more distant past in relating history to tourist audiences (interview, June 27, 2003). Stories of political conflicts of the nineteenth century appeal to tourists, whereas those of the late twentieth century may still scare them away. Nonetheless, some travelers are attracted to lingering notions of "danger." Calvet described a young European who came to the INTUR office and chatted awhile about travel in Nicaragua. As the man was leaving, Calvet was surprised to see that on the back of his T-shirt was the image of a Nicaraguan woman with an AK-47. He called the man back to say that it was fine if this was the image he chose to have of Nicaragua, but that as director of promotion and marketing, Calvet hoped that travelers would begin to have other images as well. When he described the problem as one of romanticizing the revolution, I reached into my bag and pulled out a postcard with another image of a young Sandinista with a rifle over her shoulder, this one the iconic image of a woman smiling with a nursing baby in her arms, from a photograph that has circulated widely in Nicaragua and beyond.[17] This image is found on countless postcard racks as well as on T-shirts and other items sold to tourists.

A lively conversation followed about whether with the passage of time the revolution might be considered "safer" for tourist consumption—which the director found plausible.[18] The evidence of this may be seen in the widespread availability of revolutionary images on tourist items sold in popular markets, and in the government resources recently given to turn Sandino Park into a national site to draw both Nicaraguans and tourists. High on a hill in the center of Managua, the park's towering silhouette of Sandino had been given a new lighting system before Mayor Herty Lewites inaugurated the park in June 2003. Many came to the opening, which included a photographic exhibition that recalled the presidential palace of the past dictatorship, located on the hilltop before the earthquake brought it down. The mayor had plans to build a history museum to further memorialize the site.

Around the time of the park's inauguration, I learned of a Sandinista Revolution Tour, departing from Managua and traveling to visit monuments and museums in the city of León. I attempted to track it down, going from a hotel where it was advertised to the place where the tour operator was said to be available, but like many other initiatives in Nicaragua, this one was ephemeral. Nonetheless, other solidarity tours have continued to operate in the country, including the Wisconsin sister-city project that takes activists to the country each summer and Global Exchange, which takes groups during the time of the annual July 19 march in honor of the triumph of the revolution.[19] Even Careli Tours considered offering a specialized trip in the footsteps of Augusto César Sandino, commemorating the route he and his men followed (1927–1934) in their opposition to the Nicaraguan National Guard, although this did not turn out to be feasible (Henry Urbina, interview, June 27, 2003).

An exhibition space honoring revolutionary hero Augusto César Sandino in Managua's Sandino Park

Given the turn toward neoliberal capitalism and the profit motivation of tourism in Nicaragua, it is notable that Tomás Borge, a comandante of the Sandinista revolution and member of the National Assembly, has recently served as head of the Tourism Commission. In an interview on the evening of June 30, 2003, by the pool outside a small hotel he owns, he offered a number of observations regarding what a Sandinista perspective on tourism might offer. First, he predicted (correctly) that the Sandinistas would win the next election and would not only make tourism the number-one industry but would also make it clean and healthful, free of the sex tourism and casinos that are taking hold in the country. He shared the concern of officials at INTUR that Nicaragua's image of conflict and instability has been an obstacle to developing tourism, and he imagined a tourism that would draw attention to the natural beauty of the land and the hospitality of the people.

When questioned about the historical understanding that travelers bring to Nicaragua and what they know about the revolution, Borge responded that they have little knowledge and come for the beach, mountains, and adventure. He imagined that, in the future, tourism might be reoriented toward national heritage and, within the parameters of adventure tourism, guide visitors along the routes taken by the Sandinistas during the insurrection of the late 1970s.[20] He referred often to Cuba as a model for developing tourism, expressing admiration for Cuba's success in replacing sugar export with tourism as its leading industry and in attracting numerous visitors to its famed beaches and other attractions. Borge felt certain that in Nicaragua, just as in Cuba, tourism would serve to rescue the national economy. Yet at the time of this interview he stressed that the Liberal Party government was doing little to benefit tourism. Borge was particularly aggrieved by the high-level political appointment at INTUR of a woman who held him responsible for the death of her father in the insurrection—straining their working relationship as officials seeking to promote tourism.

Although it may be surprising that Borge would make tourism the centerpiece of his political activity, he emphasized that if, for example, there were a U.S. invasion of Cuba, he would drop tourism in an instant to enlist to fight Yankee imperialism. At the end of our taped conversation, I inquired about his views of the development of Managua's Sandino Park, which had been the site of the former dictator Somoza's bunker and torture chambers. Borge reminded me that he himself was the principal Sandinista held and tortured there while a prisoner for nine months and said he supported opening the park to the public so that its history would be better known. It was clear that for Borge, tourism is an important economic venture for the country, and if it could be linked to furthering the goals of the revolution to which he remains committed, so much the better.

The fifty-four-foot silhouette of the hero Augusto César Sandino that dominates the Tiscapa hilltop overlooking Managua is an enduring icon of the revolution.[21] Created by Sandinista poet and artist Ernesto Cardenal, the work was installed just as Daniel Ortega was leaving office and Violeta Chamorro was entering as president in 1990. The symbolic value of raising the image of Sandino on that site was great, and because the military remained under Sandinista leadership, the site would remain protected. Chamorro dedicated the area around the sculpture as a national park in 1996, and Mayor Herty Lewites made improvements in 2000. Now there is a sign beckoning tourists to follow the newly paved road and visit the sculpture and well-kept park that honors the national hero and martyr. Although young Nicaraguan couples may wander there simply for the privacy it affords them and some tourists go there principally for the view of the city (and in the last few years for the featured ride on a zip line across Lake Tiscapa), some Nicaraguans and tourists I interviewed wanted to pay their respects to the chilling history that was made at the site.

Other monuments to the revolution have remained on view in the capital city. The tomb of Carlos Fonseca, founder of the Sandinista Front for National Liberation (the FSLN Party), is quietly guarded in the city's central plaza. After Fonseca's death as a martyr in 1976 and on the revolution's victory, his remains were placed at this site. However, after 1990, the tomb was left untended and its flame was extinguished, and two years later it was blown up by a bomb. Immediately, the Sandinista faithful rebuilt the tomb and a vigilant sympathizer set up camp to protect the father of the revolution. Nonetheless, in 2002 I found that the two women cleaning the site (one wearing a scarf imprinted with the U.S. flag) indicated little awareness of the tomb's history.

One more monument, highly visible in central Managua, is an immense bronze statue created by Franz Orozco to honor the "Popular Combatant," a man of exaggerated proportions raising a rifle in one hand and holding a worker's pick in the other. Often referred to familiarly as "Rambo," the statue was commissioned by the Ministry of Public Construction and inaugurated in 1985 on the anniversary of the revolution. There was an attempt to destroy the monument with sticks of dynamite in the early 1990s, but only the iron around one heel of the figure was damaged.[22] "Rambo" continued to greet travelers driving into Managua from the international airport, who might have been surprised to see so militant a monument in the neoliberal era.

The celebrated modernist poet Rubén Darío, who was born in a small town near León in 1867 and died in 1916, is not always mentioned in the same breath as the revolutionary hero Sandino, whose ubiquitous image still appears on walls and buildings around the country. Yet there are increasingly frequent references to the two together as heroic revolutionary icons—both cultural and political. Managua's prestigious National Theatre named after Darío withstood the earthquake and is only one of a number of locations where his statue is on display. For many Nicaraguans and some visitors to the country, these two anti-imperialist figures who died in the early decades of the twentieth century are recognized as distinguished national symbols of pride. To a significant degree, Sandino, like Darío, has been appropriated by the social and political elite and thus rendered safe for both domestic and international consumption.[23]

During a visit to Nicaragua in 2003, I was struck by the growing and widespread appearance of the image of Ernesto "Che" Guevara, resurfacing at a time when revolutionary icons were increasingly fashionable. I discovered an FSLN gathering in Granada honoring Carlos Fonseca, Che Guevara, and Nicaraguan-Cuban solidarity and found a new monument in central Managua with Che's famous portrait wearing a beret. His image was in less likely places as well, perhaps as a kitsch rather than revolutionary icon. A café alongside a real estate office by the central plaza in Granada, a place frequented by expatriate retirees from the United States, had the name Café Che and the familiar image painted on the wall; coffee mugs with the same likeness and logo were for sale. The waitress informed me that the café had actually been renamed "Nacho Mama's," but the familiar logo was still in use. Necklaces and T-shirts with Che's image were sold and worn everywhere, especially popular among young men who were no doubt attracted to this symbol of revolutionary masculinity.[24]

Nicaraguans I spoke with that year offered several responses to the question of why the image of Che had become so widespread. For some, it was enough to say that as Sandinistas they embraced Che's image, while others noted the internationalism of Che's politics. I have concluded that, at one and the same time, Che represents both a safer, more remote, and non-Nicaraguan radicalism, and in other instances a deeper longing at a time when Sandinista party politics are viewed as either "watered down" or contaminated by a "pact" between the Sandinista and Liberal parties. One young man wearing a Che necklace told me rather vaguely, "Some say he fought in the Cuban revolution. Others say in Bolivia." Another man was more certain that both Sandino and Che were revolutionary and anti-imperialist and added the insight that whereas Sandino represented the "national," Che was "more universal." A street vendor was eager to assure me that those who bought his Sandino and Che T-shirts were not "communists" but only wished to wear the popular images. In any event, there are many Nicaraguans and tourists alike who appear to admire both men as legendary and to sport their likenesses as broad symbols of cultural and political opposition.

What Remains: Tourism and Recycled Revolution

> Originally, I had planned to study tourism and revolution, which seemed to me to name the two poles of modern consciousness—a willingness to accept, even venerate, things as they are on the one hand, a desire to transform things on the other.
>
> **—Dean MacCannell, 1999**

As I noted in the Introduction, MacCannell did not pursue his early objective of examining tourism and revolution. There remains a need to consider the ways that tourism and revolution intersect, particularly at a time when postsocialism is heralded and globalized capitalism reigns. Some writers have discussed the desires of tourists to discover what is new, unusual, and sometimes dangerous or disastrous (Rojek 1997), but little attention has been devoted to the ways that revolutionary or postrevolutionary societies have sought to strengthen economic development and national identity through the promotion of tourism. This chapter has undertaken such a project by examining a nation that made the transition from revolutionary to neoliberal-oriented government (and back to Sandinista rule) and that has begun to contend with the practical and political aspects of refashioning the country for tourism.

A Nicaraguan-made video documentary entitled *Algo queda* (Something Remains, 2001) points to some durable gains of the revolution. A contrast to the videos mentioned earlier that excise the revolution from nostalgic historical accounts, this one is nonetheless nostalgic in its somewhat idealized representation of a revolutionary past that brought about progressive change in the interest of all. Nearly two decades ago, photojournalist Susan Meiselas brilliantly captured a "war of images" in her video documentary on memories of the insurrection, *Pictures from a Revolution* (Meiselas et al. 1992). Here, I have pointed to the contested images of postrevolutionary society as the nation prepares for the anticipated arrival of increasing tourism on its shores and in its cities. How Nicaraguans view themselves and construct themselves both frames and is framed by outsiders' perceptions of them as a people and as a nation. Whatever economic, political, and cultural advantages (or disadvantages) tourism may bring in its wake, it is also responding to and remaking Nicaraguan national identity.

So what are tourists to make of these remaining symbols of that radically different time—especially as they are often poorly informed about the Sandinista revolution of just a few decades ago? Most who stay for more than a day or two in the country venture into local markets or hotel gift shops where they find—in addition to other items targeted to them as consumers—a variety of T-shirts and postcards with the familiar image of Sandino, seventy-five years after his death. Long-reproduced photographs of triumphant Sandinistas from the 1970s—frequently including the iconic portrait mentioned earlier of a smiling young woman with rifle slung over her shoulder and nursing infant in her arms—are sold alongside ceramic bowls from the artisan community of San Juan de Oriente, paintings of traditional Atlantic coast dancers, packages of Casa del Café coffee beans, and Flor de Caña rum as "typical" gifts to show off to friends back home. Now that Nicaragua is viewed as a stable democratic nation to which tourists may safely travel, images of the revolution are no longer so threatening or undesirable and may even be a selling point for savvy travel agents.

Who knows whether Managua's Museum of the Revolution, which has long been closed, may reopen its doors and persuade more visitors to spend time in the capital before heading for the beaches and colonial towns? And who knows what recycled notions of the revolution may become part of the memories travelers take home? As Nicaragua was remade as a neoliberal nation, these memories would serve to evoke nostalgia for the brief time when idealism reigned but then gave way to the logic of the unfettered free market and the downsized state. Now, the deeply ambivalent return of Sandinista governance may signal a greater need for unifying, if cynical, narratives and symbols. Across the political spectrum, Nicaraguans and foreign visitors alike may come to embrace Sandino, like Darío, as a national hero, appropriating his image and memory as safe for public consumption and a draw for tourist dollars—conveniently enhancing the twin projects of nationalism and tourism in the new era.

Recent histories of violence, danger, war, and revolution may all serve to draw tourism once the dust begins to settle in a region. At a time when jaded tourists are becoming less fearful of the threat of terrorism and are seeking "a new thrill," they may venture to new destinations. The *New York Times* describes a tourism "boom" in Vietnam following the September 11 attacks, citing travelers' views that "the country's controlled Communist society [is] reassuring at a time of travel warnings and attacks elsewhere" (Bradsher 2003:8). Another *New York Times* article (Noel 2004:10) comments that South Africa is attracting record numbers of tourists, who may safely visit the prison cell that held Nelson Mandela for twenty-seven years and other sites associated with the brutal period of apartheid. Thus, it is not surprising if Nicaragua is seeing a new generation of visitors who wish to follow in the "footsteps of Sandino." Along with other revolutionary icons like Che, Mao, and Ho Chi Minh, Sandino may find new life as both historical figure and cultural commodity in the modern, global marketplace of tourism.

Cultural Tourism in Postconflict Andean Peru and Chiapas, Mexico

3 Forgetting the Past:
Andean Cultural Tourism After the Violence

IN THE SUMMER OF 1982, I returned to Peru five years after carrying out my doctoral research there. Several international events stand out in my mind from that time, as they captured the attention of Peruvians and many others around the globe. One was Argentina's effort to recover control of the Malvinas (or Falkland) Islands from Britain, which came to symbolize wider sovereignty and anti-imperialist struggles. Another was the World Cup soccer games that were held in Barcelona that year and, as always, drew spirited nationalist responses. These were passionate contestations for Latin Americans, sufficient to result in the rapid manufacture of T-shirts in solidarity with the Malvinas and with favorite teams in the region. For a short time, the marketers I was studying in the Andean city of Huaraz had brisk sales of such items.

A third event, this one on Peruvian soil and the most pertinent to the nation's tourism, was the Miss Universe pageant held in Lima in July that year. From the vantage point of my provincial research site, I observed the responses of women and men to the vast undertaking of this impoverished nation as it readied itself for the fanfare that would put Peru's capital city fleetingly in the limelight. Among the preparations was the concealment of a squatter settlement surrounding the Coliseo Amauta where the event was to be held, and to that end a high wall was constructed so that the celebrity guests would not be disturbed by the sight of Lima's rampant poverty. While Peruvian feminists protested with chants and posters saying "No to beauty contests!" my Andean friends watched on TV and complained loudly of the wealth and deception invested in all this foolishness at a time of deep economic and political troubles in the country.[1]

As it happened, I took an overnight flight out of Lima with a number of the contestants, still in tiaras and elegant dress, and personnel from the high-profile event. As I listened to those talking in nearby seats, I was struck by the complex politics and commercialization of the global beauty pageant industry. Aside from the fraught selection of winners representing over seventy nations and the global feminist critique of rating women based largely on their looks, there was the matter of choosing venues for the pageants. For those on my flight that night, the focus was already on the location of the next pageant, which was to take place in the United States. Several men in my aisle passed the time by offering candid comparisons of hotel and restaurant options in Lima with those of other sites where their line of work would take them.

Although the pageant was no doubt scheduled to be held in Lima long before that year, it came at a time of deep unrest in the country. Was the instability in the nation a threat to the smooth functioning of the event, or might the national promoters' eager desire to show that Peru was ready to play gracious host to such an international TV attraction be part of its appeal as a venue? The answer may be both of these, the threat and the promise. The government was keen to cultivate a welcoming image for international guests at a glamorous event that they also hoped would draw renewed tourism. The effort might have been successful in drawing larger numbers of tourists to the country had there not been growing conflict, first in the Andean region and later in Lima itself.

Peru had been dealing with insurgency since 1980, when the militant movement known as Sendero Luminoso emerged in the Andean town of Chuschi and the military began its counteroffensive (Isbell 1992; Starn et al. 1995). Espousing an extreme form of Maoism, Sendero insisted on forceful and often violent means to gain adherents and confront the Peruvian state, demolishing perceived enemies of "the people" and terrorizing the country. The movement was led by philosophy professor Abimael Guzmán from the University of Huamanga in the southern Peruvian department of Ayacucho and sought to recruit rural peasants, or campesinos, to its cause. In contrast to rural-based peasant movements of the 1960s and 1970s in Peru, and to guerrilla movements in Central America during the last few decades, Sendero opposed other leftist organizations it considered reformist rather than revolutionary and notoriously assassinated key rural and urban activists. By the time that Guzmán was captured and made a public spectacle by President Alberto Fujimori in 1992, an estimated 27,000 Peruvians had been killed by Sendero and the military (Poole and Rénique 1992:xi). Although the conflict diminished, it did not end.

When the government of President Alejandro Toledo released the findings of the Truth and Reconciliation Commission in 2003, it was calculated that the various factions responsible for killings, torture, and disappearances between 1980 and 2000 produced 69,280 deaths—concentrated in southern Peru but located throughout wide regions of the nation.[2] As recently as 2008, the Council on Hemispheric Affairs reported new evidence of political kidnappings and murders and suggested that Sendero Luminoso might be reorganizing cadres and making a comeback.[3]

Travel and Tourism in Peru

Early travelers to Peru included the prominent nineteenth-century European scientist-explorers Alexander von Humboldt and Charles Darwin, among other intellectuals and adventurers. By the first half of the twentieth century more travelers began making their way to the country, and in 1952, a young Ernesto "Che" Guevara journeyed through Peru as part of his now-famous motorcycle tour. The 1960s and 1970s saw the rising popularity of more mainstream travel to the southern Peruvian Andes, particularly to Cuzco and Machu Picchu. Tourism had become a mainstay of the Peruvian economy before it fell off sharply in the 1980s during the grim period when Sendero and the military terrified rural and urban citizens and anyone who was caught in the cross-fire. Not until tensions in Peru eased in the mid-1990s, a few years after the government capture of the rebel leadership, did travelers return once again. Some familiar strands of tourism reemerged: heritage tourism, focused on archaeological sites and museums (Silverman 2002); spiritual or New Age tourism, notably around Cuzco and Machu Picchu (Michael Hill 2007, 2008); and adventure tourism and Andean mountaineering, especially in southern Peru (Ypeij and Zoomers 2006) and in the Callejón de Huaylas (Huaylas Valley) in the north-central sierra, my main field site.[4]

Cultural tourism had manifested before the appearance of Sendero in the form of travelers' interest in the country's diverse peoples and popular arts, music, and dance; during my trips to Peru from 1977 into the 1980s, I frequently encountered tourist literature that emphasized folkways and local cultural forms. But this was notably absent from tourism promotion in the 1990s. A *New York Times* article on travel to Cuzco noted that one of the first initiatives of President Fujimori was to lend support to a campaign for a "safe Peru" and a marketing strategy that would "divorce destination from location," emphasizing the historic city and Andean region rather than the troubled nation and its people (Brooke 1990). This was designed to turn attention away from the recent killing of several tourists and the frequent bombings in Lima. One visitor was quoted as saying, "The Shining Path. . . . What's that? A religious movement?"— which would have been music to the ears of tourism promoters.[5]

Anthropologist Jane Henrici (1997) drew on promotional materials of PromPerú, the government Commission for the Promotion of Peru, to make a salient point regarding how fraught tourism was during the years immediately following the quelling of unrest in Peru. She shows that as a consequence of sensitivity around safe travel in the country there was a shift away from cultural tourism and interface with local artisans, and a turn toward craft manufacture for export. She noted the profound impact of social and political unrest in the country that extended to its tourism industry from the 1980s and into the 1990s. The evidence suggested that even until later in the 1990s, cultural imagery evoking life in the sierra remained risky insofar as potential travelers might associate images of indigenous Andean people and culture with violence in the country.

I use this point of departure to argue that over the next decade cultural tourism once again became a calling card for economic development in the country. Indeed, the number of tourists to Peru rose from just 217,000 in 1992, the year when President Fujimori gained fame for the capture of Sendero leader Abimael Guzmán, to over a million in 2001 (Baud et al. 2006:12). As the country looked to tourism as an engine for development, PromPerú judged in 1999 that Peruvian "identities and unique qualities are our principal good for the future" (ibid.:22, my translation). A significant advance was made in the growth of community-based tourism, a model premised on the assumption that for sustainable development to occur, local populations must be involved in the conceptualization and operation of tourism. Two notable works, Elayne Zorn's (2004) and Jorge Gascón's (2005) book-length studies of community-based tourism on islands in Lake Titicaca, trace the development—albeit difficult, with setbacks among campesino and mestizo (rural and town) competitors—of local initiatives that met success. Over time, some of these efforts have faltered as communities have sought not only to be participants but to retain control over their tourism initiatives (Ypeij and Zorn 2007). Later in this chapter, I discuss other local-level efforts to engage tourists in a cultural exchange and specifically consider what the parties to the tourism encounter—tourists and toured—take away from the exchange in a racialized postcolonial and postconflict context.

If Fujimori (before his shameful departure from the presidency) saw tourism as an engine for development, President Alejandro Toledo (2000–2006) saw an opportunity to gain international attention at a time when his approval rating was at an all-time low. In 2004, through his government's initiative with PromPerú, Toledo collaborated with his wife, anthropologist Eliane Karp, and a U.S. journalist to produce a documentary on tourism in Peru. As Victor Vich (2007) describes, in Toledo's *Royal Tour* he performed the role of the country's "first president descended from the Incas," wearing traditional ceremonial dress and adopting an exotic, mystical demeanor to fit the global imaginary of the Inca past. The resulting ahistorical and depoliticized representation of key sites of heritage, adventure, and cultural tourism did nothing to enhance his own reputation but may well have drawn more visitors to "the land of the Incas," as the show aired on the Discovery and Travel channels. Vich considers the powerful part the production might have on the global fashioning of Peru, or he aptly puts it, "evacuating history, selling the nation" (322).

My research in highland Peru dates back three decades (Babb 1985, 1998, 2008), and I made return trips in 2006 and 2007 to examine more closely how the nation is remaking itself through tourism development in the period following the violence. Having argued that cultural tourism and the marketing of so-called authentic and traditional Andean people and culture are on the rise, I consider two other important travel destinations before turning to the Callejón de Huaylas. There, I offer the example of experiential tourism in the community of Vicos, made famous in the 1950s and 1960s when the Cornell-Peru project leased the Hacienda Vicos with the objective of transferring power to the local people and modernizing culture and the economy (Dobyns et al. 1971; Stein 2003). Ironically, today the community plays host to tourists seeking to participate in the everyday lives of "traditional Indians." Although the region has been deeply affected by dramatic change in recent decades, we will see that tourists are most impressed by the apparent timelessness and "authenticity" of their experience in the community.

Sites of Andean Tourism

Tourism in two locations in highland Peru provides a contrast with that in the Callejón de Huaylas, the main focus of my research. Taken together, the three sites offer support for my argument that today we find not only deeply rooted cultural history but present-day cultural life on the tourist circuit—in this case, a circuit that I myself made to obtain a fuller grasp of tourism's return a decade after the decline of violence in the country. The first, Cuzco and the nearby megasite of Machu Picchu, draws the greatest number of tourists in the country, averaging about two thousand every day. The second, Ayacucho, receives only a small fraction of the number who travel to Cuzco, about ten to fifteen daily, but like many parts of the country it is counting on tourism development to boost the economy. Most significantly to this work, tourism in the Cuzco region is steeped in reverence for its cultural heritage, encompassing archaeological sites, architecture, and festivals, while tourism in Ayacucho recognizes a rich archaeological past and impressive churches but seeks to conceal its recent history of violence.

Cuzco is the tourist destination favored by some 80 percent of those traveling to Peru. The Inca city and the spectacular Machu Picchu a few hours away by rail bring a broad range of tourists, from the mainstream to high end, from backpackers hiking the Inca Trail to those opting for the luxurious Hiram Bingham Train (named for the Yale University "discoverer" of the archaeological site). When I traveled to Cuzco in June 2007, I timed the trip to avoid the enormous crowds that would gather for the annual Inti Raymi Festival of the Sun, but even the week before, traffic in the city was slowed by constant processions and events leading up to the main festivities. In three trips to Cuzco over the

Selling to tourists as they board a train to Machu Picchu

decades, I have observed the steady climb in number of tourists, cost of travel by train, and admission to Machu Picchu. My first visit, in 1984, was at time of low tourism due to the political conflict in Peru, particularly in the southern region; by the time of my second trip in 1997, tourism was returning and tour operators were optimistic. Ten years later, like many others I was shocked by how difficult it was to obtain train tickets and by the inflated fares (about 130 dollars round-trip from Cuzco)—and then by the high rates charged by hotels near the site (running into the hundreds of dollars per night) and by what guides were charging for a two-hour tour (about 40 dollars).

The appeal of Cuzco is far more than its status as the gateway to Machu Picchu, as it offers impressive Inca walls in its own right along with an array of hotels, restaurants, shops, and other cultural venues. Van den Berghe and Flores Ochoa (2000) argue that ethnic tourism and *incanismo*, "reverence for the Inca past and for all aspects of indigenous culture," account for much of the appeal; yet they acknowledge that the local urban elites and tourists who often hold such views frequently overlook or even disdain the impoverished people who populate the area today. Cadena (2000) has also made the point that as urban "indigenous mestizos" and foreigners have appropriated Inca cultural history as their own, contemporary Quechua-speaking Andeans have been "de-Indianized" as a consequence. During the last decade or so, this nostalgia for an idealized past as written onto the present can serve to conceal the realities of recent violence and current underdevelopment. Thus, cultural heritage has been marketed by those savvy enough to see the potential it has for branding the city and attracting tourism dollars. That many are willing to pay a premium for luxury as they travel to the area has not escaped their notice.

Michael Hill (2007) has shown that in the present context of neoliberal development, Cuzco figures as an ideal location for the promotion of spiritual tourism, not only by the tourism industry in this part of Peru but at the national level by PromPerú. Thus, the Cuzco brand is introduced through the advertising slogan "Pack Your Six Senses," promising the delivery of authentic Andean culture and religious practice in a way that is appealing to twenty-first-century travelers. Much of the effort to attract ever-greater tourism to the area plays on the desires of travelers to acquire and consume the presumed esoteric knowledge of the Incas, stemming from ancient tradition, yet all as part of a modernization and development scheme (438).

The relatively high cost of travel to Cuzco and Machu Picchu is no doubt the result of high demand, which in turn must be explained both by virtue of the area's historical importance and breathtaking beauty and by the prodigious marketing of Machu Picchu's cultural and spiritual significance. The recent campaign to promote spiritual tourism uses images to convey a New Age mystical appeal.[6] On the day I spent at the site, I saw worshipful tourists with their hands poised over the stone altar of the Temple of the Sun, in an effort to absorb its energy, and others who were meditating or using incense to enhance their experience. As Hill (2008:252) has noted, the New Age Andean movement often employs essentialized and racialized notions of Quechua speakers' cultural history, and even if the local, indigenous population stands to benefit from the growth of this tourism, the exchange remains an unequal one insofar as foreigners and nonindigenous Peruvians control more of the industry's resources.

As visitors completed their pilgrimage to the crowded site and prepared to leave, they were encouraged to approach several computers and vote online in the (profit-motivated) international competition to select the "New Seven Wonders of the World." Indeed, on my final day in Peru it was announced that Machu Picchu was among those picked as representing "our common heritage." Even though it is often hard to know what will attract tourists or keep them away

Spiritual tourism at Machu Picchu's Temple of the Sun

(during research in Peru in 2006, I heard that tourism was down because people wanted to stay home to watch World Cup soccer), it is likely that the additional attention to the icon of Peru's proud heritage, already recognized officially as a UNESCO World Heritage Site, will bring still greater numbers to Cuzco and Machu Picchu. It is also more than likely that the increasing commodification of the site will contribute to its "Disneyfication," presenting past and present in Peru as packaged brands for global consumption (Cortés 2007:303).[7]

Peru has of course long depended on its world-famous archaeological sites to draw visitors, but Helaine Silverman shows that in recent times the country's archaeological past has been "converted into a vast tourist project, contradictory, negotiated, and contested relationships are played out in a constantly changing drama, with ruins, indigenous people, ordinary city residents, foreign tourists, the Peruvian government, and the private sector as the actors" (2002:881). She makes the important point that we must examine local contexts and entrepreneurship and not simply the role of nationalism if we are to understand these developments. Elsewhere, she goes on to discuss the deployment and valorization of the archaeological past and of "indigenized localisms and regionalisms" for specific political purposes, such as turning attention from the 1997 Peruvian hostage crisis,[8] or economic ones, as when President Toledo advocated "selling" the greatness of Peru's history "so that three million tourists arrive by 2006" (Silverman 2005:153). And, again, renewing interest in the distant past helps obscure the recent violence and contributes to the safe image that Peruvians seek to present in order to draw tourism in the postconflict period.

As Cuzco and Machu Picchu have loomed large as icons of Peruvian national identity, they have also appealed to travelers eager to engage with present-day indigenous peoples. At times tourists appear to be most intent on gazing upon the "living past," encountering cultural heritage on contemporary display. To preserve the romance of this imagined past in the present, historic centers like Cuzco (and, for example, Quito, Antigua, San Cristóbal de las Casas, and Old Havana) may be "sanitized and stripped of all disturbing signs of crime, poverty or inequality, including the people who symbolize these things" (Baud and Ypeij 2009:11). Nevertheless, and as we find in the case studies presented in this book, tourism can be a means by which marginalized groups seek to become more prominent actors in the wider society. Contestations over the rights to space, cultural representation, and livelihood are commonplace in transitional societies that are self-consciously remaking themselves through strategies of tourism development.

Areas of the country that benefit from the spillover of tourism in Cuzco include parts of southern Peru that are well linked by roads and direct air service; this favors Puno and Arequipa in particular and, to a far lesser degree, Ayacucho, for those intrepid travelers willing to take a long and nerve-wracking bus ride. My decision to travel from Cuzco to Ayacucho was hardly related to ease of travel, as there were no direct flights and I needed to return to Lima and fly out again the next day. Nevertheless, I wanted to visit the area most affected by conflict and violence in the 1980s and 1990s, and Ayacucho was the center from which Sendero Luminoso emerged. No doubt to divert attention from more troubling images of the departmental capital, Ayacucho is described in tour books and by government promoters as a picturesque city of many churches—in Cuzco, nearly all who heard I was going there volunteered slightly exaggerated numbers of churches that I would find.

When I had visited the offices of PromPerú in Lima the year before, I was shown some new TV spots, including one that evoked Ayacucho's religious orientation and mystery, and I was eager to see how far the area had come in capturing a part of the tourist market. The answer, I discovered, was not very far. As residents of one of the most underdeveloped regions of the country, people in Ayacucho were quick to complain that since the time when violence and terror gripped the area, the government had done little to rectify the conditions that originally sparked unrest. Roads in the largely rural, agricultural area remained poor, and the region had been bypassed by economic development initiatives. While local efforts were made to be ready for a growth in tourism, the average number of tourists arriving in Ayacucho remained very low. Most foreigners in the city were volunteers, like the medical mission staying at my hotel and a group of young people working with the New York City–based organization Cross-Cultural Solutions. A Vanderbilt University archaeological field school was also based there. Yet it was nearly impossible to find conventional tourists.

The presence of even a few tourists may be notable in light of the recent history of violence in the area. Overcoming a negative image and the infrastructural problems of transport were obstacles that stood in the way of tourism development. Those who made their way to the area were generally attracted by the less-trodden character of the city, the charm of its churches, and the nearby Wari archaeological site that was a standard tour option provided by tourism offices. The pace was slower than in most tourism destinations, and the emphasis was on becoming acquainted with long-established cultural and historical traditions in the region. When I found tourists, talked with them, and gave them questionnaires, I was interested to learn what they knew of the recent history in the region, specifically of Sendero Luminoso. In general, their slight knowledge of the conflict and turbulence was based on the guidebooks they had with them (similar to what I had found in Nicaragua).

It was only because I entered every one of the handful of tourism offices I came across walking around the city that I happened to learn of a place to visit that had not yet made its way into most travel guides. The Museo de la Memoria (Memory Museum) was the result of the efforts of members of ANFASEP (Asociación Nacional de Familiares de Secuestrados, Detenidos y Desaparecidos del Perú—National Association of Families of Abducted, Arrested and Disappeared of Peru). This group of (mainly) women had come together in 1983, and two years later began operating a *comedor* (communal dining hall) for orphans who had lost their parents in the violence. The group protested publicly, demanding truth, justice, and reparation. Finally, with the release of the report of the Truth and Reconciliation Commission, the group inaugurated a museum two years later, in 2005, to memorialize those who were lost, "para que no se repita" (so that it is not repeated). As the orphans grew up, they formed a youth group that is active in giving tours and reaching out to others in the community. A German nongovernmental organization (NGO) was instrumental in launching the project, assisting the Quechua-speaking members to have attractive booklets available in several languages and to tell their story and publicize the program (DED 2005).

The wider community has only slowly accepted the work of ANFASEP, as many citizens of Ayacucho have clung to the notion that the members are mothers of fallen "terrorists" rather than of those unjustly targeted by Sendero or the military. When I asked those staffing the Memory Museum whether their visitors included more tourists or locals, I was told tourists, yet it became evident to me that tourists would be hard pressed to find their way to the museum. Only one tour office seemed to have brochures on display and available for tourists, and my efforts to inquire about whether the museum was part of the advertised city tour met surprised reactions. A tour operator who was highly recommended by several travel books and with whom I took tours of the city and of the Wari site, even knowing of my research, exclaimed, "But it's so violent!" Despite my insistence on my serious interest in getting to the museum, he would only drive by on the way to visit other museums and artisan workshops. He took my group to visit the Pampa de Ayacucho, the battleground outside the city where South America's last battle for independence was fought in 1824, but

A *retablo* at Ayacucho's Memory Museum showing scenes of violence and of the Truth and Reconciliation Commission

I needed to make my own way to the Memory Museum, where the more recent and sorrowful conflict was commemorated.[9]

The museum is an impressive cultural resource in the city, though it does not draw much attention. Located in a quiet part of town, the Memory Museum occupies the top floor of a three-story building that also houses ANFASEP's offices, a small store selling commemorative items made by its members, and a comedor. On the exterior walls, a large and vivid mural by local artist Wari Zárate viscerally depicts those slain in the violence and the organizing efforts of women in the aftermath. Inside the museum are informative and evocative displays, photographs, and personal effects of those lost to the violence. Visitors first encounter a striking five-tiered *retablo* (reliquary box) with scenes of conflict and of the Truth and Reconciliation Commission. Guides show them other bold and haunting artistic works featuring ceramics and other media, a rare departure from the artesanía that is ubiquitous in local markets. The exhibition relates the history of the conflict of Sendero and the military and of those detained and disappeared, including a re-created torture site and exhumation of mass graves in the region. The photographs and testimonies emphasize ANFASEP members and their families, which has made the museum somewhat controversial in the community. This explains in part why the museum goes largely unrecognized by Ayacuchanos and why it is shielded from the tourist gaze, despite its riveting physical presence.[10]

While the abundant churches were on prominent display and the deep cultural history represented in archaeological sites and museums in the region was celebrated, there appeared to be a level of fear that more knowledge of the recent violence would scare away tourism. Given the difficulty that Ayacucho has had in attracting even a modest number of tourists beyond Semana Santa (Holy Week), renowned in Peru and a draw for tourists as well as for migrants from the coast who return to visit family, it is not surprising if many residents and tour operators wish to forget the troubled past and emphasize what is more benign in the region.

There is a premium on calm and peaceful Ayacucho now—in fact, in Cuzco a woman selling textiles had told me not to worry, "There's nothing happening there now." Although this dictum might be anathema to most tourist destinations, it is what many travelers to Ayacucho may prefer to hear. It will likely take time before the Memory Museum has a place as a commemorative site on the tourist circuit—and as a destination for domestic pilgrimages. I anticipate, however, that if roads leading to Ayacucho are improved, foreign and national tourists will one day desire to come and learn more about the region's (and the nation's) unsettling past. This would parallel the recent valorization of heritage and memorial sites in other postconflict and postrevolutionary nations where, with the passage of time, tourism industries have begun to appreciate their historical significance as well as their market potential (Babb 2005; Bilbija and Payne 2011).[11]

Nature, Culture, and Experiential Tourism in the Callejón de Huaylas

If Cuzco calls mightily on its Inca heritage and Ayacucho seeks refuge from a bitter recent past by calling on Wari culture and abundant churches, the Callejón de Huaylas in the department of Ancash might be said to live more in the moment and to embrace present-day culture, people, and nature. Best known for its stunning mountain ranges, the Cordillera Blanca and Cordillera Negra, the area draws climbers and adventure tourists of many descriptions. The natural environment is celebrated as a leading attraction, but culture is a draw as well, as visitors tour the towns throughout the valley and its uplands. My past experience in the department capital of Huaraz was spent in large measure in the city marketplaces, where cultural encounter and sociality are paramount. Tourists are attracted to marketplaces for just this reason, because they are lively gathering places, contact zones for all manner of people who come to buy and sell. License is given to outsiders who wish to engage in the social exchanges, if only through nonverbal communication, which marketers are willing to indulge in that public domain. Some of my earliest observations about tourism were from the vantage point of the marketplace.

Tourism in the Callejón de Huaylas is highly accessible, as there is a good road from Lima and comfortable buses make the trip to the city of Huaraz in about seven hours. Recently, air service from Lima has added to the possibilities for travel there. The low cost and ease of travel by land have made this area extremely popular with domestic tourists, many coming from Lima for weekend trips or for longer trekking vacations in the Cordillera Blanca—where they join international tourists coming largely from Canada and Europe. The region is known principally as a center for adventure tourism (trekking, kayaking, mountain biking, and camping) and for enjoying the crisp mountain air and beautiful natural environment. A host of businesses in Huaraz serves the needs of those who have come for mountain trekking and other sports, providing equipment, maps, and guides for hire. Huaraz, long my field research site, is often viewed as a way station—fairly unattractive, rebuilt in haphazard fashion after a massive earthquake in 1970 destroyed most of the town.[12] Nonetheless, Huaraz offers creature comforts and a sufficient number of good restaurants and cafés to appeal to travelers whose main destinations will take them outside the urban center.

As a point of departure to other parts of the Callejón, Huaraz's downtown is dotted with tourism offices offering three standard day trips: to nearby Lake Llanganuco, to the Pastoruri glacier, and slightly farther away, to the important pre-Inca site Chavín de Huantar. I have made trips to all three destinations, which bring both domestic and international travelers lured by the low cost and fairly well-run tourism services. For those who are not on mountaineering trips and who have the time, these day trips often frame and define their visits. A small office of iPeru, a division of PromPerú near the Plaza de Armas, provides information and guidance to tourists and participates in festivals geared toward enhancing tourism. Those staying longer in the city sometimes visit the local archaeology museum and lithic garden, hike a short distance to the ruins of Wilcawaín, or take a twenty-minute ride to the thermal baths. Whereas my past research interests kept me closely tied to life in the city, during my last two trips I joined those making use of travel services and had the opportunity to observe, interview, give out questionnaires, and accompany tour operators and tourists. The tourism venues mentioned so far are physical settings, a lake, glacier, and archaeological site, and not principally areas in which to meet Andeans, who are more frequently part of the scenery on package tours.

When travelers do meet local residents along the way on these day tours, it is generally in encounters staged for tourism. Artisans sit along streets in towns of the Callejón with crafts spread in front of them, awaiting tourist vans and buses for fleeting sales, before tourists move on to their next destination in the valley. Locals make and sell homemade ice cream and other sweet confections that tourists desire during day trips to Llanganuco. Women and children pose in traditional dress with llamas at scenic points along roads where travelers will stop to take their pictures and leave them tips on the way to Pastoruri. There are, surprisingly enough, campesinos ready to carry weary gringos on their backs up the glacier when they cannot make it on their own steam—an intimate service that painfully evokes the colonialist past. Opportunities to get to know local people rarely go beyond a simple exchange of greetings and a negotiation to take a photo or two.[13]

Nevertheless, tourists may come away from these interactions with quickly formed impressions of Andean character and identity. Notions of unchanging lives are reinforced by perceptions of language, dress, religious practice, and cultural traditions. Such snapshot images—often decontextualized and based on scant knowledge—can add up to deep and lasting opinions about places visited and people met. Of course, impressions are generally formed well in advance of actual encounters through reading guidebooks and promotional literature, talking with other travelers, and so on. The desire to have a more profound experience with local people, and especially those viewed as rural, indigenous, or peasant people, has led to a growing market in community-based and experiential tourism—forms of cultural tourism that are gaining ground.

I turn now to an exemplary case of cultural tourism or, as it is often called in Peru, *turismo vivencial* (experiential tourism) in the region. The host community in question, Vicos, is introduced here and discussed further in Chapter 6.[14] According to one source, there are currently over forty experiential tourism projects in the country, evidence that cultural tourism and an emphasis on Andean people and culture have returned and are growing in Peru, sometimes taking new forms (Viviana Quea, personal communication). This includes areas that were marked by violence a decade or so earlier, among them the Callejón de Huaylas. People in the region are beginning to talk more than before about that difficult time; apparently, it is far enough behind them in this part of the country that they are more secure in revealing the terror they experienced. I found that this was so in at least some instances, particularly with individuals who had come to place trust in me over my years of research, but also among others I had met more recently.

The community of Vicos,[15] less than an hour from Huaraz, began to host tourists a few years ago as a development initiative supported by several NGOs: the Mountain Institute (TMI), with offices in Lima and Huaraz as well as outside Peru; Yachaqui Wayi and Urpichallay, both in the region; and Crooked Trails, a nonprofit, community-based tourism organization located in Seattle. The Vicosinos, long known for their proactive (and some outsiders say aggressive) approach to economic opportunity, came up with the idea, and with some outside assistance seven families who are spread throughout the community elected to participate. The male heads of household became *socios* (members) of the tourism project and used building materials provided by TMI to construct attractive guest lodges adjacent to their own homes. The men took part in workshops to learn the social graces of hosting tourists, while their wives, it appears, were counted on to prepare the lodging and meals for guests. My host in 2006, when I was a guest for several days, related that his family and particularly his wife were anxious about how well they could meet the expectations of foreign guests. Two young scholars who conducted research on the tourism venture in Vicos reported similar concerns. Rowenn Kalman (2005:57), an anthropology student from the United States, found that the socios feared "that foreigners would not like their food or find their customs interesting." And Guido van Es (2003:6), a researcher from the Netherlands in development studies, assisted Vicosinos in their tourism project and wrote about their difficulty in overcoming the distrust between the community and those living in the surrounding area. He suggested that this distrust could impede tourism and concluded that the best prospects for the future reside in cultural tourism and "the authentic intercultural experience Vicos offers."

The community has long been subject to interventions of foreigners as well as more powerful nationals (Stein 2003). After the arrival of the Spanish and several hundred years of servitude to mestizo hacienda owners, they had grown suspicious of newcomers who treated them as "dirty and ignorant Indians." When anthropologists from Cornell came in the early 1950s, Vicosinos remained largely unconvinced that these administrators would be different from those who exploited them in the past—even if today many Vicosinos testify that the community was set free when Allan Holmberg and Mario Vazquez, the most prominent of the applied anthropologists, came to Vicos with the Cornell-Peru Project. In the 1980s, Vicos was subjected to the aggression of Sendero in the region, and those years are remembered as a time of great suffering when several community leaders were killed (Kalman 2005:20). Given the ambivalent and disturbing interventions of the past, it is not surprising if some Vicosinos are worried that tourism might also usher in new relations of inequality.

Notwithstanding their concern, the socios and their families play the part of generous hosts to the modest number of tourists who have come to stay in Vicos, and who have by all accounts gained much from the experience. The owner of Crooked Trails estimates that since 2001 her organization has taken two to three groups, each ranging from eight to ten people, to Vicos every year (Tammy Leland, personal communication).[16] A few individuals contact TMI or Yachaqui Wayi directly in Huaraz, as I did, to make arrangements to participate in the tourism program. Two other visitors (a medical student and a graduate student, both from the United States) and I made our way to Vicos; on arrival in the community the socios, including our hosts, warmly welcomed us in the main plaza. We were then asked to step inside the Casa de los Abuelos (Grandparents' House), a small information center on the plaza that opened in 2002 at the beginning of the tourism project.

There, we were oriented to Vicosino history, economy, political organization, spiritual life, and culture. Pablo Tadeo Cilio, who serves as coordinator of the socios and divides his time between Vicos and Huaraz, gave us a tour of the center. The Cornell-Peru Project was highlighted, with photographs on display by the entry showing the Vicosinos in the 1950s with Allan Holmberg, Mario Vazquez, and others. The images and information emphasize Vicos history from the time of the hacienda, agricultural life and calendar (month-by-month work cycle), geography, political structure, education, *cosmovisión* (Andean harmony with mountain gods and nature), traditional medicine and healers (curing with guinea pigs and eggs), music, dance, fiestas, and dress. The last display suggests possibilities for activities and hikes during the visit and offers thanks to the Mountain Institute.

After this orientation, our hosts escorted us to our guest lodges. Since visitors are spread out among hosts in the community, each host family is responsible for providing the activities that the tourism program promises. Guests are asked to join in agricultural work, help prepare bread or meals, and take walks in the area; and in certain households they have opportunities to spend time with a beekeeper-host or attend special events such as a wedding (as in my case). All visits to the community are expected to include conversations about cosmovisión and local beliefs in Pachamama (Earth Mother) and the *apus* (mountain gods), to have demonstrations of traditional weaving, and to conclude with a *pachamanca*, the traditional Andean feast cooked in an underground fire pit. These practices were developed with the assistance of the NGOs mentioned earlier and conform to what both the Vicosinos and the NGOs believe will be of interest to tourists.

All these elements were included in my own visit. My host, whom I call Tomás, was known for his bread making, and we worked together, with some help from his wife, whom I call Dora, during my first morning there. When we were ready to put the small breads in the oven, he suggested that I get my camera and capture the activity for a souvenir photograph. I had some momentary difficulty with the digital camera, and he showed some disappointment—being able to share pictures with the hosts is something they value, and they also recognize the tourists' passion for taking photos home with them. Thankfully, I had the camera working in time for Tomás to stage a photo of the breads going into the oven. He then invited me to put on a hat and *pollera* (wide, gathered Andean skirt) belonging to Dora, and I accepted the hat for another photo. While the bread baked, I helped Dora and her mother with meal preparation and the couple's children played nearby. I learned that some families, including my hosts, recently had electrical power delivered to their homes, though not to their guest lodge. Therefore, the lights and radio in use by the family were not available to their guests. Although the guest lodge was set up to have water, there was none during my visit.

Tomás and the children showed considerable interest in me, but Dora used little Spanish and we spent long periods in silence, though I tried to engage in some simple conversation in Spanish (I know only a few phrases in Quechua). It was not until the evening when Tomás accompanied me to the guest lodge to build a fire and tell me about Andean beliefs and rituals that I made a greater connection with Dora. She came in and sat quietly on the floor by the doorway while Tomás and I continued talking. I was asking him about the practice of "trial marriage" in the Andes, which is understood as having a year together before a marriage becomes permanent. When he told me that this was an opportunity to see if the woman was going to be suitable, I responded half in jest that it was also a time to see if the man would be suitable—Dora erupted in knowing laughter at this, and I concluded that I was right in sensing that she understood a fair amount of Spanish even if she used little.

During my second day in Vicos, much of our time was spent at a church wedding and the party that followed for a Vicosino groom and his bride from a neighboring community. The general expectation seemed to be that I would blend in and be part of the event, learning to eat politely with my hands, and so on. There were humorous moments, as when the bench I sat on tipped over and left me sprawled on the ground, to the amusement of the Vicosinos. The most challenging for me, however, was the long distances we walked in the community, up and down at an altitude of around twelve thousand feet, high enough that I became very short of breath.

I was relieved on the third day to spend time around the lodge observing the elaborate preparations for a pachamanca, carried out by Tomás and the other socios of the tourism project who came over to join him. The men had replaced their everyday clothes, western dress, with *traje*, the traditional homespun black wool pants and vest, along with sandals and hats, for the occasion. They checked to see if the earth oven was hot enough, and when it was time to put the food on to cook, they layered potatoes and yucca with beef and chicken wrapped in banana leaves and put beans on top of the oven where they would not burn. Finally, they placed light branches with leaves, plastic sheets, and dirt all around the oven. While we waited for the food to cook, the men invited me to ask them questions, and I was glad to have the chance to inquire about changes in Vicos, as well as their goals and preoccupations relating to the tourism project. Several of them expressed their concern about natural resources, especially access to water in the community; about tourism, they seemed more confident of a positive outcome that would benefit socios and the community.

About forty-five minutes later, the food was ready to be served. The women came on the scene, placing great piles of food in bowls and passing them around. *Chicha*, maize beer, was offered as the customary Andean drink, and we all fell silent as we enjoyed the abundant food. Later, after the pachamanca and a display of weaving, all the men gathered around to make short speeches about the significance of my visit to them. I was honored and could well imagine how

Women serving food that men have prepared for a pachamanca in Vicos

moving this would be to other guests, especially those unaccustomed to Andean hospitality.[17] After that, we quickly carried out the business of my making payment for my visit; then several of the men accompanied me to the main road to wait for transportation back to Huaraz.

When I returned to Vicos in 2007, I spoke with others who had just participated as guests of the community. As a project in experiential, or cultural, tourism, this one is characterized by its authentic aspect, set in a community that has retained many cultural traditions and livelihood practices and does not appear to have become jaded by hordes of outsiders (even if it has a long history of intervention). It is also a fairly rustic experience, offering guests simple meals and lodging, often with no running water or electricity, at the modest cost of about twenty-five dollars per day, everything included (even a 10 percent contribution to the Vicos community). While there was general agreement among the visitors that the hosts had a full agenda they wished to adhere to, urging guests to move from one activity to the next, and that they expected tourists to be duly prepared with cameras ready, there was little complaint that authenticity was "staged" (MacCannell 1999). For their part, the socios expressed that they were simply offering what was most important in their cultural repertoire. Although there may have been a performative aspect to this experiential tourism, with guests urged to "try on" local identities in the form of costume, diet, and worklife, the tourists agreed to "play along," making this a two-way exchange. For the Vicosinos, despite their initial worries, host families expect that tourism may not only acquaint guests with their traditions and lives but will raise the self-esteem and broaden the horizons of their own children, who often have limited experience beyond the community. Thus, they hope for more than the economic success of the tourism project so that a certain cultural capital in the form of exposure to new opportunities may benefit them in the long term.[18]

Such an intercultural exchange is of course the objective of experiential tourism. A writer in the Huaraz publication entitled *Desarrollo, cultura y turismo desde la Peripheria* (*Development, Culture, and Tourism from the Periphery*), which since 2005 has come out about three times each year in bilingual Spanish-English format, has this to say: "Turismo vivencial comes from ecotourism and cultural tourism. We can define it simply as the sharing of a different lifestyle . . . depending less on the material world." The author goes on to recognize this kind of tourism as part of "that network of meanings we call 'culture'" and cautions that relations of power may infuse encounters with the Other. He concludes that "thoughtful analysis of these generated power relations must be part of vivencial tourism as it can create a space for intercultural understanding" (Aquino 2005:21). Engaged scholarship must also take into account, as Hill (2008:442) expresses well regarding Andean race relations, that "tourist contexts are powerful arenas in which identities and bodies become marked and differentiated" through practices of consumption.

The promotional brochure for Experiential Tourism in Vicos (TMI n.d.) in both Spanish and English versions describes the community's project, called Cuyaquihuayi, as "a direct experience with families that live in the Andean mountains." The community of around six thousand residents has attracted young travelers and students, one of whom is quoted in the brochure: "To get acquainted with places where people once lived in ancient civilizations and to share a few days of their daily lives, all this will help you understand this part of the world's richness which one never imagined existed far away from the cities." Without question, the project has enjoyed success in introducing visitors to a very different way of life, but there is evidence that tourists feel they are "seeing back in time" when they travel to Vicos, potentially coming away with a rather static view of a place that has in fact experienced great change.[19] To avoid such a view, tourists might be well advised to read from the recently published material from the Vicos oral history project, undertaken by TMI and Urpichallay in collaboration with Cornell University, which offers diverse perspectives on the community's past. Florencia Zapata, who gathered the oral history, emphasizes the "plurality of voices" in the Vicosinos' collective project of remembering and interpreting their past and the enormous changes during their lifetimes (Comunidad Campesina de Vicos 2005:7).

The Andean Tourism Encounter—
Embracing Cultural Difference?

It is evident that tourism is reviving in Peru and that cultural tourism in particular has made a comeback. Many questions remain unanswered, however, as the tourism encounter may be mirroring the "development encounter" of past decades in seeking to bring about "modernization" in the global South—but even more, to benefit local elites and the global North (Escobar 1995). In Vicos, tourism may pick up where the Cornell-Peru Project left off, introducing modern ideas and desires to Vicosinos even as tourists are most impressed by the community's cultural traditions and lifestyles (Dobyns et al. 1971; Babb 1985, 1999; Stein 2003; Avila Molero 2005:420–422; Vicos, a Virtual Tour 2006). Thus, in contrast to Cuba and Nicaragua, where tourism may be viewed as taking up where social revolution left off, in Peru we might say that tourism has returned as part of a revalorization of traditional culture on the one hand and of a broader modernization project on the other. In all these cases, it must be noted, racial and other minorities continue to face social exclusion despite such revalorization.[20]

Will tourism development in Peru occasion the sort of refashioning of the past and consolidating of present inequalities that have been well documented by scholars critical of tourism as "a form of imperialism" (Nash 1989) and of "the tourist gaze" (Urry 1990; Pratt 1992; Hanna and Del Casino 2003; Van den Berghe 1994; Bruner 2005)? Will Peruvian tourism begin to incorporate the recent period of violence in its narratives, or will historical tourism deal only with conflict and rebellion of the safer, more distant past in order to sanitize the present? Will cultural tourism, promoted as offering an honest and open exchange between hosts and visitors, provide a space for discussion of the recent past and problematic present, or will the parties to the cultural tourism exchange collaborate in a shared, nostalgic fiction of timelessness and unchanging tradition among "authentic" indigenous Peruvians? Finally, will community-based tourism like that in Vicos have a chance of succeeding, or will it falter for lack of adequate support or because of competition in an increasingly crowded field?

Some critical voices in tourism studies have commented with interest on the postmodern turn in the global travel industry, wherein more cynical tourists question performances and identities that are offered up on the commodified tourism market (Castañeda 1996; Rojek and Urry 1997; Little 2004).[21] In some cases, the toured are also acknowledging the staged aspect of authentic cultural production and exchange. This rather jaded, if good-humored, attitude could be seen during a procession in the streets of Cuzco. In the busy week leading up to Inti Raymi, it was not clear whether the procession was intended more for locals or tourists, but my traveling companions were amused to see its imaginative lineup of floats and themes. A gigantic papier-mâché, bare-chested Pachamama passed by with her attendants dressed as dancing meats and vegetables, including the national dish of guinea pig and potatoes. Then, viewers on the sidelines were treated to a float that included performers dressed as prototypical trekker tourists carrying backpacks and cameras. These "tourists" focused their cameras on both the larger masquerade and the spectators, who included foreign visitors, locals, and officials seated in a reviewing stand in front of the city's baroque cathedral (Mary Jo Arnoldi, personal communication). Turning the gaze around from tourists to locals acting as tourists was a clever way of acknowledging Cuzco's ambivalent relationship to the hordes of visitors who fill its streets on an annual basis.

A cartoon strip entitled "Backpacking Pat," which ran for several issues in 2005 in the back pages of the Huaraz magazine *Peripheria*, seemed to have a similar friendly posttourist sensibility. The Pat of the title was a bearded young man, clearly a gringo, who was decked out in heavy trekking gear for his first trip to Huaraz. The strip's story lines include tips for the new arrival, with serious-minded advice on how to get to know and respect the environment as well as lighter-toned hints on where to dine on the best-prepared guinea pig or to find late-night bars. Humorous drawings of young tourists in shared quarters of a hostel and on the dance floor of a club show the hapless Pat fumbling his way through city and countryside in the Callejón de Huaylas (Durante 2005). This sort of playful parody of gringo ways by a Peruvian cartoonist suggests that tourism in the region may have entered a new phase. Will savvy tourists be culturally and environmentally conscious and still express ironic pleasure in discovering themselves in unlikely places? Or will they take an easier path to knowing the Other only as bearer of tradition, against which their own modernity is measured?

We may wonder whether those who make their way to Vicos as experiential tourists will make sense of persistent tradition alongside desires for electricity and water, new technologies, digital photos, cell phones, and other consumer goods that are in ample evidence today in the community. Perhaps some will have the sort of experience related by a young woman from the United States, who wrote to me with both insight and nostalgia about her most memorable time in Peru a few years ago. She recalled that it was after a day of hiking outside of Vicos, "dancing in a little saloon (no plumbing, only endless bottles of imitation Coca Cola and a few bottles of beer) . . . with three Vicosinos (guys) . . . and other gringos from Vicos. I don't speak any Quechua and only survival Spanish, and they didn't speak English, so when another gringa and I ran into them at this saloon . . . we gave up on conversation and decided to just dance. All the people passing by were baffled by these two gringas dancing with the Indians."

On my last day in Huaraz in 2007, at the popular gringo hangout California Café I was surprised to find a small stack of professional business cards bearing contact information for Pablo Tadeo Cilio, the Vicosino socio of the tourism project who works most closely with the Huaraz NGO Yachaqui Wayi. Offering services in turismo vivencial as well as animal husbandry and carpentry, he included on the cards his cell phone number and e-mail address. A week after I returned home, I received an unanticipated e-mail greeting from Pablo offering to be of further service to me or others who might wish to visit Vicos. In this case, a Vicosino is embracing modern means to attract visitors to experience traditional Andean life in his community.

In the end, the joke may be on those of us who are surprised by such developments in Andean communities, where culture and identity have long been in flux and have taken innovative and hybrid forms. Some knockoff Barbie dolls I found on the tourist market in the Callejón de Huaylas, some dressed as *cholas* (between the status of indigenous and mestizo) with long braided hair and bright-colored hand-knit outfits (*de pollera*, referring to their full skirts) and others as their city cousins in urban attire (*de Lima*), are a final example of the unexpected offerings available to tourists who seek out the culturally ambivalent, ironic, or simply funky.[22] Whether the same tourists will notice or desire the still harder-to-find T-shirts and tapestries depicting past and present social injustice and violence in Peru is another matter.

Whereas tourism in Cuba and Nicaragua may be built on the scaffolding left by social revolution, we have seen that in Peru tourism builds on past dreams of modernization and hopes of recovery from violent memory and economic need. Next I turn to Chiapas, Mexico, to consider a case of tourism development in a setting that, far from concealing a recent and turbulent past, presents visitors with ample opportunity to sample its more inspiring and romantic aspects.

4

Remembering the Revolution

Indigenous Culture and Zapatista Tourism

The development of Mexico's tourist industry offers an entry point into understanding the role that economic development played during the years of evolutionary reconstruction and state building.
—**Dina Berger,** *The Development of Mexico's Tourism Industry*

IN THE WAKE OF THE MEXICAN REVOLUTION OF 1910–1920, tourism made a grand appearance as part of a nation-building project. This chapter examines the early development of tourism at the national level before turning to consider the growth of tourism in the southern Mexican state of Chiapas in more recent times. I trace the gradual return of tourism to Chiapas after the Zapatista uprising in 1994 in order to suggest that the romantic appeal of an indigenous revolutionary movement has helped to drive both solidarity and mainstream travel in the region. I present ethnographic material from my research in Chiapas to show that the colonial town of San Cristóbal de las Casas is at the center of an expansion of cultural tourism that draws attention to indigenous peoples and traditions as well as to the contemporary context of revolutionary practices and politics. Finally, I discuss the marketing of Zapatismo, as well as of "authentic" indigenous culture, and conclude with an account of a Lacandón jungle tour.

Historian Dina Berger (2006) has written of the development of Mexico's tourism industry from the 1920s through the 1940s. She argues that revolutionary elites were able to market the image of revolutionary Mexico and make it compatible both with the goals of the revolution and with desires for "good neighborliness" with the United States. Indeed, Mexico's neighbor to the north has been the main source of its tourists, so creating an image of a modernizing and safe, yet exotic, destination within easy reach of U.S. travelers was essential to building its industry. The rise of tourism during the first half of the twentieth century was supported by efforts to refashion the Mexican nation as a place in which diverse desires might be satisfied—where tourists could enjoy "pyramids by day, martinis by night."[1] Thus, the Mexican case is exemplary of those Latin American nations that I contend have used tourism development to pick up where social revolution left off in contributing to political and economic stability and in fashioning nationhood. In Mexico, as elsewhere, "tourism was an expression of revolutionary personal advancement" (Berger 2006:3) as well as a lever for social transformation.[2]

Mexico would need to compete with Canada and Cuba, which were the main sites of U.S. tourism following World War I. Following Cuba's lead, Mexico sought to develop infrastructure and entertainment to attract tourism. Well before the Cuban revolution curbed tourism (and the United States imposed its travel blockade), the Mexican Revolution sought to pursue its objectives precisely through the advancement of the tourism industry. As we have seen in earlier chapters, this would be the aspiration of Cuba in the Special Period as well as of Nicaragua in the period following the Sandinista revolution. Mexico was a forerunner in finding that the apparent contradictions between tourism and revolutionary ideals need not be obstacles and could actually be turned to good advantage. That is, tourists might be lured by the romance of revolution, and tourism could in turn be used to promote economic development and political stability.

Despite historical differences, there are similarities between Mexico's and Cuba's early efforts to appeal to both the familiarity and the exoticism of their nations and peoples, and to both modernity and antiquity. Consider the slogans advertising travel to the two nations: "Visit Mexico—The Egypt of the Americas—A Foreign Land a Step Away" (Berger 2006:21); and "Visit Cuba. So Near and Yet So Foreign" (vintage travel poster from the 1950s). Images of historic sites and dancing "natives" mingled freely in posters and ads that played on tourists' desires for both the old and the new, offered up on the growing market.

Located in the difficult terrain of southern Mexico where there were still few paved roads, Chiapas saw only limited tourism during the 1920s and 1930s. After infrastructure and services had improved, including construction of a portion of the Pan-American Highway, tourism took off in the 1960s and 1970s. Anthropologist Pierre van den Berghe (1994) carried out a short, systematic study of tourism in San Cristóbal in 1990, building on three decades of his own travel and research there. Interviewing tourists from nineteen countries (including Mexico), he focused on "ethnic tourism," similar to cultural tourism and referring to travel that emphasizes cultural difference—particularly native peoples and places. His book provides a baseline study of tourism in the area just before the Zapatista uprising.

As Van den Berghe shows, San Cristóbal and the Chiapas region appeal to tourists who travel to somewhat out-of-the-way places and who wish to have a more authentic experience of a colonial Mexican town set in a largely indigenous part of the country. The town itself has a mainly Ladino, or mestizo, population that grew from about twenty thousand to more than one hundred thousand over his three decades of travel there. Increasingly, indigenous peoples (especially Chamulas who were expelled from their community after they converted to Protestantism) have settled in the town, giving it an unusually "picturesque" character for tourists seeking the culturally different. These visitors, whom he describes as ethnic tourists, are so intent on seeing Indians that the town itself is often just a quaint backdrop or jumping-off point for visiting surrounding communities (70).

Van den Berghe observes that "San Cristóbal had the good fortune of remaining a backwater until the 1960s and owes much of its development to being a tourist attraction" (55). By the 1970s, the town was thriving with new guesthouses and hotels, restaurants, and cafés that attracted a countercultural clientele rather than the mass tourism that was starting to head for Cancun and other Mexican resort areas. Van den Berghe emphasizes that "ethnic tourism is, by nature, a fragile commodity. . . . [It] is intrinsically self-destroying unless carefully controlled" (147). Although tourism in any area can become saturated, places that are known for their unspoiled and exotic character may be viewed as suffering disproportionately from overexposure to travelers. This concern resonates with what I have heard in Nicaragua, where tourism promoters say that the Sandinista revolution protected the country from excessive tourism development—and now they are ready to cash in on the unspoiled "product" they have to offer.[3]

Chiapas may have attracted fewer tourists from the United States than other more accessible parts of Mexico, even if the study sited here found that the largest single nationality group in the sample of 175 was 50 individuals from the United States. Canadians and Europeans numbered 108 in Van den Berghe's sample from 1990, and today there is still a substantial European presence among tourists in San Cristóbal.[4] This was so even in the postuprising period, when a reduced number of tourists were there in solidarity with the Zapatistas and as critics of the North American Free Trade Agreement (NAFTA) and globalization—many of them U.S. citizens.

The Zapatista Uprising and Tourism

On January 1, 1994, the day when NAFTA went into effect, several thousand indigenous Mayan peasants led by "Subcomandante Marcos" rose up in rebellion against the neoliberal trade agreement, briefly seizing and holding San Cristóbal and several other towns in the region.[5] The Chiapas uprising found fertile ground in one of the poorest states in Mexico, where rural people stood to lose the most in the open market of competitive trade across borders. The predominantly indigenous population believed that their marginalization would be still greater under the new terms of global trade. Military troops came in swiftly, and a cease-fire was called after twelve days, but tensions continued and the region was militarized. Two years later, the Zapatista Army of National Liberation (EZLN) and the government signed the San Andrés Accords outlining a plan to address land rights, cultural rights, and indigenous autonomy, but negotiations foundered. In a tragic incident in 1997, forty-five indigenous people, mainly women and children, were massacred by paramilitary forces (including indigenous recruits) in the community of Acteal—an investigation was stalled, and in the view of many, justice has not yet been served.

Thanks to the Internet and other media, antiglobalization activists around the world responded quickly and enthusiastically to the Zapatistas' remarkable example of grassroots rebellion. Along with journalists, many activists began traveling to Chiapas to participate in international delegations that found inspiration in and wanted to support the Zapatistas. While mainstream tourism fell off in the aftermath of the uprising, solidarity travel from the United States and around the globe grew to impressive proportions. One analyst who made two brief trips to Chiapas in 1994 to assess the effects of the rebellion on tourism commented that the violence, militarization, and human rights abuses had consequences similar to those in other areas where political violence had held sway, notably in Nicaragua and Peru in the 1980s (Pitts 1996:217). Despite the depressive effect on tourism as a key economic sector in Chiapas, Pitts noted, "Some entrepreneurs took advantage of the excitement and sold guided tours of the 'Zapatista homelands' for around US$500" (221). He went on to describe other opportunistic responses:

> War souvenirs also became popular among both journalists and war tourists. Zapatista dolls, Mexican Army dolls, black ski masks, T-shirts, lighters, pens and other conflict ephemera could be purchased at often exorbitant amounts. The sale of such items was particularly meaningful to local market and street

vendors. . . . Not only were there huge drops in tourist numbers, but the composition of visitors also changed dramatically. Because of its "ethnic ambience," and the perception that the Zapatistas represented a much larger dissatisfied Indian population, journalists from around the world flocked to the city. In addition to the journalists, "conflict" or "war tourists" also abounded.

While this observer concluded that tourism would not return to earlier levels in the region until the area was once again viewed as safe for travel, he found evidence that some journalists and activists were lured precisely by the developments in southern Mexico; as one Canadian woman put it, she had come to Chiapas in 1994 for "journalism, a tan and revolution" (quoted in Pitts 1996:224).

British travel writer Isabella Tree described her encounter with the Zapatistas during a trip to Chiapas a couple of months after the New Year's public emergence of the insurrection. One of the political "pilgrims" who arrived to partake in the exhilaration of the time, she was moved by the distinctly autonomous nature of the indigenous-based Zapatista movement in formation and by the forward-thinking (some said postmodern) sensibility of its leadership, known for its nimble use of global communication technologies. Like many others, she embraced the Zapatista call for respect for diversity and inclusion in a world that was increasingly homogenized through hegemonic capitalism. Tree (2005:253) quoted the well-known words of Marcos: "We are you. Marcos is gay in San Francisco, black in South Africa, an Asian in Europe, a Chicano in San Ysidro, an anarchist in Spain, a Palestinian in Israel, a Maya Indian in the streets of San Cristóbal, a Jew in Germany, a Gypsy in Poland . . . and, of course, a Zapatista in the mountains."

Tree described the mix of travelers to Chiapas at that time who were in awe of the rebels' "epoch-making resonances" and "mythical portent"—and who hoped to meet and take photos of them (256). She herself was entranced by the participation of Mayan groups (including Tzotzil, Tzetzal, Tojolabal, and Chol) and by the legendary and endangered Lacandón. She stayed at Na Bolom, the former home of Danish archaeologist Frans Blom and Swiss photographer Trudy Blom, who had done much to support the Lacandón and whose home-turned-museum was a guesthouse for both indigenous people and tourists. The Bloms have been credited with drawing responsible tourism to the area when it was little known to most travelers; they brought a concern for, and a romanticized approach to, indigenous cultural preservation and environmental protection.

The Zapatistas were mindful of those tourists who happened to be on the scene at the time of the uprising. Indeed, during the capture of San Cristóbal on New Year's Day in 1994, Subcomandante Marcos was said to have called out to a group of tourists, "We apologize for the inconvenience, but this is a revolution" (Mancillas 2002:153),[6] while writing out safe-conduct passes to another group who had been planning to visit the archaeological site at Palenque (Martín 2004:121).[7] This courteous treatment of tourists reassured the foreign visitors, who were concerned to know if they might continue their tour of Chiapas. Although mainstream tourism dropped off after the insurrection, there were few incidents to signal a danger to visitors. Nevertheless, in one case that received international media attention, about one hundred indigenous sympathizers of the EZLN invaded and peacefully occupied an ecotourism lodge near the town of Ocosingo that was owned by a U.S. couple (Martín 2004:107). The Zapatistas may have confronted tourism that they felt was linked, despite its eco-friendly orientation, to efforts to take land away from local communities in the service of corporate interests, but they benefited from international solidarity tourism and from their own deployment of the trope of tourism.

After years of waiting for implementation of the 1996 San Andrés Accords, the Zapatistas in 2001 launched their March for Indigenous Dignity, or "Zapatour." This was a two-week caravan from Chiapas to Mexico City that ended with 250,000 supporters gathering in the capital city on the occasion of the Zapatistas' appearance before the national Congress. The historic significance of the event drew international activists like Canadian writer Naomi Klein, who was inspired to travel to see for herself the mythic, masked, and "unknown icon" Marcos and the movement that inspired so many to think differently about building nonhierarchical democratic societies that would respect cultural difference and give voice to the voiceless (Klein 2002).

There has been considerable scholarly attention to the continuing Zapatista struggle and to the local conditions of entrenched inequality that motivated it, including rich ethnographic accounts (Nash 2001; Stephen 2002). Several scholars have examined the global activist response and the emergence of international Zapatismo, which has been important to the success of the struggle in Chiapas (Olesen 2005).[8] Political scientist Clifford Bob (2005) argues that it was the exceptional ability of the Zapatistas to communicate with and help mobilize a global solidarity network that accounts for their successes where so many other local and regional movements have failed to gain wider notice and support. His transnational analysis may go rather far in placing more emphasis on the "marketing of rebellion" than on the resonance of Zapatista thought and politics with other contemporary social movements, but there is no doubt that this movement has gained enormous respect and built up stunning networks of support worldwide.

A study by sociologist Abigail Andrews (2007) based on research she undertook as part of a U.S. New Year's 2004 delegation to Chiapas provides a valuable perspective on the activist-tourist experience. Beginning with her self-reflection on the way that activists sought both to preserve and reject their social privilege in the process of engaging with Zapatista individuals and communities, she went on to examine the diverse ways in which those she observed and interviewed strove to make sense of their revolutionary sojourn. She describes the evident longing of group members—who generally came with romantic notions of the Zapatistas—for intimate experience with indigenous rebels, even if only through meaningful looks and other exchanges, often without much common ground, linguistic or otherwise. She notes, "For activist-tourists, revolution and even danger provide a means of accessing a political and social 'other'" (4). Some self-aware participants were critical of the consumerist outlook, implicit voyeurism, and, as one young man put it, "Orientalist" gaze of internationalists within the host communities (44). Other delegates fell into competitive efforts to outdo one another in their exemplary activist comportment or treated the Zapatista communities "like an 'activist Disneyland'" (18). Ultimately, many came to recognize that as paying guests in the communities "their main form of solidarity was tourism" (39) and that "a delegation was a packaged, purchasable experience" (40). We saw evidence of this sort of postmodern orientation to tourism in the chapter on Peru, and I will discuss its appearance in the Latin American and Caribbean region further in the Conclusion.

Chiapas Tourism After the Uprising

This chapter explores a point made in earlier ones: mainstream as well as "revolutionary" or "conflict" tourism is often enhanced in the aftermath of a period of unrest or social transformation, becoming a development objective for diverse parties. After an initial period of uncertainty when tourism industries seek to reassure prospective travelers that they can offer safe and welcoming visits, there can be an acceleration in consumer interest. We have seen this in the case of Cuba, Nicaragua, and Peru, despite their differences, and I would argue that we see it as well in Chiapas, Mexico.[9]

My visit to Chiapas in 2005 was part of a travel circuit that included Merida and Oaxaca as well as a week's stay in San Cristóbal de las Casas and visits to surrounding communities. Given the previous decade's developments in this state in southern Mexico, I felt that Chiapas would be an important complement to my other areas of research. Certainly it was an area sought after by solidarity tourists, and recent reports indicated that mainstream travelers were rediscovering the charms of the colonial city and its surroundings.[10] I returned to Chiapas to take part in the 2006–2007 New Year's tour offered by Global Exchange, which operates "Reality Tours" in many parts of the world. That trip, which included more time spent in Zapatista communities, gave me added insight into the expectations and experiences of travelers who identify with Zapatista politics and cultural practices. In 2008, I made a third visit, based in San Cristóbal, and traveling into the Lacandón jungle to explore tourism to that area's archaeological sites, indigenous villages, and natural environment. My most recent trip was in 2009.

Like any other traveler to Chiapas, I had my expectations when I went there for the first time. As an anthropologist, however, I had read about the region over the years, as it was the focus of many classic studies, and I had paid closer attention since the Zapatista uprising in 1994. Before traveling to Chiapas, I was in the city of Merida in the Yucatán and visited several shops operated by Chiapanecos, individuals and families originally from Chiapas and identified as such by their appearance and dress. One shop was brimming with items from that region, including traditional clothing as well as postcards with photographs from the insurrection. Most eye-catching were the many T-shirts with EZLN themes, one with text reading "EZLN: www.radioinsurgente.org," usefully offering the Web site for news of the Zapatistas, followed by words in Spanish for "peace, land, justice, food, education, health, liberty, housing, democracy, equality." The iconic image of Subcomandante Marcos was prominent, as was the image of a Zapatista woman in mask and braids, both of which I later found to be ubiquitous in San Cristóbal. When I asked about Zapatista dolls,[11] the young woman working there pulled several from under a table. Apologizing that she had only larger ones that were not in high demand by travelers, she showed me both Marcos and companion Ramona dolls, the latter honoring a revered indigenous woman and Zapatista whose recent death elevated her to an even higher status.

In Oaxaca, I asked other travelers making a circuit in the direction of Chiapas what they expected to find there. Many carried the Lonely Planet guide, which offered some brief discussion of the recent unrest in the area, but several I met told me that they were going for the traditional culture and history and were not much concerned about political events of the past. I encountered more European than U.S. travelers, bearing out the general view that those from the United States more often head for the mass-tourism sites like Cancun and not for more remote destinations.[12] While waiting for a delayed flight to Tuxtla Gutiérrez, the capital city of Chiapas, I spoke with a French couple who planned to rent a car and use their Michelin guide to have a self-styled tour of the Chiapas region. Both had some acquaintance with the Zapatista uprising, though the woman had a rather negative impression and the man was open to learning more about the situation, saying that he had also traveled to Syria, as if to explain his attraction to conflict zones.

On the drive to San Cristóbal, my driver described working with journalists, researchers, and tourists who came to get firsthand knowledge of the political developments in the region.[13] He was most curious about those outsiders who came to exploit the rich natural resources of the area, particularly of the Lacandón forest, and contrasted the wealth of the land with the poverty of the people. He figured that these interests, academic and entrepreneurial, appropriating knowledge as well as resources, were interlinked, though he was not sure about the motivations of the researchers and whether or not they were innocent. When I later learned more about the scale of biopiracy in Chiapas, I understood better why he and the local population might be suspicious of those scientists and others who came in search of new knowledge—and in some cases, new business opportunities. They often saw a fine line between appreciation of indigenous knowledge and practices on the land, and a rapacious desire to possess the same. Despite his broad concern about the self-interest of outsiders, he expressed the wish that his son would learn foreign languages and be prepared for work in the tourism industry.

Early on in my first visit to San Cristóbal I met the director of the state tourism office, Marco Santiago Sánchez, who described tourism over the last decade. He told me that just after the Zapatista uprising, "tourism was finished." But he went on to say that the conflict had put Chiapas on the map and drew international attention to the area—and "that has been positive for tourism." When I asked what sort of tourism the area attracts, he said that it is mainly "cultural tourism" (interview, May 13, 2005). He noted that many tourists come from France, Spain, Italy, Germany, and Canada, with fewer from the United

States. By the time of our conversation, more tourists were coming annually than in 1993 before the insurrection, showing that tourism had recovered and indeed increased. He wanted to see tourists stay longer than the typical two or three nights they often spent in the city before moving on, but in general he presented an optimistic outlook.

In another conversation with Sánchez, he spoke about how the city's tourism offices attempt to "sell" or "brand" San Cristóbal, calling on its colonial character and also promoting its reputation for excellent dining and night life. A new road would enable them to provide better and quicker transport from the Tuxtla airport. Because the past conflict might worry some tourists, those working in the tourism industry do not mention it unless visitors express interest, but overall it has served to enhance tourism (even if there is no official marketing of the revolution). He was glad to see tourism studies and training offered locally, for example, at the Universidad Mesoamericana, and viewed its popularity as an auspicious sign for the future (interview, May 16, 2005).

Despite the recent growth in tourism, not everyone was pleased with the changes brought about by the Zapatistas. The American owner of a local bookstore catering to tourists seeking English-language reading conveyed her annoyance. She moved to San Cristóbal in 1994, soon after the uprising, and complained that the indigenous supporters are violent, seize property, and settle on the *zócolo* (central plaza), making it unappealing for residents and visitors. She was vexed that there would be a demonstration that day, saying that I would see for myself. The demonstration, it turned out, did not involve indigenous Zapatistas at all but rather laid-off workers from local tourist bars; two hundred employees had been dismissed as a result of new restrictions on locations where alcohol could be served, and they were threatening to have a hunger strike. The bookstore owner appeared to be dismayed by any political activity that might interfere with business.

My introduction to the city of San Cristóbal included my discovery of a place up one of the main streets with a small complex of tourist venues: Madre Tierra (Mother Earth) restaurant, which offered natural foods and a laid-back attitude; a bakery selling bread, pastry, and pizza; a small Cine Club that had mainly Zapatista fare, then showing *The True Legend of Subcomandante Marcos* (French, Tessa Brisac 1995) and related offerings like *The Motorcycle Diaries*; and, upstairs, the office of Zapata Tours. The restaurant and Cine Club proved to be good places to give people my questionnaires, and I was able to strike up conversations there while people waited to be served meals or to watch videos. The

Zapata Tours office was named for Emiliano Zapata and appealed to Zapatista-focused tourists. Later, I would take the half-day tours they offered to nearby communities and a customized tour of Zapatista communities.

Whereas this locale on Insurgentes Street had a number of attractions for tourists, particularly a younger clientele of cultural and solidarity tourists, the town itself offered a wider array of choices. As Van den Berghe observed in 1990, San Cristóbal remains small enough that its main areas of interest to tourists can be visited by foot in an afternoon. There are a few principal streets that branch out from the zócolo. Insurgentes turns into Utrilla and leads in the direction of the landmark Santo Domingo church and main artisan market. Perpendicular to Insurgentes is Real de Guadalupe, a street filled with restaurants and tour offices, a Spanish-language school and the cultural center Kinoki (venues for still more video showings), and shops of all kinds. In recent years more Internet cafés have opened; one in particular, TierrAdentro, attracts visitors to its courtyard café-restaurant with wireless access, Zapatista-friendly ambiance, and small shops and cooperatives that surround a wide, open space.

Tourists at café TierrAdentro, a popular gathering place that provides commercial space to Zapatista cooperatives

Items for sale range from posters and embroidered clothing and tapestries with political messages and EZLN stitched on, to jewelry, Zapatista dolls, postcards, and ashtrays featuring Comandanta Ramona.[14] Nemizapata, another store on this street, sells exclusively Zapatista items, including posters, embroidered clothing and wall hangings, organic coffee beans produced in the region, and more dolls of every dimension. Other streets are beginning to have more tourism venues, notably 20 de Noviembre, which is closed to traffic so that tourists may walk freely past its many restaurants, shops, theater, and other attractions.

San Cristóbal is a well-preserved colonial city making efforts to be named a UNESCO World Heritage Site. The town's historic charm and its modern conveniences have attracted a number of expatriates who have settled there. The historic downtown has experienced some of the same vulnerability to foreigners buying up property as the colonial city of Granada in Nicaragua—causing concern among local residents who find that prices are rising in response to this development. For the substantial indigenous population that lives in the outskirts of San Cristóbal, the rising cost of living is even more problematic. Despite the city's appeal to foreigners, many travelers pause only briefly—long enough to spend money on hotels and restaurants—and use it as a point of departure for travel to more "exotic" areas of Chiapas.

The two most frequently visited places outside San Cristóbal are the towns of San Juan Chamula and Zinacantán.[15] Nearly every tourism outlet, large or small, offers these trips, often to both communities within a half day, as they are scarcely thirty minutes away. Chamula, with a Tzotzil Mayan population of over forty thousand, has the makings of an ideal indigenous village for tourism: strikingly different from Ladino towns, with a narrative of loss stemming from internal religious conflict, a spiritual practice uniting traditional ritual and Catholic faith, and a lively marketplace. When tourists enter the church, they must agree not to take photographs and must walk quietly among those who have come seeking *curanderos*, or healers. Visitors are mesmerized by the scene they encounter, with clusters of indigenous people sitting on an open floor spread with pine needles and candles, breathing the pungent scent of copal incense. They are intrigued by the use of both *posh* (cane alcohol) and Coca-Cola (Pepsi and Coke have monopolies in the region and are used ritually and as a beverage of choice) and a bit startled by the sight of roosters being sacrificed for curing.[16] Ladinos in the region say that this indigenous community is particularly entrepreneurial at the same time that it is fiercely possessive of its traditional culture.

In contrast, the Tzotzil Mayan town of Zinacantán is smaller in population, with about thirty thousand residents, but more socially diverse; outsiders laud its more open and modern outlook. This town was a focus of anthropological attention during the time of the Harvard Chiapas Project dating to a half century ago, and I visited it with interest. Tourists are generally brought to one of a few textile-producing workshops where they can observe women weaving, sample a little posh and a typical snack, and conclude by buying souvenir textiles. During one tour, our guide emphasized the authentic character of the town, narrating the Mayan legend of maize and its symbolic relation to human diversity. He urged us to try on indigenous dress and enact a traditional wedding ceremony in the workshop we visited. He himself put on traje to play the part of a Mayan priest and then coaxed a Mexican woman in the tour group to play the bride and a young French man to play the groom, with a woman from the United States performing as the *madrina*, or godmother. These willing members of the group were rewarded with some posh "lite" (with added flavoring for tourists) and picture taking. Our guide proudly emphasized that it is only on his tours to the town that this bit of pageantry is featured and is followed by a generous sampling of warm black corn tortillas wrapped around fresh cheese and avocado—making a bid for offering a coveted "insider's" experience. The group appeared to be well satisfied with this chance to "try on" local culture, all the while taking little time to engage with the women artisans who were offering us items for sale and food that they had prepared.

Van den Berghe described the indigenous presence in San Cristóbal as key to its broad appeal to ethnic or cultural tourists. Since the 1994 uprising, we find the added presence of Zapatismo in the city not only in the form of literature and other media such as videos produced by the Chiapas Media Project, or Promedios, but also in ubiquitous craft souvenirs. An abundance of Chamula vendors in the market outside the Santo Domingo church sell Zapatista dolls in indigenous dress, masked and carrying arms: tiny ones on earrings, small ones on key chains, medium-sized dolls for display, and larger ones on horseback. Turning Zapatista icons into folkloric craft or kitsch has particular appeal for some solidarity tourists and for others whose sense of irony may be more "post-tourist" than postrevolutionary. The dolls, T-shirts, shoulder bags with EZLN embroidered into the design, ski masks of the sort worn by Zapatistas, and so on give this tourist destination a cachet that may surpass that of Cuba, where Che T-shirts and other paraphernalia are found everywhere.

Venues like the Bar Revolución capitalize on this deterritorialized revolutionary status as well, with bartenders wearing T-shirts with the name of the bar and a large star, matching the one on the sign outside. The décor includes large portraits of Zapata (smaller ones of Che and Gandhi) on the wall, a Cuban flag hanging prominently over the door (a Mexican flag was on a wall inside), CD covers for Buena Vista Social Club, and nostalgic film paraphernalia.[17] The fact that the Cuban revolution was launched in 1956 by Fidel Castro's group setting sail from Mexico may account for the affectionate and proud references to that quintessential revolution. The natural-foods restaurant Casa del Pan features a wall-sized mural representing past, present, and future with images of Zapata and the Mexican Revolution, an indigenous woman carrying baby and corn, and then Marcos and other Zapatistas. Far more restaurants and hotels call on the region's indigenous peoples and cultures as a local brand to attract tourists, who are presumed to expect references to the iconic brand at every turn (along with modern amenities).

One local entrepreneur was somewhat wistful though pragmatic as he described tourists' longing for images of revolution. He produces T-shirts with images of Che (for Americans, he said) and Marcos (for Europeans), pointing to the latter group's greater familiarity with recent politics. He expressed his doubts about the manifestation of Zapatista politics in the area, saying that it was too aggressive. It had slowed business, discouraged investment in the area, and driven away tourism. "It was a good dream but now it is history," he told me. "Now it's just something interesting for tourists." He implicitly acknowledged that what had stalled tourism has also brought it back, and he appeared unabashed as he capitalized on the global popularity of the revolutionary figures.

On the final night of this trip to Chiapas, I had dinner at Na Bolom, where dinner guests are seated together at one long table in order to promote conversation. On this occasion, I joined a middle-aged couple from Florida who were in the process of buying a ranch in southern Chiapas. They had learned of this opportunity through the stream of Chiapanecos who travel to Pensacola to work in landscaping. The woman had lived in Mexico for a couple of years in the past, teaching English and never acquiring more than the present tense in Spanish. She felt that despite the past conflict and the Zapatista rebellion, she and her husband would come with open minds and make a go of it. Aware that Chiapas was a poor state in the midst of ample resources, she espoused no particular political perspective on the evident inequality. However well meaning they were, this rather naïve frontier outlook could certainly lead to cultural misunderstanding and greater tension in the future.

The Reality Tour

Just as I had traveled with Global Exchange groups to Cuba, I joined a group going to Chiapas to experience solidarity travel to the area more than a decade after the uprising. This Reality Tour was among the organization's "educational, socially-responsible study seminars [that] offer our participants an opportunity to truly examine the political, social, economic, cultural, and ecological realities of communities in the region."[18] The tour was planned to coincide with the 2006–2007 anniversary of NAFTA and of the Zapatista uprising and brought together individuals from around the United States. After a late connection in Tuxtla, I joined group members on December 26 at the Casa del Pan restaurant in San Cristóbal. The group included one teenager with her mother, who was an alternative medical practitioner, several recent students and young activists, and a few retired professionals—a typical mix for solidarity travel, with me in the minority category of middle-aged professional. All came with prior knowledge of Chiapas and the rebellion and had liberal to more radical leftist leanings, several with a longtime desire to "know the revolution."

For the most part, San Cristóbal was a home base for this group and only of direct interest insofar as it offered opportunities to visit NGOs, human rights offices, alternative media outlets, and centers of indigenous activity, such as the Mayan Medicine Museum with its medicinal herb garden. We spent our first days in meetings in the city to acquire the background we would need for the remainder of the trip. All appreciated the convenience of Internet cafés, restaurants, and shops, but the group's main focus was on getting out beyond the city to visit a coffee cooperative and alternative school and, most important, to spend time in the Zapatista autonomous communities—which we did for several days. We were prepared for travel to the Zapatista communities by our group leader, "Marit," a European woman who had lived in Chiapas for a decade. She coached us to observe and listen, not to interfere; to be considerate when taking photographs and not to give personal gifts; to invite our hosts to ask us questions just as we would ask them questions. She warned us that "Oventic is almost a tourist site," with travelers going there throughout the year and not just during the anniversary celebrations. Marit also advised us that we could expect state military to be present, and that if we met a roadblock, we should "act as tourists." There is a way in which "we" are "internationalists" (solidarity travelers) and never "tourists," though other activists may be; nevertheless, it would be the safe identity to fall back on in case of any difficulties.

We traveled to Acteal, the site of the 1997 massacre, where we would spend a night camped out on the floor of a simple guesthouse. We were welcomed by our hosts, a pacifist group connected to the Catholic Church who refer to themselves as Las Abejas (The Bees) because they are active and organized. They offered us a hot meal and an opportunity to learn about their recently fractured community as they recounted their efforts to pursue peace and justice and develop a stronger foundation in the midst of hardship. As we sat talking with a group of men from Las Abejas, a number of the older ones wearing traje and huaraches drifted off to sleep. The younger men spoke about retaining the tradition of fiestas and cargos in the face of modernization and about resolving conflict in a time of neoliberalism and globalization. We were invited to visit their sanctuary, built under a large gathering space after the massacre. The following day, we went to Oventic, the principal *caracol*, or Zapatista administrative center, visited by internationalists in Chiapas. This activist sojourn was to be the high point of our trip to Chiapas.

Arriving by van in Oventic on December 31, we entered the designated Zapatista "Liberated Territory," which elicited an enthusiastic "Right on!" from one of our group members, an earnest young man from Ohio who was a social worker and anarchist. We would be taking part as observers in what was billed as a four-day "Intergalactic Gathering" (or "Intercontinental Encuentro for Humanity and Against Neoliberalism") of an estimated two thousand Zapatistas with many hundreds of international activists from over fifty countries. We all needed to register to attend, a requirement for visitors to the caracols, and we received colorful identification tags with EZLN and "Encuentro of Zapatista peoples with the peoples of the world," along with our names handwritten by our hosts to hang in plastic cases from cords around our necks—sure to be coveted keepsakes back home. The sign welcoming us read "Bienvenid@s," a convention used in parts of Latin America to be inclusive of women as well as men, avoiding sexism in the Spanish language.[19] We were allowed through the gates by masked individuals, who wore either the full balaclava (ski mask) or a bandanna tied to conceal their lower faces. Walking down the steep, wide brick path leading to the center of activity below, we saw a reception center, a small health clinic, a simple restaurant, and the office of the Junta de Buen Gobierno (Good Government Council), where our group was allowed entry.

We had an audience with several men and a woman from the council in a room decorated with images of Zapatistas and of Che Guevara, with a sign reading "Viva EZLN" and a world map on the wall. They described their work in resistance and their "Other Campaign" to establish "other" systems of self-governance, education, and health care "for a world where those who command, do it by obeying." Their dream and an inspiration for this gathering, they said, was that "one day we would have a real democracy, justice, and liberty." This would be "a world in which many worlds fit." The woman comandanta, who spoke only Tzotzil and not Spanish, contributed little until we asked about the part women play among the Zapatistas; she then told us, with translation, of the role of women in the junta and the municipality. She related that women have equal rights but added that they meet separately to address machismo, violence against women, and women's right to choose when to have children (this received applause from our group).

Later, we divided up to take part in several workshop sessions on health, education, and women's issues. The sessions would continue January 1 on

A woman and three men in the Good Government Council during a 2006 encuentro that drew international visitors from over fifty countries

communication, art and culture, commerce, and land rights. The workshops I attended were lively, with many indigenous Zapatistas seated in the audience carrying on spirited discussion with the panelists on the stage. An objective was to prepare for further mobilization and to build stronger linkages with other social movements. As the day wore on, people drifted in and out and eventually scouted for food and drink, for sale at several stands set up for the occasion. Clusters of people spent time talking or buying mementos from vendors. One group from Portland, Oregon, sang a song that identified with the teachers' struggle then playing out in the neighboring state of Oaxaca, with the lyrics "Go home, go home turista, es una revolución anti-capitalista."[20] There was dancing, a high-wire act, rap and punk rock music, and speeches. I met a number of Mexicans who had come from Mexico City and were as captivated as the internationalists by the gathering. When the power went out temporarily, the misty night air bathed the place in a foggy, mysterious haze that suited the "magical" quality that the experience had for many in attendance.

The moist, romantic haze of cloud surrounded the tired but excited participants who were gathered across a vast area facing the large stage as we waited through the hours leading toward midnight. Marcos and his entourage were expected for the New Year's Eve celebration, and that kept all of us in thrall that night—even those of us who would be heading back to San Cristóbal in the wee hours. Security lines of Zapatista men and women had moved through the crowd, allowing only the participating Zapatistas to move to the front and keeping internationalist observers in the space behind. *Conjuntos* (bands) played traditional Mexican music with Zapatista lyrics, then the Zapatista anthem, and the Mexican national anthem—making the point that while they want autonomy, they also desire recognition as Mexicans. A few firecrackers and fireworks kept the crowd entertained. Finally, around 12:20 a.m., a procession of some dozens of people marched to the front of the space and then to the huge stage (I overheard the mother in our group telling her teenage daughter that the stage was the size of "the one at Woodstock").[21] People in the crowd had jumped to their feet to look expectantly for Marcos, who appeared, identifiable when he lit his pipe, and strode with his companions onto the stage to great fanfare.

First, Comandanta Yolanda spoke a few words, emphasizing the importance of women in the Zapatista struggle. Then Marcos spoke, soon switching from Spanish to Tzotzil to deliver his prepared remarks. When he had finished, another indigenous woman comandanta, Hortensia, presented the translation in Spanish, a linguistic reversal of symbolic power relations emblematic of Marcos and the Zapatistas, which made an impression on the gathered crowd. Marcos's speech emphasized the current stage of Zapatista mobilization: the importance of collectivity in confronting the *mal gobierno* (bad, capitalist national government) and of developing the Zapatistas' worldwide network composed of many diverse movements sharing common cause in confronting the force of globalization. Around 2 a.m., after the speech but before Marcos and the others had left the stage, our group reached exhaustion and reluctantly made its way back to our van to return to San Cristóbal.

Our tour group, like other activist groups that travel to Chiapas, was most inspired by the promise to "dialogue with indigenous peasants who have been working for the right to own the land upon which they live and work, and govern their communities according to indigenous traditions and customs [and to] take advantage of this opportunity to meet people involved in grassroots movements and exchange ideas with them while learning more about the unique history and culture of Chiapas."[22] Several group members expressed middle-class alienation from their own society and a desire for the sort of authenticity discussed by MacCannell and others. One wrote in my questionnaire: "I wanted to witness the Zapatista revolutionary model. . . . I expected to find a communal atmosphere that is removed from the consumer mentality in the States." Another wrote: "I love the Zapatistas and their whole approach to revolution. Also, living in Bush's America is so hard to live in (spiritually speaking— I am not suffering physically as so many are) that I came here to be re-inspired with hope." Although activist groups like this one share something in common with more mainstream cultural tourists coming to the area, they typically want to distinguish themselves as more serious than tourists and view themselves instead as political pilgrims on a quest to build a global movement. Nonetheless, within such groups there are inevitable tensions over socially and politically appropriate conduct. In our group, all U.S. citizens, there were times when a few members seemed to want to distance themselves from others they viewed as behaving like tourists. One of the senior women exclaimed during a moment of exasperation with her fellow travelers, "Americans are such a pain!"

From Archaeological Sites to Jungle Tours

During a trip to Chiapas in spring 2008, I again made San Cristóbal my base and spent time in some of the tourist venues there. I traveled once more to the nearby communities of Chamula and Zinacantán (this time, on a day when President Calderón was making a rare visit to the area). I sought out any opportunity to go on a "Zapatista tour" but finally needed to hire a guide to take me out to two Zapatista communities, including Oventic, where I had an opportunity to meet privately with members of the caracol's Comisión. I was struck on this third visit to Chiapas by the number of free spirits—I might call "seekers"—I encountered, rather like the spiritual tourists around the Cuzco area in Peru. As I met people who agreed to fill out my questionnaires, the conversations that followed were often more revealing than what they expressed in writing.[23]

At the café TierrAdentro I spoke with a woman from the United States who had been living in Mexico for some time and who confided to me that in a past life she "must have taken an anthropology course"; she had a keen interest in knowing more about the nearby communities and what had caused some of them to experience religious conflict. Similarly, at the restaurant Casa del Pan, where tourists looking for natural foods congregate, I gave a questionnaire to another young woman from the United States with long blond hair in dreadlocks, and she later asked to join me at my table. She told me she had just come from a Rainbow gathering in Veracruz and had had an amazing experience.[24] At age twenty-seven, she had already taken part in Rainbow gatherings in India and Thailand, and for this extended visit to Mexico she had saved up thousands of dollars from her earnings as an artist. She raved about the positive energy she was discovering and the faith she had in the people she met. Later, in Chamula, I noticed the gringos who were sitting on the bare church floor among the indigenous healers and those who came to be healed—who also had the appearance of New Age seekers.

Here, however, I want to focus on a three-day trip I took to eastern Chiapas, my first to the Lacandón jungle, considered the birthplace of Zapatista politics and an area rich in its natural environment and cultural history. I had worked with a tourism outlet in San Cristóbal and planned three sequential day trips with tour groups going to the Palenque, Bonampak, and Yaxchilán archaeological sites and then on to Lacanjá, for an overnight stay in a Lacandón community and a "jungle tour." Those of us whom the driver picked up to leave at dawn on the first day included a German couple, a Mexican mother and daughter, a Mexican couple, a Romanian woman, and myself. We made stops along the way to Palenque to visit scenic waterfall areas, Agua Azul and Misol-Ha. By the time we reached the famed archaeological site of the ancient Mayan city of Palenque, it was midday and extremely hot. We had traveled from the cool highlands to the tropical lowlands, and it was energy draining just to walk around under the blazing sun.

Nevertheless, our group rallied together and agreed to share one of the many guides who briskly approached our van. An Israeli couple joined us on the spot, and we negotiated payment with our guide, "Víctor." As we set out toward the site, Víctor established his credentials and made a bid for later tips by telling us that he had worked for years with archaeologists and had insider's knowledge about Palenque. He assured us that much of what passes for information about the place is mistaken and that he would set the record straight. Leading us through surrounding jungle to the site, he entertained us by pointing out the dense plant life, insisting that a volunteer swing on the vines before moving on. Then, acting as site historian, he took us to see some key points of interest, telling us that the site was much older than reported in most sources and that there was a more complex mix of cultures that came together at Palenque than commonly understood. He offered a host of theories, and when he showed us the Temple of the Dead and its red- and blue-tinted tombs, he noted that archaeologists talk about the age of the tombs but New Agers who visit talk about their positive and negative energy. Víctor seemed open to considering either "theory" and said that scientists were still studying these questions "in Miami." His efforts to present the inside story and engage our interest were rewarded when thanks and tips were offered at the end of the tour. Whether the group, hot and tired from the visit, felt they took away new knowledge was hard to say, but group members did seem to leave with a sense of awe about the site and the people who built and populated it, suggesting that the tour had its intended result.

On the second day, my group was collected from various hotels to travel by van and later by boat to Bonampak and Yaxchilán. The van was crowded with a collection of mainly young travelers, including a woman from Australia, a couple of men from Holland, a Japanese couple, and the large backpacks of those who would be going on to Guatemala. The driver was ill-humored and seemed to enjoy keeping us all in the dark as to the day's plan, just telling us brusquely when to get out of and back into the van. The mellow young man from the Netherlands sitting next to me passed the time telling me about his two years "traveling the world" and going to whatever places "chose him." Back home he had experienced a string of bad luck until he found God and now evangelizes if people are open to it. Besides the personal life stories exchanged among travelers thrown together, there was the friendly competition of swapping tourism tales. In our van, two who had recently been in India complained of the rigidity of some locals there, and one of them offered, "Well, you know why it's called India? I'll Never Do It Again!" Their Chiapas travels would no doubt provide still more ritualized stories of triumph over everyday adversity in unfamiliar surroundings.

Some of us were directed to board a boat on the Río Usumacinta, which divides Mexico and Guatemala, to travel for about an hour to the Classic Mayan site of Yaxchilán. This group of us, eager to learn more about early cultures in the Chiapas jungle, also banded together to hire a guide once we got there. Like Víctor, this guide spent time telling us about the natural environment as well as the site, quipping about one tree that is popularly known as "turista" because its bark peels. He led us through the site, comparing it to Palenque and disagreeing with some of what Víctor had said the day before. After the return trip by boat followed by lunch, we traveled by van to still another ancient Mayan city, Bonampak, a smaller site best known for its murals. Four Mexican tourists and I hired a Spanish-speaking guide, who held our attention with his narrative of the mysterious discovery of the site surrounded by jungle and then directed us to its famous painted walls. When our visit there concluded, the van took just two of us to meet up with a man who was to be our Lacandón host at Lacanjá.

"Gina," the Australian woman, and I were taken in our host's car to his Campamento "Tomás," where his extended family played host to a steady stream of tourists. Tomás came across as having both traditional and modern attributes, not surprising given his reliance on retaining "authenticity" even as he has acquired the skills and efficiency needed to run his business. Wearing his hair long and dressed in the simple white gown historically worn by the Lacandón, he chauffeured us in his car and handled the financial end of the family's tourism enterprise. He showed us quickly to our cabins and to the nearby bathrooms and showers and asked if we wanted chicken or quesadillas for dinner. Then, just as quickly, he told us that we owed him money, Gina for her meals and I for my jungle walk the next morning. We had each paid in full at our tour agencies before the trip and were firm about it; he later agreed that we were paid up, but we were left wondering if the van driver had turned over to our host all the money that was due to him.

The *campamento* was made up of a series of cabins and campgrounds along a narrow river stream, where we cooled off by taking a swim amid the chickens and guinea fowl on the riverbank. Two young Mexican couples we had met earlier set up tents by the river, then had a swim. Later in the afternoon walking around the camp, I saw that the men and boys wore traditional dress while the women and girls were for the most part in Western dress. A young girl, one of Tomás's grandchildren, was riding a bicycle and wanted to show it off. I was

A Lacandón host at a tourist encampment in Lacanjá

struck by these gender practices, so far suggesting that girls and women might have freedom in their activity. Some of the older Lacandón were self-conscious about their use of Spanish, which made them reticent, but the children seemed comfortable talking with us visitors. I learned that a group from France was there and would be staying one more night. Their tour leaders were a French woman living in San Cristóbal and a Nicaraguan-French man living in Paris. The group had been traveling together for nearly two weeks and appeared eager to talk to me, as someone from outside their small orbit. I shared stories of travel in Peru with one man, who seemed to believe that as an anthropologist I possessed exclusive knowledge.

When I spoke privately with the French woman tour guide about Zapatista-focused tourism, she drew me away from the Lacandón who might overhear us and not be sympathetic with Zapatista politics. She told me that although Zapatismo is a sensitive subject in the area, she herself was a sympathizer and admired the Zapatistas for being very conscientious. She said that in comparison the Lacandón are out to make money and are now charging more than they used to (and, by implication, more than they ought to) charge. Even though

Tomás's extended family lives at the campamento, it is not like other communities; she noted the supply store and Internet facility for tourists and for some locals with the resources to use them. She implied that much had changed in the lives of these indigenous people (similar to what I had heard about Chamula, described by some as "capitalist-indigenous").[25]

Indeed, I found myself comparing my brief experience in Lacanjá with my days spent in the community tourism project in Vicos, Peru. Was it only because the Vicosinos were at an earlier stage of tourism development that the stay there felt more "genuine" and welcoming? Was Vicos, like Lacanjá, destined for a more commercialized practice of hosting tourists in the future? These questions reflect, of course, certain idealized expectations of travel to culturally different, exotic locations that visitors imagine to be uncontaminated by the forces of the capitalist market economy.[26] In both Vicos and Lacanjá, the cost of a visit was quite low in fact, and if tourists object, it may be that they expect "Indians" to provide services at little cost. Also similar in the two communities, an objective appeared to be to offer apolitical cultural tourism, in contrast to the highland area of Chiapas where political tourism captures a good part of the market. This cautious approach may reflect the cultural logic of more vulnerable populations catering to tourism.

The work of tending to multiple groups of tourists in Tomás's campamento must certainly be great, particularly as it is carried out by just one large family. Much of the labor remains hidden from view and is performed by women: for example, the preparation of large quantities of food for meals that are offered in a dining hall with long communal tables and the laundering of sheets and towels without modern equipment. The men, as in Vicos, act as official hosts and guides, presenting the public face of the Lacandón to visitors. Thus, when I had dinner as well as breakfast the next morning with the French group, women served us food but did not stay or try to engage in conversation, perhaps because of limitations in use of language. Traditional gender relations and practices seemed to be at play, though that may actually be a Mayan response to postcolonial gender relations, which often lack the greater autonomy associated with indigenous societies.

On my second day there, Tomás's son "Roberto" came to meet me as my guide for the jungle walk. After a breakfast of scrambled eggs, tortillas, and coffee, we would set out for between three and five hours of hiking through rather rough terrain, though we would follow paths cut through the jungle. Roberto, a man in his early twenties who told me that a year ago he decided to cut his hair and wear Western dress, carried a machete in case it was necessary to clear a path in the ever-growing vegetation. I grabbed a bag of a few things I considered necessary for such an expedition, and we set off into the *selva*, or jungle. Roberto explained that we would see the Cidro River and waterfalls, a variety of plants and possibly animals, and some ancient ruins. He didn't converse much as we walked but was friendly in answering my questions. He told me about his family, the twelve of them who live at the campamento, including his wife and three children. When I asked about Lacandón staying on the land, he said that virtually all stay on the Montes Azules reserve in this part of Chiapas,[27] but that there is competition from other indigenous groups who want to come and take away their resources, trees and animals, though it is not their right to do so. Roberto's wider experience, having traveled to Mexico City and San Cristóbal on matters relating to tourism development, had not diminished his strong indigenous identity. Indeed, an individual's or group's indigeneity is often defined precisely through contact and travel and may be both local and cosmopolitan.

Trekking across streams, climbing up and descending hills, and stumbling on roots and rocks in the path, we made our way. We occasionally met up with the French group, led by an older Lacandón man in traditional dress who was moving along at a good pace. They stopped to swim in the largest falls area where I rested before heading back to the camp. There I gave questionnaires to a number of the French tourists and chatted with the guides before their departure. Gina had already left on the next leg of her journey, so my final hours at Lacanjá were spent on my own, having a lunch of beef and tortillas served in the otherwise empty dining hall.

When I returned to my cabin, I found a young girl I had talked to before, who appeared to be around five but might have been eight years old, waiting to see me. She told me in a confident way that I should pack up my things because someone would be coming to clean my room. I was surprised, since I had a few more hours before I was to leave, but she informed me that the message came from Tomás and that if I wanted to rest, I could go to another room with hammocks available. She was so fully in command that I did as she said and left my packed bags in the dining hall.

After visiting with Tomás and his family, it was time for him to drive me to get my transportation back to Palenque. As we drove, he told me more about his life and the changes from the time when he worked more in the fields, until now, when he devotes himself full-time to tourism. They still have land to farm, as the reserve belongs to all Lacandón, giving them the advantage of community control. Other family members farm corn and yucca, mainly to eat themselves but occasionally to sell. Although Tomás had not been to school and did not read or write, all of his children had gone to primary school and would have more options for work in tourism and the wider market economy. As we neared my pickup point, he let me know that visitors sometimes gave him a tip for gas, and he seemed satisfied when I offered him one. We said brief good-byes, and then I thanked him and got my ride to Palenque.

Tourism in Postrevolutionary Chiapas

I have argued that tourism can be spurred by revolution and uprising, in this case by the early twentieth-century Mexican Revolution and by the recent Zapatista rebellion, as a result of the added interest and attention that accompanies the opening or reopening to tourism in areas where there has been social unrest.[28] In addition to the allure of places previously off-limits, postrevolutionary settings generally have been protected from overexposure to commercialized travel, making them that much more attractive for tourism. Even in cases where the benefits of tourism's absence is dubious, tourism industries may construct these areas as newly ready for business and put out the welcome mat. As we have seen, tourism can serve some interests of revolutionary movements by promoting stability, peace, and justice; moreover, in postrevolutionary times tourism can serve to showcase new regimes. Thus, in many cases tourism can become a key sector for economic development and political refashioning. In concluding this chapter, I note some of the telling contemporary ironies that I have observed in this transitional and still uncertain period in Chiapas as a revolutionary social movement continues to stand up to a powerful state. Parallels with the areas discussed in earlier chapters should be evident.

During a recent trip to San Cristóbal, I heard about a dance and musical performance at a small theatre on the *andador*, the tourist walkway through town. *Palenque Rojo*, the mythical story of the Mayan city in the jungle and the demise of its ruler Kan Joy Chitam II, was playing to sell-out crowds, as tourists purchased high-priced tickets outside the theater during the busy daytime hours. The Canadian woman who sold me my ticket told me she came to San Cristóbal a few years ago after a period of illness to find a curandero. Now settled here with a partner and their young daughter, she is struggling to get by and dreams of launching a spiritual tourism service for those interested in alternative medicine and indigenous practices and beliefs. Her identity as a seeker meshed well with selling tickets for this performance.

That evening, a multinational crowd waited eagerly for the theater to open as people read the program notes, which began this way (translated into five languages):

> In the extraordinary lands of the Maya, embraced on all sides by the jungle, with its exoticism, wild beasts and magic, there was an age which gave rise to two great city states: Palenque and Toniná. These two cities fought to control the commercial route from the Gulf of Mexico to the heart of the Petén. Here in Palenque Rojo, we present one of the most important moments of this power struggle as related in a beautiful bas-relief: the kidnapping of the Ruler Kan Joy Chitam.

The performance incorporated time travel and illusion, with a striking set design, costumes, and choreography that seemed to mesmerize the audience. The Mayan Kan Joy Chitam entered carrying a flaming torch while actors disguised as exotic jungle animals made their way around the stage floor. Dancers, musicians with drums, and a smoky haze of copal incense set the mood. Suddenly interrupting that mood were the sounds of cars honking and alarms going off. The Popol Vuh and hieroglyphs appeared on a screen at the back of the stage, adding to the dissonance of sounds and images. Men with painted faces and long hair, elaborate headdresses, and warrior spears danced energetically, while several women played supporting roles. Another man and woman entered, this time latter-day European archaeologists with jungle gear and knapsacks, coming to explore the area.

The images and narrative suggested the nobility of indigenous people and culture, and (to my mind) satirized the European intervention. Toniná and Palenque were represented through more images on the screen, as men appeared in animal-skin loin cloths, displaying toned bodies and prowess as hunters. The archaeologists reappeared to discover Toniná, as loud drums and war shouts seized our attention and the near-naked men ran through the aisle, causing spectators to draw back into their seats. Toniná attacked Palenque, and Kan Joy Chitam was kidnapped; the vanquishing warrior was revealed to be a woman, adding a note of gender transgression to the story. The archaeologists appeared once again with their cargo pants and packs, this time to discover the area's people and culture. The audience responded enthusiastically as the encounter concluded with a lingering image of Palenque in the background.

An actor in the production *Palenque Rojo* posing in costume outside the theater to attract ticket sales

What do tourists take away from this theatrical event and other cultural displays they consume and enjoy in Chiapas? An appreciation of the long-term political conflicts in the region, or fodder perhaps for their travel narratives relating the exoticism of those they encountered in this vibrant and sometimes volatile area in southern Mexico? Whatever doubts we have might be tempered by the views of the indigenous performers in *Palenque Rojo*, whom I had a chance to interview a year later. While one woman expressed concern about the commodification of Mayan culture, others, including the Lacandón man who has played the leading role for several years, judged the work to revalorize the culture for Mayas as well as international audiences. Summing up his own commitment, he said simply, "It's my life."

Snapshot images form quickly, as most tourists spend just a few days in the region and then move on. A British man who responded to my questionnaire in April 2008 offered his first impression of travel to the area: "Only arrived yesterday from Guatemala. San Cristóbal is as described to me, i.e. like Antigua, Guatemala but with Zapatista souvenirs." Chiapas is on the map once again as a desired destination for tourists interested in indigenous peoples and cultural heritage as well as for activist travelers. This may expose the region to the tourist gaze and to the commodification of the area's culture and politics, threatening its perceived authenticity. Yet it is clear that local populations in Chiapas and elsewhere are often able to make good on tourism's promise by furthering their own well-defined interests.

Tourism and Its Discontents

Gender, Race, and Power in Transitional Societies

5 Sex and Sentiment in Cuban and Nicaraguan Tourism

IN PARTS 1 AND 2 of *The Tourism Encounter*, I presented individual case studies of tourism in Cuba, Nicaragua, Andean Peru, and Chiapas, Mexico—postrevolutionary and postconflict societies that have embraced tourism as they have undergone political transitions and have undertaken nation-building projects. In Part 3, Chapters 5 and 6 offer comparative perspectives on these nations and regions to illuminate the particular challenges that more marginalized sectors confront in the tourism development process. In this chapter, I bring together discussion of Cuba and Nicaragua as each has experienced gendered and racialized consequences as a result of its growing dependence on tourism. In the next chapter, I turn to Andean Peru and Chiapas in order to reveal how indigenous women are positioned as either highly vulnerable or as well suited for success (and sometimes both) as they command specific forms of cultural capital in the tourism market. In the Conclusion, I draw further comparisons among these four nations in an effort to sort through the ambivalent and contradictory forces of global tourism in the lives of various actors discussed in this work.

Travel Snapshots

HAVANA, CUBA. When I arrived in Havana's airport in December 2003, just before tighter restrictions were imposed by the United States on travel to Cuba, I was swept along with others going through customs. As our movement slowed and we formed lines, I noticed a large-screen TV showing Cuban women dancing provocatively in skin-tight clothing. The images were distinctly sexualized, but it was unclear to me if they were intended to be a welcoming diversion, cultural heritage on display, or even perhaps an advertisement for beer. In a country that has expressed official concern over rising sex tourism and that prohibits advertising, this seemed to present a curious contradiction, albeit one of many encountered on a daily basis by travelers in Cuba. What struck me, however, was that among the many attractions this Caribbean island offers, this one was put on prominent view for visitors entering the country.[1]

MANAGUA, NICARAGUA. Similarly, when I arrived in Managua's airport on a visit to Nicaragua in summer 2004, I discovered a desk with smiling hosts greeting tourists, answering questions, and offering free travel literature. A glossy magazine entitled *Between the Waves* attracted attention through the use of a cover photograph of a young woman wearing a bikini and perched suggestively on a boat. The magazine's business manager later told me that the advertisers wanted every issue to have such a cover photo of a tanned Central American beauty, since "sex sells" (Reinhard Holzinger, personal communication). *Between the Waves* is given away free at the airport and in a number of hotels and restaurants catering to tourists in Nicaragua, and advertisers are clearly banking on the cover images enticing potential consumers of their goods and services.

Intimate Encounters in Transitional Societies

In my ethnographic research in Cuba and Nicaragua, I have found that the tourism industries in these nations often mimic those in other tropical tourist destinations in offering "sand and sea" vacations with optional visits to colonial cities and towns. Although Nicaragua and Cuba have much in common with other nations using "branding" techniques to define their appeal and compete for a share of the global tourism market, they differ from the mainstream in attracting a significant category of travelers who seek out travel in postconflict and postrevolutionary locations. The gender-related tourism I consider in this chapter is less directly linked to Cuban and Nicaraguan histories of social and political upheaval,[2] though these travel destinations are often selected because they have recently been considered off-limits (in the Cuban case, this pertains particularly to U.S. citizens), making the countries alluring to those seeking less-frequented sites that are known to a select few. Travelers expressed to me their desire to visit Nicaragua and Cuba before they lose this quality and become overdeveloped tourist sites like neighboring areas of Central America and the Caribbean.

Of course, the substantial differences between the two nations should not be overlooked. Notably, after little more than a decade in power, the Sandinista revolutionary government lost the 1990 elections and the country made a sharp turn in the direction of neoliberalism. Cuba's government, meanwhile, held to its revolutionary commitment through its most difficult period following the loss of Soviet support, albeit with a number of concessions to a mixed economy (Eckstein 2003). Whereas resources have been scarce in both nations, Nicaragua lies at the poorest end of the economic continuum in the region and Cuba is much more highly developed. Now, both countries are again in a transition process, since Fidel Castro transferred power to his brother Raúl, and Sandinista Daniel Ortega returned to power in Nicaragua; to date, however, there is little sign of change for tourism and its gendered effects.

Despite their differences, the two nations have in common an increasing number of international tourists coming to enjoy a range of travel opportunities in these sites of social revolution, ranging from backpacker, eco-, and adventure tourism to higher-end heritage and leisure tourism. At the same time, other forms of tourism have appeared in the wake of the countries' recent economic uncertainties. As in many places where populations coping with inadequate resources find that tourists provide a ready source of income, prostitution, sex work, and "romance" tourism have flourished (not least in the Caribbean—see Brennan 2004; Cabezas 2009; Padilla 2007). Often in the tourist encounter, under conditions that favor the commodification of social relationships, there is no strict line between intimacy that represents a brief exchange of sex for money (sex tourism) and that which leads to longer-term involvement in exchange for gifts, including cash or, in some cases, love and marriage (romance tourism).[3] I consider the forms the phenomenon takes in these postrevolutionary nations and how the nations attempt to manage contradictions of official policy and everyday practice.

In these postrevolutionary societies, where government and industry officials have expressed a desire to go a different way from capitalist market-driven economies and to cater to more "wholesome" tourism, the emergence of sex and romance tourism is notable. Fidel Castro was effective in curtailing prostitution in the years following the 1959 revolution in Cuba but made a weaker gesture to do so when tourism was revived in the 1990s (Facio 1998–1999). In Nicaragua, the revolutionary government of the Sandinista National Liberation Front confronted the sexual exploitation of women in its early years; more recently, Tomás Borge, the Sandinista head of the Commission on Tourism, opposed casinos and nightclubs in Nicaragua that encourage sexual exploitation (interview, June 30, 2003). Nonetheless, there appears to be some ambivalence in efforts to curtail the growth of prostitution, doubtless because it provides foreign revenue. I do not mean to suggest that the only gendered effect of tourism is the rise of prostitution and sex tourism, and, indeed, women workers are active in other sectors of the global tourism industry (Bolles 1997; Ghodsee 2005). Even so, my comparative research demonstrates the value of examining the transition from the Cuban and Nicaraguan revolutionary governments' earlier success in reducing the socioeconomic and gender inequalities that promoted sexual exploitation and prostitution to the present commodification of sex and intimacy that accompanies dependence on tourism to rescue these nations' economies.

Because sex tourism generally receives little official notice in Cuba and Nicaragua, falling below the radar screen or considered too controversial to address publicly, there is little in the way of formal data to draw on in this research. Studies on the subject have more often relied on qualitative rather than quantitative research methods. Although the narratives and descriptive material that provide support for such research may appear somewhat impressionistic, I would argue that there is a need for more detailed ethnographic studies that examine the nuances of socially and historically situated sex and romance tourism. The case studies that follow include accounts, or stories, from my field research that should illuminate the broader processes at work. I offer illustrations that I consider representative, as well as findings from existing social research and media reports, in order to ground my comparative analysis. I will examine the Cuban case in some detail before I turn to the Nicaraguan case.

Love for Sale: Sex, Sentiment, and Tourism in Contemporary Cuba

My reflection on the widespread phenomenon of sex and romance tourism in Cuba begins with a short narrative to set the scene. Several years ago in Havana, I found myself unwittingly complicit in what appeared to be solicitation for prostitution or, perhaps, for a longer-term romantic interest. As a middle-aged man from the United States struck up an acquaintance with a young Cuban woman, he sought my help in translating between Spanish and English and I became both an observer and a broker for a brief and unconsummated encounter.

Late one evening in December 2003, I went out walking from my hotel in Old Havana, the Ambos Mundos, famous for having played host to Ernest Hemingway during the 1930s. My companion, whom I'll call James, and I were part of the same group sponsored by Global Exchange, and we had agreed to go out for a drink and to enjoy one of our last nights in Cuba before returning to the United States. We walked along well-known Obispo Street heading in the direction of Havana's Central Park. As usual, we were approached by a number of jineteros selling cigars "straight from the factory" at unbeatable prices, and James was momentarily distracted by a man who insisted on showing us to his place along the way, near the Floridita, one of the bars celebrated as a former Hemingway hangout.

We walked past the upscale Hotel Sevilla and farther along the promenade known as the Prado to an unpretentious outdoor bar in the direction of the Malecón, Havana's oceanside drive. As we chose a table, we noticed a young woman—pretty and looking a bit self-conscious—alone at the next table. I was a bit startled when James asked her if she wanted to join us, and she came over to sit down as we ordered drinks. The young woman, whom I will call Marta, made a point of asking if we were married or together; we explained that we were just friends. We began talking, and I translated quite a bit for James, who had only elementary Spanish and wanted to ask a number of personal questions. Where

Bars and restaurants catering to tourists on Obispo Street in Old Havana

was she from, what was she doing, how old was she, and did she have a husband or boyfriend? She told us she was from the provinces, from Camaguey, and had come to Havana to help her sister with her newborn baby before she would return home at the end of the month. She was twenty-three and studying at the university in Camaguey. She might take up computer courses or economics, or something else. Marta said she lived with her mother and two brothers and did not have a boyfriend. Her father lived in the same city and was remarried with a young child. She did not have to work, she said, since she lived at home and the university was free. When we asked if she liked Havana or Camaguey better, she quickly said Camaguey because Havana is *muy agitada* (very busy). James wanted to know if life was harder in Havana or Camaguey; she said Camaguey, because there are not as many resources and things cost more.

James asked if Marta liked to cook, and she said yes, and wash and iron too. She asked him (through me) whether he was married; I explained to her that his wife had died recently. He asked if she liked to dance, and she asked him the same. As the conversation continued, he commented that she had pretty hair and her perfume reminded him of his wife. I found the situation disconcerting; I was sure that Marta must have the impression that James was quite interested in her. She seemed to be getting this message as she looked demurely downward frequently (perhaps because I was there), sipping the piña coladas that replaced the can of cola she had when we arrived. When he asked if any of her family members lived outside Cuba, she said no and that, except for her sister, all were in Camaguey. At one point Marta asked him to take off his glasses and commented that his eyes were very blue. She asked his age (fifty-one) and said he looked forty-five or forty-six, politely adding that I too looked younger than my age. She addressed me since I spoke Spanish and he spoke little, but otherwise she focused on him.

At one point, James asked the waiter for a *cenicero*, an ashtray, for his cigar. That somehow turned the conversation in the direction of La Cenicienta, Spanish for "Cinderella." When I related a bit of the story line to Marta, she said she knew of it and added that she was very romantic. I commented that often in life there isn't a Prince Charming, but she did not let on if she agreed with me. I wondered if she might really be hoping for her Prince Charming to come and take her away.

After we had each had two drinks, James suggested that it was time to leave and Marta seemed surprised. She said to me somewhat reproachfully, "Va a dormir solo?" (Is he going to sleep alone?) I had been thinking for a while that

I might appear to be complicit in setting something up between them, even though I had tried to signal to her that he didn't mean anything by his questions. Before we stood up, James paid the bill of about ten dollars and passed her a five-dollar bill. She looked disappointed at the outcome, but we parted in a friendly way, with the customary embraces. As James and I left, I told him of my discomfort with the situation, and he disclosed that he was aware of the expectations he had raised in Marta.

The Romance of Cuba in the Popular Imagination

As we saw in Chapter 1, tourism in Cuba takes a number of forms, from holidays on world-famous Varadero Beach, to architectural tours of Old Havana, to health tourism, to cultural and educational tourism. The Cuban government announced a campaign several years ago to eliminate sex tourism, but it never got off the ground (Berg 2004b), and today sex is on the market in Cuba. In addition to the brief encounters of clients and jineteras or jineteros in Havana and elsewhere in Cuba, some travelers, most often middle-aged men, seek longer commitments with Cuban women who enjoy the men's attention and access to their dollars (or, now, convertible pesos). In some cases, women travelers seek sexual and romantic involvement with Cuban men who, like Cuban women, enjoy the flirtation and the relative luxuries that tourist dollars provide. Gay tourism is likewise in evidence, as male travelers find Cuban partners for a quick encounter or a more lasting affair.[4] Although I have observed these forms of tourism, for the most part they are beyond the scope of this work, and I will focus on the more widespread presence of Cuban women who are sought out by foreign men.

During five visits between 1993 and 2009, I observed the sexual, affective, and monetary exchanges that occur with great frequency in the city of Havana. I argue that in postrevolutionary Cuba, particularly since the Special Period of the 1990s, sex and love provide not only a diversion and relief from economic problems but also a bit of hope for many Cubans seeking both sensual and sentimental encounters. While the desires of travelers to Cuba may be fueled by media-enhanced longing for youth, beauty, and the "exotic,"[5] the Cubans involved in these entanglements are also motivated by yearnings to be swept away by romance to new places and new lives.

As noted earlier, tourism, including sex tourism, is hardly a new phenomenon in Cuba. Tourist travel to Cuba dates back well over a century and reached a high point in the 1950s during the Batista dictatorship. When the revolution triumphed in 1959, tourism fell off and sex workers were considered to be in need of rehabilitation, so prostitutes were given training as seamstresses and in other professions. The loss of Soviet support produced severe economic need in the 1990s, and a new strategy was ushered in to make tourism the leading industry in the island nation (Schwartz 1997; Scarpaci et al. 2002). Today, even if many sex workers engage in one-time arrangements with foreigners, many others aspire to have longer-lasting relationships that could lead to a week-long holiday, future remittances, or even marriage and a visa to leave Cuba.

A 1991 *Playboy* article by Jeff Cohen may well have inspired men in the United States and elsewhere to dream of travel to Cuba. With the Cuban government's blessing, the author was pleased to find willing models for the pictorial in a country in which "ninety-two percent of [women] belong to the Federación de Mujeres de Cuba, the Cuban Women's Federation," which he described as an alliance of feminists working to end macho attitudes. He and his French photographer, Patrick Magoud, turned to the forbidden paradise to discover the beautiful women who were making tourism "the best hope for the island's economic future" (73). Notably, while Magoud photographed seductive "top models" in Cuba, he fell in love with one of them and took her back to Paris with him.

Nearly a decade later, *Playboy* published another article on Cuba, this one, interestingly, by Cuban American feminist writer Achy Obejas, and instead of photos there were evocative drawings by LeRoy Neiman (Obejas 2000). While this piece proclaimed that "Cuba is hot, Cuba is ready," in reference to the "fabled island of pleasure and eroticism," it nonetheless went further in showing how the nation was getting ready for rising tourism. The nation was optimistically preparing English-language menus and road signs, anticipating the end of the U.S. blockade, which was expected to open the floodgates of travel from Cuba's near neighbor. Obejas observed that ordinary Cubans were rarely the beneficiaries of all that was offered up to tourists in the form of luxury and leisure; for example, the opening up of the economy to private enterprise, home restaurants, and independent shops favored only those Cubans with access to the hard currency of the tourism sector. Those Cubans who could tap into the tourist economy were doing so, often leaving poorly paid professional jobs for the better earnings found in tourism's service sector. Her article comments on the widespread prostitution and black market that have thrived since the early 1990s.

This side of tourism should be understood in historical context, as it has emerged in large part from conditions that were not of Cuba's making, the dismantling of the Soviet Union as well as the U.S. embargo on trade and travel to Cuba. The nation experienced the consequences of the Special Period and of the rapid development of tourism, but the hardships have been felt differentially, with women, Afro-Cubans, and those of more marginal socioeconomic status bearing the heaviest burdens (Holgado Fernández 2000; Safa 1995:166). The Cuban government has regarded the resulting jineterismo with some embarrassment as "a visible symptom of a moral crisis of the nation" (Berg 2004b:49). The view that tourism, along with private enterprise and creeping inequalities, is a necessary evil—first expressed by Fidel Castro—was repeated to me by Cuban citizens. In a conversation with Elena Diaz, a feminist scholar at the University of Havana, she used the term "mal necesario" to describe the significant, and gendered, downside to this economic development strategy, which is bringing jineterismo, including sex tourism, in its wake.

Silvio Rodríguez, the famed Cuban singer-songwriter, has written and sung songs of the Special Period, including several that evoke sad disillusionment over the growing appearance of sex tourism. His song "Flowers" is a lament for the "disposable flowers" that wither when they pass through forbidden doors, and his "Fifties Club" looks back on a time when anything could be bought for a price and "even desire becomes an object of consumption" (Rodríguez 2003:599–603).[6]

The same metaphor is used by writer Andrei Codrescu, whose *New York Times Magazine* article "Picking the Flowers of the Revolution" asserts, "In the waning days of socialism, Cuba is succumbing to an erotic imperialism, as men from the United States and other countries buy up its youngest, most beautiful women at bargain-basement rates" (1998:32).[7] The piece relates the case of "Jack," a fifty-two-year-old man from the United States who began going to Cuba in 1993; that year, many men traveled to Cuba "for the women," and it was likely not just coincidental that this was during the worst time of the economic crisis. Like a lot of foreign men, Jack found a young Cuban woman, just fourteen when he met her, with whom he fell in love. Although Cubans are generally not allowed in the tourist hotels, Jack and his girlfriend found ways to be together, and with her parents' blessing, he continued seeing her; when he was back in the United States, he sent her one hundred dollars each month through a Canadian bank. They waited to see if he would move to Cuba and join her— if the embargo lifted. This sort of romance between foreign men and Cuban women has become commonplace in the last decade, and matchmaking services are on the rise. As Codrescu notes, "The romantic range spreads from lust and money to love and marriage" (1998:32).

Gender, Race, and Cuban Tourism

Several scholars have described the desires of foreign men and Cuban women, clients and jineteras, for something more enduring than the usual fleeting encounter. Julia O'Connell Davidson (1996) discusses the emergence of sex tourism, particularly since 1993. Although the Cuban government initially tried to keep tourism and the Cuban people separate, the desire for dollars resulted in many Cubans besides those employed in the tourist sector trying to sell goods or services to the increasing number of foreign travelers who came to visit. An informal economy directed to meeting tourists' needs and desires was tolerated during this time.

Davidson notes that among the growing number of European men coming to Cuba for the women, many prefer "to spend several days or even weeks with the same woman and are keen to conceal the economic basis of the relationship from themselves" (1996:43). The men derive considerable benefits from the arrangement, including not only sex but also cooking and cleaning services and the assistance of a guide and interpreter. The sense of mutual attraction may mask the fact that the man pays for all expenses and helps his girlfriend meet her economic needs. The relatively low cost to the men helps maintain the illusion that she must feel genuine attraction and affection for him. Thus, both may desire a holiday romance, even if the exchange has very different meanings for each of them.

Whereas supporters of the Cuban revolution have lamented the advance of sex and romance tourism, the development holds special interest for those eager to see the demise of socialism in the country (Cabezas 1998). There is for some a wish to discover the market economy taking over production and consumption and even extending to personal relations. It is difficult to say whether men and women who appear to be smitten are in fact so, or whether women are performing their desire for men who are often older than their fathers, and the men are falling for it, but there are clearly sexual "scripts" at play (Marrero 2003).[8] In spite of the difficulties faced by the Cuban economy since the fall of the Soviet Union, not all Cubans are eager to find romance with foreigners and leave their country, benefiting as they do from higher levels of health care and education than elsewhere in Latin America and the Caribbean. Nonetheless, both parties can stand to benefit from these relationships, whether they are of short or long duration.

Racial differences often increase the potential for exoticizing. Anthropologist Nadine Fernandez (1999) describes the connection between the racialized and sexualized identity of jineteras on the one hand and the infusion of international capital in Cuba on the other. She draws attention to the growing so-cioeconomic separation between Cubans and tourists to the country, as well as the problems this produces (83). Moreover, she finds that whereas Afro-Cuban women are more often identified with sex tourism, white Cuban women more often are perceived to be involved in "romance tourism" (88).

Writer and artist Coco Fusco (1998) made a foray into Cuba to learn more about the place of women of color in sex tourism. As a Cuban American, she gained access to Afro-Cuban, or mulata, jineteras and found that many were seeking a source of longer-term support, as she put it, a "sugar-daddy," since the state was no longer providing the safety net that they needed. Mulatas, con-sidered particularly desirable by many tourists looking for sexual liaisons, may capitalize on their racialized sexuality as they offer themselves "as temporary partners or potential wives to foreigners" (154). Fusco notes that many mixed-race women are themselves the "love children" of Cuban women and white foreign men. She found that the tourists who approach them tell them it's for "love" and the women are "sophisticated traffickers in fantasy as much as sex" (157–158). Jineteras she met knew of women who had left with men for Europe, some happy with the outcome and others finding themselves in difficult situa-tions, including continued prostitution.

Another Cuban American, Alysia Vilar (2003), wrote a series on Salon.com that was a somewhat florid account of her personal experiences joining Cuban jineteras and earning some money while she tried to locate her Cuban father. She came to understand the perspective of women who sleep with foreign men for payment, often in the form of clothes, perfume, or money, and who do not regard this as prostitution. She writes that the women are "seeking out a rich boyfriend, either for marriage or regular remittances." Those who do so "are the hopeful light of their supportive families. For to jockey [be a jinetera] is to dream of a successful future, to dream in a country that feels so bereft of hope, of promising careers, of stable relationships. It's also the only way for many to make dollars, in a country where lawyers earn $18 a month and a meal in a restaurant costs twice as much." And according to her Cuban friend, "These men here aren't looking for a one-night stand, they want a Cuban girlfriend while on holiday."

For Money or Love

In Cuba, I have found ample evidence of both sex tourism and romance tour-ism. The presence of young Cuban women approaching men, particularly in the Old Havana area, often saying quite simply "Llévame" (take me away), was unmistakable. Women travelers also appeared eager to link up with Cuban men; frequently, the men were Afro-Cuban and the foreign women were white. Among the women I met who were staying in Cuba for several weeks or longer, many went out night after night, to bars and clubs, to listen to music and to dance. One went to matinee dance clubs where she enjoyed treating Cuban men to drinks and flirtation; several found boyfriends with whom to go out for a few weeks; another was making a return visit to Cuba to see the musician she had fallen for six months earlier; and another, a young, white Canadian woman, had married an Afro-Cuban and was trying to arrange for him to leave Cuba with her. The practice of women tourists seeking romance during their travels and local men enjoying the benefits is fairly common elsewhere in the Caribbean, as Joan Phillips (1999) has discussed in relation to the "beach boys" of Barbados.

My interest in the more common practices of male tourists and Cuban women seeking one another was a hot-button issue for many Havana residents. In summer 2005, a Cuban woman employed as a tour agent expressed to me the common view that jineteras are involved in sex work *por gusto* (for their own pleasure) to support their superficial desires and needs. This reflects the official party line in Cuba, that real poverty does not exist in the country and that young people engage in hustling activities to support artificial yearnings for consumer goods (Facio 1998–1999). Yet the diverse women I encountered who were involved in sex and romance tourism (or who were presumed to be) pose a challenge to that view.

I was outside the Floridita bar in Central Havana one afternoon when I saw a rather professorial white-haired gringo in conversation with a younger mulata Cuban woman. As the two stood on the sidewalk about fifteen feet away from me, she touched his arm as they spoke and then turned to walk in my direction. As she approached me, she began asking for my help, and rather than offering or refusing a handout, I told her I would be interested in talking with her. I commented that I knew that a lot of Cubans have a hard time getting by and head for the streets to make a living. The woman, whom I will call Sandra, quickly told me that she was not a prostitute, but yes, she has to get by. She said that it was dangerous for her to be seen talking with me, and we should go somewhere else.[9] I offered to buy her a cup of coffee, and she accepted, though she proceeded to take me to a bar on Obispo Street—La Escabeche would become a familiar place to me in the weeks ahead. I agreed when she suggested that we order mojitos, the well-known Cuban rum drink. Having established that I was a researcher and interested in her story, I took out my notebook to record notes, and she unselfconsciously told me about herself.

Sandra was thirty-one, with two children, aged four and six; the children's father had left, and her parents were retired. There were ten siblings in her family, and she left school after sixth grade to look after the younger ones. She told me that she gets by through the sale of used clothing given to her by tourists and Cubans who bring back clothing from other countries. Her earnings are better than before, when she worked as a chambermaid. She emphasized that she did not deal in drugs or prostitution. When I asked what she thought of girls and women who go into prostitution, she said that she does not pass judgment since life is hard, but she made it clear it was not for her (or at least she wanted to give me that impression). She told me that some women earn about one hundred dollars per night with one or more men and that some tourists also bring drugs and sell them through Cubans. She had friends who were enticed to leave Cuba with men as a result of sex and romance tourism and who were then used for prostitution in Italy, Spain, Russia, Canada, and Holland. She described these as cases of sex trafficking, saying that she had five friends who left with men and suffered for it; at least one had returned to Cuba.

Sandra went on to tell me that she had been sent to prison for four years but was released early for good behavior. She told me that she was sent there on a trumped-up charge of prostitution after she refused to have sex with a police officer.[10] While she was in prison, her mother cared for her young children. She told me this story in a straightforward way, and I wondered if she was attempting to impress me with her difficult life conditions, even as I admired her ability to narrate a painful past. She soon changed the topic to point out to me that this bar was known to attract Cubans and tourists who want to hook up together. I saw that there were indeed several examples of this: a gringa who might be in her thirties warming up to an Afro-Cuban man, and a young Cuban woman hanging around a gringo and a couple of young gringas. I commented that I knew of gringas who were just looking to have fun with Cuban men, to go out dancing and flirt a little. Yes, she said, and "para pagarle la pinga" (a crude reference to the women paying for "the penis"). I persisted, saying that it was interesting that gringas would rarely pay for going out or having sex with gringos, and she quickly responded that if women pay expenses or offer gifts, they do so because "el Cubano es caliente" (Cuban men are hot). There was no doubt in her mind that tourists were after sex with Cubans.

Sitting nearby was a young man with bongo drums, who told me his father was Jamaican and his mother came from the United States to support the revolution. He wanted to know what I thought of the country where he had grown up, and then he proceeded to tell me that nothing was right in Cuba. He said that this was where he likes to hang out and concurred when I said I had heard about Cubans and tourists linking up at the bar, saying "This is the place." Back in my hotel later that evening, I met with a Cuban sociologist and described that day's encounter with Sandra, asking if her story seemed plausible—which she said it did. This underscored for me the difficult and ambivalent mix of tourism with sex, romance, and politics in Cuba.[11]

Over the following weeks, I would pass this bar and glance inside as I walked through Old Havana. Then, after I began working on an occasional basis with an Afro-Cuban woman I had met on an earlier visit to Cuba, whom I will call Claudia, I suggested we go in to learn something more about the workings of sex and romance tourism. A female vocalist was singing with a band, and the mood was easygoing. Within minutes, we met Ana, who would become a key interlocutor on questions of Cuban flirtation and romance. In this small establishment on a busy corner of the old city, with its five tables in addition to the bar itself, Ana stood out as she sat alone at the table next to ours. A tall and slender mulata with long blond *trenzas* (braids), she was strikingly beautiful and self-possessed. She wore stylish jeans, a close-fitting black top, and strappy pink sandals, had painted nails, and held a silver purse. When Claudia engaged her in conversation and told her of my research, Ana joined our table. She introduced herself as a Cuban dancer living in France, just back for a visit. Her mother was Cuban and her father Syrian, which explained her good looks, she said with a wink. She had a sixteen-year-old son, who seemed to be mainly in the care of her mother. She told us that she gave classes in salsa and danced in Havana at the Tropicana nightclub, the famous venue for extravagant shows.

By this time I noticed that there were aspects of Ana's story that did not add up. I commented that I had been to a show at the Tropicana a couple of nights before and asked if she would be dancing there that night, but she avoided the question. Her account of living in France (referring to the city of Nancy) seemed vague, without many points of reference. Yet she was more than willing to talk and adopted the role of intimate friend from that first meeting, giving me her address and phone number and insisting that I must call and visit. The relationship we formed over my remaining time in Havana that year never went further than going to a couple of bars along Obispo Street, but she intro-

A dancer performing at the celebrated Tropicana nightclub

duced me to the culture of foreigners and Cubans hanging out, hooking up, and building connections that might endure for a night or for years.

That first time in the bar, Ana attracted the attention of a man who soon joined us. He explained that he was from France and had a Cuban girlfriend he had returned to see after a year apart. That did not stop Ana from playfully but persistently flirting with him, as best she could, given his limited Spanish and her apparently nonexistent French. While he and I had a conversation in English about how he met his girlfriend and how the long-distance relationship was going, she periodically tried to steal his attention with provocative queries, like "Francia [Frenchie], would you like to have a massage?" She motioned with her hands to be sure her meaning came across. He responded in English that his girlfriend had spies out everywhere and would kill him, which I translated into Spanish for Ana. She admonished him that she was asking an innocent question, but then her words were belied when she stood up to dance in place to the music, shimmying in a precise and subtly seductive way. He commented to me that 99 percent of men would go with Ana in spite of having a girlfriend, but he was different. He announced that he would be going to another bar on the circuit, the Café Paris—and, soon afterward, Ana proclaimed that we women (Ana, Claudia, and myself) should also go to that bar.

We soon headed off to the next bar, just a few blocks away. The place was crowded, and we found a table in the back. Across the way from us was a solitary man whom Ana invited to join us. He had a sad look and somewhat reluctantly came over with his beer to sit down. He told us he had just arrived from Finland, spoke English but little Spanish, and would stay in Cuba for a month. As he finished what turned out to be his fourth beer, he pulled out a photograph of a woman he had tucked in his copy of the Lonely Planet guide to Cuba and confessed that a difficult breakup with his girlfriend back home had prompted him to travel. He told me that he needed to be alone for a while, which I dutifully translated for the others. Nonetheless, Ana insisted that he needed our company and proceeded to mimic his long face, trying to make eye contact and coax him out of his low mood. Claudia and I finally left the two at the bar, talking about our interesting evening and speculating about whether the two could possibly be linking up.

After several visits to La Escabeche, where I would often see Ana, I felt like a regular there. Over time, I watched Ana attract the attention of a number of men and engage their interest over the course of an afternoon or evening. Even with limited ability to converse in the same language, she would let men know she liked their eyes or their smile, inquire as to whether they had girlfriends or liked massages (a repeated ploy), though I never observed her going off with anyone, if only because I did not stay out as late as she did. In our early conversations, Ana showed off her new jewelry and boasted of how expensive it was. She never told me exactly where her money came from, though Claudia was quite certain that Ana was indeed a jinetera; she guessed that Ana earned well at times but spent her money heedlessly, then had an urgent need for more. By the end of my visit, she had become an affectionate friend, saying we should always remain in touch—though I never doubted the opportunism of our relationship. She also spoke about being low on money and asked if I would send her gifts after I left Cuba. On our last evening together, she persuaded an Italian living in Havana to go with us to a restaurant and told him up front that she needed some money in order to eat; he quickly complied by handing her some cash, demonstrating to me how adept she was in getting by in an economy driven by tourism and need.

Certainly, not all Cubans get along as well as Ana, and she herself, at age thirty-five, would not command the higher earnings of younger Cuban women on the tourist market. There is much diversity among women I encountered in the tourism scene. I once noticed in the Escabeche bar a most unlikely Cuban woman come in, wearing loose-fitting and conservative shirt and pants, looking more like a missionary than a woman on the make. Yet she sat at the bar and soon struck up a conversation with a burly American man (who very likely traveled illegally through Mexico to get to Cuba), somewhat nervously asking the usual getting-acquainted questions: Where do you live? Where are you staying? and so on. I left before I could learn more about where this was heading, but it reminded me that all manner of Cubans are struggling to improve their livelihoods, support their families, and get ahead, even if it means entering into precipitous intimacies.

With the sudden arrival of Hurricane Dennis, my departure from Havana was delayed for two days and I was relocated to the Ambos Mundos Hotel. During that time I remained in the hotel, as it was one of the few places in the city with power. I passed some hours in the crowded lobby, where tourists were stranded and a number of Cubans had gathered with them. Normally, Cubans are not allowed past the lobby, but I observed some Cuban women accompanying tourists in elevators—perhaps having offered a tip to the staff or just finding that the rules were relaxed due to the extreme circumstances. Among those passing time in the lobby, I saw the same heavy-set and amiable American man mentioned previously, engaged in rapt conversation with several Cuban women.

Research on sex and romance tourism in Cuba has advanced in productive ways, though to date only a few Cuban researchers have published works on sex work or prostitution in their own country.[12] The international "Cuba boom" (Behar 2002) has Cuba aspiring to host up to 2.5 million tourists annually.[13] Further research on the intimate encounters of tourists and those toured may tell us more about the paradoxes of travel to Cuba. My broader interest in the cultural politics of tourism on the island focuses on the coexisting cultural-historical tourism that continues to reference the revolution and the nostalgic tourism that is typified by longings for the prerevolutionary days of Hemingway, old American cars, and extravagant shows—and sometimes for the imagined sexual licentiousness of the past.[14] Contemporary tourism reveals the tension between these two sides of Cuban experience. Even an "enlightened" tourist like James—who carried around with him a biography of Che Guevara—in seeking my help translating with Marta at the bar, revealed his desire (only somewhat suppressed) for the other, romantic Cuba of his imagination.

Innocence for Sale: The Double-Edged Sword of Tourism in Nicaragua

Whereas Cuba had a long history of tourism before the revolutionary government shunned it for three decades (and then economic necessity made tourism a priority once again starting in the 1990s), Nicaragua figured much less significantly as a travel destination in the years before the Sandinista victory in 1979.[15] Both countries saw solidarity travel in the postrevolutionary period, but Nicaragua has only in the past decade attempted to fashion itself as a tourism competitor along with Costa Rica and other Central American nations. Known as the second-poorest country in the hemisphere and considered unsafe during the Contra war of the 1980s, Nicaragua has had "image problems" to overcome. Yet after the Sandinista electoral loss, by the mid-1990s visitors began coming in growing numbers to the country, as discussed in Chapter 2. A New York Times reporter described the changes in the country at that time as "enormous" (Rohter 1997:10).

Even so, several years later INTUR personnel were concerned that it was still hard to shake the notion of Nicaragua as a place of political conflict and danger. Managers in the departments of marketing and international relations told me in 2003 that they must strive to overcome the old views and to present a "positive impression" (Raúl Calvet and Regina Hurtado, interview, June 27, 2003). Around this time, a new INTUR director, Lucia Salazar, was appointed, and in an interview that appeared in promotional literature for Linblad Expeditions (which had begun operating cruises stopping in Nicaragua) she described her personal motivation for promoting a fresh image for Nicaragua. During the time of the revolution, her father was killed in conflict with the Sandinistas and her family lived in exile in the United States for fifteen years. Now she views tourism as "one of the only ways that Nicaragua can counter the negative image it was branded with in the 1980s" (2004:6). As noted earlier, she worked closely with the Sandinista head of the Tourism Commission in the National Assembly, Tomás Borge, whom she held responsible for her father's death (7). When I interviewed Borge on June 30, 2003, he mentioned their decidedly uncomfortable working relationship and emphasized his own desire to look to Cuba as a model for successful tourism development.

Despite their ideological differences, Salazar and Borge agreed that a "healthy" and "clean" national image would help to develop Nicaraguan tourism. In my interview with Borge in 2003, he told me, presciently as it turned out, that the Sandinistas would win the next election, and he predicted that they would not only support tourism as the number-one industry but would also "make it clean and healthful, free of the sex tourism and casinos that are taking hold in the country." For Salazar's part, she advocated for a safe and clean environment for tourism so that there would be no more talk of "plastic bags being the national flower" (Sánchez Campbell 2004:9A). Both lauded the second annual convention on tourism held in Granada, Nicaragua, in August 2004 (Sánchez Campbell 2004:9A) with the theme "For a clean and safe Nicaragua" (Zambrana 2004) as helping to establish a secure experience for tourists coming to the country.[16] Whether or not the tourism industry one day achieves its stated objective of projecting a more clean and wholesome image to mainstream tourists, I have found that for now it presents mixed messages to prospective travelers.

That same year, I discovered that INTUR had developed five 30-second television spots to run on CNN's Headline News with the slogan "Nicaragua: It's hot!" This "brand," or product-marketing device, was identified as a way of selling the country to potential investors and international tourists. One thing that travelers to the country know is that Nicaragua's climate is steamy, relieved only during the rainy season when the humidity lets loose in torrents. So, when I had a preview of INTUR's new ads, I had to assume that they were intended to invoke another meaning of the word *hot*.[17] Indeed, the spots offered fast-paced and colorful images of the country with captions like "Culture," "History," and "Adventure," implying that Nicaragua is a new and exciting place to visit and that it is *de moda*, in fashion. But the ads' fleeting images of young women frolicking in bikinis also conveyed a not-so-subtle message that Nicaragua is "sexy" and that visitors would discover tan beauties eager for the company of foreigners with money to spend. When I commented on the ads' sexual innuendo, I was met by a rather innocent response from the assistant in the marketing department, who had not considered this possible reaction (María Eugenia Sabella, interview, July 20, 2004).[18] This, notably, in a nation where one of the first official acts of the revolutionary government in 1979 had been to ban the use of sexualized images of women in the media.

My most recent visit to Nicaragua, in 2008, came two years after the return of FSLN candidate Daniel Ortega to the nation's presidency. Since the electoral loss in 1990, Sandinista politics had been fraught with compromise and pacts with the political and religious right (which had caused many to part ways and join the Sandinista Renovation Movement, or MRS). Nonetheless, Ortega's comeback was viewed throughout the region and much of the world as signaling a move leftward as part of the so-called pink tide in Latin America. Although Nicaraguan critics have recently likened his populist refashioning as a sort of New Age caudillo to past dictatorships that crushed their opposition,[19] the U.S. media prefer to link him with Venezuelan president Hugo Chávez. In the current context, tourism has taken a slightly different form but still holds pride of place as a leading industry along with coffee production.

Now, with the return of Sandinista leadership, visitors to the country have a lingering impression of national heroes Augusto César Sandino and Rubén Darío as they pass between huge portraits of these men on facing walls at the international airport. Sandino, in particular, has recovered his place of honor as national and historical icon and is not so closely linked to the controversial decade of the 1980s. INTUR is announcing the prospect of promoting a Sandino tour that would follow a circuit from Sandino's birthplace to the areas where he fought his anti-imperialist campaign in the 1920s and 1930s until his assassination by Somoza's forces.[20] In addition, to assist the rural sector there has been an emphasis on sustainable and communitarian tourism, drawing tourists to coffee cooperatives and other sites where they enjoy the natural environment and contribute to local economies (Cañada et al. 2006; Cañada and Gascón 2006). Tourism may conceivably be moving in the direction of the sort of wholesome activity that Tomás Borge and others talked about in earlier years.[21] Even so, we will see that less wholesome strains of tourism are also present and have deeply gendered effects.

Women, Youth, and Tourism

In the capital city of Managua, there is much talk about the rapid proliferation of casinos and nightclubs. Since the first casino, Pharaohs, opened on the Masaya highway in 2000, a number of others have appeared in Managua and other cities. Some Nicaraguans express national pride in this hallmark of modernity and in the amount of money invested in the development of casinos. One writer effused that "visitors will think they have arrived in Las Vegas, in the United States" (Bravo 2004:4A). Others, however, like Tomás Borge, are more concerned that the expansion of casinos as well as nightclubs will serve to attract a growing clientele in search of sexual favors.[22]

I was told that one well-known club called Lips, owned by an American, charges over twenty dollars for a single drink because it is assumed that men asking for a cocktail wish to have the service of the lap dancer that comes along with it. The club is centrally located across from the Crowne Plaza (formerly, the InterContinental Hotel) and demands attention with its neon sign displaying large, red lips. My visit at midday during off-hours did not dispel the notion that the club offers far more than a bar to its clientele; a woman employee nodded silently when asked about the practice of charging high prices for drinks, with sexual "extras" provided.

By 2008, the Masaya highway in central Managua had become far more developed as a commercial area with malls, casinos, hotels, restaurants, and clubs. Several venues, like the Elite and the Diamond Clubs, are known for their strip shows, and the women who perform there may leave with clients who pay the club a fee for their time.[23] More women, and sometimes *travestis*, transvestites or transgendered individuals who have found a niche in the market, can be seen

Outside the Elite strip club in Managua

along the road later at night, selling sex to both nationals and tourists. Several NGOs send out young people regularly to carry condoms and encourage the use of clinics for regular health exams and sexually transmitted disease (STD) testing. Nicaragua's sexual culture is more evident today than a decade ago, and the return of the FSLN has not diminished its presence in the country.

A middle-aged man from the United States who has lived in Managua for some years commented to me that he believes that "all Nicas" have their price and are willing to provide sex for money. He mentioned being approached by a teenage boy from his neighborhood who offered sexual favors in exchange for a small sum. This man's perception is surely conditioned by stereotyped generalizations regarding sexualized and racialized Others, though it points to a commonly held view. Based on my past observations, the actual practice of exchanging sex for money appeared to be more widespread after the transition from revolutionary to neoliberal government in the 1990s. The transition meant higher unemployment, growing disparities of wealth, and the elimination of the state provision of basic foods and health care.[24] Even though tourism has contributed to economic development at the national level, it has also introduced new social inequities and new, often unattainable, consumer desires.

Over the years carrying out research in Managua, I lived in one barrio that became a home to me. There, I observed evidence of the sex trade and of the occasional longer-term relationships that formed between Nicaraguans and foreigners, whether visitors or residents. From the early 1990s, I saw the growing number of women and travesti sex workers on the streets near the Inter-Continental Hotel and elsewhere in the city. In the working-class neighborhood where I stayed, I knew young mothers still in their teenage years who dressed up and went out to seek work that would pay better than informal services like taking in laundry or cleaning homes, which they also performed. A nineteen-year-old with two young children, whom I had known for some years, seemed embarrassed when I saw her one day wearing a faux leather miniskirt and close-fitting laced bodice, though I could not bring myself to inquire where she was going. Several young women living with their mother across the street from me made little secret of their livelihood, as clients called for them in luxurious vehicles with shaded windows to go off to motels for amorous and reportedly well-rewarded trysts (Babb 2001a:256–257).[25]

The lives of most sex workers are far from glamorous, however. In an interview I conducted with a woman from the barrio Acahualinca, a particularly impoverished area of Managua, I heard about her experience of low pay and episodes of violence. At Girasoles (meaning "sunflowers"), an NGO that provides services to sex workers, I met with "Elvia" in an examination room where we sat and talked. Self-possessed and wearing a long, slim, dark skirt and matching blouse with deep V neckline, she asked me to guess her age. She revealed that she was fifty-two and had been a sex worker from the time she was twenty-five, when she was abandoned by an abusive husband, the mother of five young children, and recently arrived in the city. She later had five more children, though two of them died. Now, her sister cares for the youngest ones, who do not know how she earns the income that helps support them. She meets men at a bar and negotiates a price based on the services offered, sometimes providing sex on credit until the men's payday on the fifteenth and thirtieth of the month. She commented that in her barrio it is not uncommon for women to work this way, and she does not feel particularly stigmatized, though it is not work that she would choose if she had other options. She prefers to go to the bar with other women, as protection against possible violence when men drink heavily. Some sex workers in Nicaragua are starting to organize, but Elvia just counts on the support of sex workers she knows and Girasoles (interview, June 5, 2008).

The colonial city of Granada has become one of the primary sites of tourism in the country, particularly since foreigners started buying and renovating properties in the city center. There are language schools, fine restaurants and hotels, and an abundance of tourism offices. Horse-drawn carriages and a quaint look combine with modern comforts at relatively low cost. A number of retirees from the United States have come to purchase homes in Granada, especially since discovering that the cost of living is substantially lower than in neighboring Costa Rica. Some older men have sought out young Nicaraguan women as their mates and housekeepers, an arrangement that could be viewed as a form of sexual servitude. Several of these men manage real estate and sell properties to other newcomers to Granada and the region. Speaking to them in the company of their timid young wives, it was impossible to avoid the impression that these men were exploiting the physical, emotional, and sexual labor of highly vulnerable Nicaraguans. Nonetheless, these women had their own expectations, which often included their husbands' support of their mothers and siblings, and in several private conversations the women suggested that they would not put up with abusive behavior over the long term.

Granada's central park, just across from the historic Hotel Alhambra, has become notorious for attracting male tourists seeking young women for a single night or longer. Most perniciously, some seek out children and adolescents, and young people may be seen waiting in the park for potential clients. A longtime resident estimated that about 60 percent of unaccompanied male tourists may be coming to Granada for the purposes of sex tourism. In 2001, a segment of a weekly television program *Esta Semana* (February 23, 2001) entitled "Inocencia en venta" (Innocence for Sale) made the public aware of the situation of adolescents, mainly girls, between the ages of eleven and thirteen who are sought out for sex tourism in Granada. With their identities concealed, young girls described being taken to hotels or houses where they were paid for sex, with no questions asked. Until this recent attention, there was little control over such practices, but following national media coverage the city mayor called for legal intervention. In one heavily publicized case in 2003, a pedophile from the United States who recruited children for sex and pornographic photography sessions was arrested and is now serving time in prison.

In recent years, Granada has developed a long corridor with little city traffic, La Calzada, which is dedicated to expanding tourist options. Besides the hotels, guesthouses, restaurants, and tour offices, the street has also attracted some of the youthful sexual commerce that city officials would like to discourage. Women working at an AMNLAE Casa de la Mujer (women's center) on that street expressed concern about the children and adolescents who sell candy to tourists and who are also known to be sought out for sexual services (Olga María Marenca, interview, June 6, 2008). One of these women told me that she was once surprised to be approached by a man who simply assumed that as a young-looking woman she would be available to him. A recent study of the sexual exploitation of children has shown how pervasive the problem is in Granada and elsewhere in the country. The researchers identified several forms of sexual commerce involving youth, and a commission has been organized to educate those in the tourism industry and to call for greater support from the legal system to penalize offenders (Karla Sequeira, interview, June 12, 2008). The feminist NGO Puntos de Encuentro has published a booklet directed to young people and their allies to inform them of their rights and to empower them to resist sexual exploitation (*La Boletina* 2007).

Highly visible cases, often linked to tourism, have prompted action at the national level. INTUR, along with the Nicaraguan Ministry of the Family (MiFamilia) and the National Police, held a forum in the city of Masaya on exploitative sexual commerce of children and adolescents (Linarte 2004:13B). Experts found connections to family violence and sexual abuse, poverty, and a weak legal system. This kind of sexual exploitation has been increasing in border areas of the country as well as in tourist centers. Officials have called on service providers in the tourism industry to serve as watchdogs so that perpetrators of sexual exploitation of minors may be brought into compliance with the law. Those service providers either directly or indirectly participating in the sexual commerce of children and youth would be stripped of their licenses under Article 72 of the General Tourism Law.

The Pacific coast town of San Juan del Sur has become a better-known site for tourism in recent years, attracting those seeking the beach, sea diving, surfing, and other water sports. Cruise ships now stop in the formerly sleepy town, adding only a little revenue since the travelers are cautioned against consuming local food and drink. But the presence of so many travelers has had an impact on the town. Residents are concerned that their youngsters will adopt the ways of "hippie" and other foreign youth, viewed as sloppily dressed and groomed, often with bad manners. Prostitution, although not on the scale found in Granada, is on the rise according to longtime residents. In even the best hotels and restaurants, middle-aged male tourists are accompanied quite openly by young Nicaraguan women. A local woman commented perceptively that tourism is an "espada de doble filo" (double-edged sword), bringing the good and the bad to San Juan del Sur. As wealthier outsiders, both Nicaraguan and foreign, discover the charms of the coastal town and buy property there, locals like her find it impossible to afford the higher cost of living.[26] She told me that she would like to see a group of women get together to defend the town against the pernicious effects of tourism, which could threaten their cultural identity. Despite her misgivings about the impact of tourism, however, she is putting her own daughter through a college program in tourism studies and hopes that her son will pursue the same path once she has the resources to send him to college. She remarked ruefully to me that it is no wonder if women are entering prostitution, given the high cost of living and limited employment opportunities.

I interviewed one young woman, "Margarita," who at twenty-three was widowed with eight-year-old twin daughters in the northern city of Matagalpa and had come to San Juan del Sur for a few months; she planned to earn enough money in sex work to return home and open a small dry-goods shop. Every week she made the lengthy trip back to her family, who thought she was working at a bar, and to take a class to become a beautician. Pretty and smart, Margarita was hedging her bets by preparing for a couple of different employment opportunities, and in the meantime she worked in a family-run *putería* (whorehouse) in the seaside town. Margarita came to her workplace through a friend who worked there and had clients both on-site and elsewhere in the town. The latter commanded much higher rates, but a good part of the payment for her work outside went to the owner of the putería. She spoke appreciatively of the kind man and his evangelical wife and their toddler son but made it clear how important it was to her that she work there only a few months and that her work remain unknown to her family and community.

I had made contact with Margarita through an employee at one of the town's more expensive resorts, where I knew the owners well enough to ask candidly about how guests hook up with sex workers. According to an obliging concierge, or "arranger" as he was called, he tries never to disappoint a guest; if someone wants "a girl" or drugs, for example, his attitude is that he can manage it in a discreet way that is safer for both the resort and the guest (and he always keeps condoms at the front desk). He makes sure that sex workers are escorted to the correct accommodations and that they leave quietly and inconspicuously afterward. He assured me that every hotel in the area provides such services, often for generous tips. He and other employees at the resort told me that with so many tourists coming to San Juan del Sur, local men sometimes feel that their women are being "stolen away" from them (interviews, June 10, 2008).

Besides those women who choose sex work, others simply prefer to date foreign men, whom they find attractive and often better mannered than local men. I met several young women, frequently with some professional training, who are holding out for an *extranjero*, a foreign man, who has better prospects than the Nicaraguan men they know. Some local men are similarly interested in foreign women, often for the advantages that these tourists offer in the form of money to spend, desire for a good time, and so on. Such men may be not only *mujeriego* (womanizers) but *gringa-iego* (specifically seeking women travelers), as one local observer expressed it. This may be a result of the Americanization of youth that has accompanied the growth in tourism from the north. The possibilities for romance, short or long term, are appealing to many Nicaraguans, and some spend time around language schools and other places that draw tourists in order to meet them. I learned of young Nicaraguans (more often male than female) who had dated a series of foreign students over a period of years, apparently hoping for a long-term commitment or marriage (Aynn Setright, personal communication). Although romance tourism is not as well known in Nicaragua as in Cuba, it is found in places frequented by foreign travelers—in seaside resorts, retirement communities, and study-abroad programs—raising questions about gender and power in these relationships.

The Hidden Side of Tourism Development

In Managua, video maker Rossana Lacayo spoke with me about her 2003 work, *Verdades ocultas* (Hidden Truths), which traces the stories of several sex workers in Nicaragua. The narratives in this award-winning video relate the difficult conditions that propelled the women and one travesti into sex work—inadequate incomes to support their children, histories of violence, and too few choices. She described *trata de blanca*, the trafficking in people, mainly young girls. Lured away from their families and networks of support, young women from Nicaragua's rural sector are particularly vulnerable to abuse and are sometimes taken to other Central American countries for sex tourism.[27] In other cases, adolescent girls are offered to truck drivers traveling through Nicaragua and along the Pan-American Highway as a form of *comercio sexual* (sexual commerce). She noted that sex tourism is even more hidden than this form of sexual commerce, so it has received less attention (interview, July 28, 2004).

Several NGOs are documenting this phenomenon and working to offer alternatives to impoverished families that sometimes encourage daughters to provide sexual services to men in order to put food on the table. The feminist director of the NGO Xochiquetzal, an activist organization working in the area of sexuality and human rights,[28] was more passionate on this subject than on any other when I interviewed her. Hazel Fonseca (interview, July 23, 2004) emphasized that her organization's work centers on bringing attention to many of the areas of sexual injustice that occur beneath the surface in Nicaragua, calling for an end to these forms of exploitation and discrimination. Thus, the NGO's publication *Fuera del Closet* (Out of the Closet), best known for supporting gay rights, aims to bring all manner of previously hidden sexual exchanges into public view. Fonseca regards sexual commerce that targets vulnerable youth, whether a result of sex tourism or of sexual predation more generally, as one of the most urgent social problems needing to be confronted—and she advocates for youth empowerment in the process.

If we find greater attention to sex work involving young people than to adults in Nicaragua, this may be due only in part to the more compelling nature of their situation. It may also be explained in terms of the potential for damaging effects on tourism in Nicaragua's economy. Whereas child prostitution as flagrant criminal activity detracts from the image the country would like to project, adult sex workers and entertainers provide some of the revenue the nation has come to depend on. Writing on neighboring Costa Rica, Rivers-Moore (2007) describes the broad and critical attention given to child sex tourism in contrast to the "blind eye" turned to more mature sex workers, even when their rights are violated. She accounts for this by noting the reliance on "gringo" tourism, a part of which seeks out sexual encounters, as well as the vulnerable migrant status of many sex workers—a great number of them Nicaraguans who are undocumented and unprotected, suffering racialized opprobrium they would not experience at home and turning to sex work as available employment.

Staging Sex and Love in Postrevolutionary Nations

Tourism in postrevolutionary and postconflict nations reveals the highly ambivalent ways in which gender, sexuality, and race figure in these countries' efforts to develop their economies by refashioning themselves for international visitors. Sex and romance tourism is just a part of what I have observed in Nicaragua and Cuba, but it gets at some of the most vexing problems that often accompany tourism, particularly in the neoliberal era in the global South: the encounters of foreigners who are seeking "exotic" and even intimate experiences with locals, who for their part may desire the financial, and sometimes emotional, support that travelers seem willing to offer. These two countries are far from alone in attracting this kind of tourism experience—we see it in many developing countries that play host to tourism—but these cases are striking insofar as revolutionary ideologies seem to fall by the wayside. My research on this phenomenon contributes to our understanding of the particular dilemmas faced by postrevolutionary nations as tourism looms large as their principal industry; the ethnographic material presented here reveals the deeply gendered and racial consequences of tourism in these societies in transition to more market-driven economies.

There are certain striking similarities in the Cuban and Nicaraguan cases, including the desire, or ideological commitment, to offer "wholesome" tourism experiences even as the market pushes these nations toward a tolerance of commodified sex and intimacy. A young Nicaraguan woman I met, a domestic worker who was studying nights to try to enter tourism administration, told me that her dream was to leave Managua and join forces with another woman to own and operate a guesthouse in the provinces. She was aware of sex tourism in some parts of the country, including Managua and Granada, but, she volunteered, "it's not as bad as in Cuba." This points to the question of whether Nicaragua will follow the direction taken in Cuba, tolerating sex and romance tourism as the tourism industry expands and more pleasure seekers arrive. Although it is true that at present the phenomenon is far more pronounced in Cuba than in Nicaragua, it is also arguable that among those involved, Cuban sex workers tend to have greater control over these practices than their Nicaraguan counterparts, who are often targeted as highly vulnerable due to their youth, poverty, and lack of social support. When Nicaraguans lost the safety net of social services provided by the revolutionary government prior to 1990, they began relying on NGOs to provide support. While some access this support, many others do not, leaving them to fend for themselves. Cubans, even if they face social and political restrictions and shortages of needed or desired consumer goods, continue to benefit from state guarantees of education, health care, and other basic rights and resources.

In the last half century, Cuba and Nicaragua drew wide international attention as a result of their broad programs of social transformation. Although Cuba's revolutionary process has been far more sustained than Nicaragua's, both countries share a legacy of concern for their citizens' social and economic well-being. Without a doubt, their triumphant social revolutions put these nations on the map, in the Latin American region and in the world. Thus, I was startled when a travel agent in Managua told me that with tourism development, "Nicaragua is becoming a place on the map" (Careli Tours, interview, July 22, 2004).[29] Although this at first seemed to be a reflection of the nation's historical amnesia, it could also be a manifestation of the hopes of many Nicaraguans, like Cubans, regardless of political orientation, that tourism will do for the future what social revolution accomplished in the past.

However, in an era of neoliberalism and globalization when social inequalities are in great evidence, we should be less sanguine about the distribution of benefits from tourism. We must be chastened by the words of the Cuban feminist who told me that tourism is a "necessary evil" and the Nicaraguan woman who described tourism as "a double-edged sword." Cuba is featured in such publications as *Fantasy Islands: A Man's Guide to Exotic Women and International Travel* (Wilson 1998:147–149). Along with Vietnam, Cuba is described as a "communist" nation where the government seeks to prohibit tourists from taking local women to hotels, but the author assures readers that it is one of the best places to find women with whom to become sexually or romantically involved. He writes, "In Havana, beautiful young women stroll around looking for a man like you." Moreover, "the asking price is likely to be shockingly low." He goes on to offer the best venues for meeting women who dream of having European or American husbands. Could the unofficial "branding" of Cuba as a haven for sex and romance tourism be in Nicaragua's future as well? The political and economic vicissitudes in both countries and the sexualizing of previously "forbidden" lands suggest that this is possible. Nevertheless, both countries have histories of women's active social and political participation, and we could see other currents of change in the future.

The opening up to tourism in Cuba and Nicaragua paves the way for the sort of "staged authenticity" conceptualized by MacCannell (1999) and discussed in relation to sex and romance tourism by Brennan (2004). Men and women perform their desire and stage intimacy, offering at least the illusion of authentic experience, insofar as there are mutual benefits in doing so. When postrevolutionary nations no longer provide the safety net of the past and economic livelihood is no longer a certainty, sex and love appear to be the means by which to grasp opportunities that are otherwise unattainable. The trafficking in question is not only in sex but in fantasy and in hope. Tourists as well as local women and men collaborate in this staged exchange of intimacy with money and other gifts. The nations I have considered here reveal the profoundly unequal terms of tourism's encounter with gender and power, race and nation, as realities fall short of expectations. More often than not, sex is fleeting, promises are broken, and romance remains elusive—just as elusive as the dream of economic advancement and well-being promised long ago in these postrevolutionary nations.

6 Race, Gender, and Cultural Tourism in Andean Peru and Chiapas, Mexico

It is in the intimacy of everyday relations in the street, marketplace, and village that implicit decisions and identities are made about who is, and who is not, Indian. . . . Modernization has reinforced the Indianization of women, while opening the option of cultural mestizaje to most men.

Marisol de la Cadena, "Women Are More Indian"

WELL OVER A DECADE AGO, Marisol de la Cadena wrote these words to describe the gendered and racialized identities of Andean people in southern Peru and to show how women, in contrast to men, have come to be viewed as "more Indian." Since then, this approach to identity formation has resonated among scholars working in the region, as it calls for a more subtle reading of cultural meanings and practices that are laden with differences of gender, race, and power (Weismantel 2001:96; Canessa 2005:16). Others have examined the politics of race in colonial and postcolonial times in Andean Peru (Orlove 1993; Poole 1994) and in Mexico (Mallon 1995)—the two nations under discussion here—but Cadena's intervention was notable for pointing to the need for a closer scrutiny of gender just as it called for a more nuanced interpretation of indigeneity.[1]

The intersectionality of gender, race, and nation is a familiar framework for feminists working around the globe and has found considerable acceptance among social analysts and cultural theorists more broadly; yet intersectionality has not often been historicized so as to allow us to observe the uneven manner in which change occurs. Under the terms of engagement now emerging in Andean Peru and Chiapas, Mexico, I want to suggest two things: first, tourism has become a particularly robust site for reexamining what is at stake in the notion that "women are more Indian"; and second, we may find that what has been a social liability, being both female and indigenous, has become in some cases a new form of cultural capital.[2]

In the introduction to his recent collection on gender, indigeneity and the state in the Andes, Andrew Canessa (2005:4) notes, "'The Indian' has become an international commodity, and Indians are widely recognized around the globe for their 'traditional' lifestyles and as guardians of the natural environment." An essentialized notion of indigenous people may be a form of Orientalism (Said 2003) or imperialist nostalgia (Rosaldo 1989:69–74) imposed from outside indigenous societies. However, under the terms of international tourism indigenous women and men themselves deploy notions of traditional or authentic cultural difference as a strategy to attract more tourists. In other cases, as we will see among indigenous Zapatistas, they may defy conventional expectations and display more rebellious identities, which may also draw a select tourism niche market. Thus, it is critical to consider the active ways in which, as Canessa and his collaborators show, indigenous people on the margins play a part in making the nation by becoming stakeholders in their own identity construction. Women, most visibly through their use of dress and language, once again are shown to be the principal signifiers of traditional culture, the indigenous, and Other.

Following periods of political upheaval in Andean Peru and Chiapas, there has been a tourism revival in these regions. As we saw in Chapters 3 and 4, well-established tourism industries were stalled for a decade by very different political movements in these areas—in Peru during the 1980s and into the 1990s by ruthless forces of Sendero Luminoso and the military, and in southern Mexico by the state's response to the antiglobalization Zapatista uprising that surfaced publicly in 1994. Now tourism is thriving once again as conflict has subsided and the two nations have sought to promote economic development and to refashion regional and national identities in a time of neoliberalism and globalization. Together, these regions present some marked historical similarities, but the different characters of their recent conflicts extend to rather different prospects for indigenous women involved in tourism.

I argue here that tourism has gendered and racialized effects, as romantic or exoticized images are used—by the state or by indigenous people—to entice travelers, who expect to find cultural difference prominently on display. This chapter examines the consequences, whether intended or not, as cultural tourism in Andean Peru and Chiapas draws travelers seeking locally authentic experiences with indigenous women and men. As part of my broader project, I have considered the stories of those who are toured as well as of other individuals whose lives are intricately linked to the growth of tourism, from government and industry officials, to informal-sector workers, to global travelers. In Peru, tourists often desire to experience "safe" and "remote" indigenous communities, whereas in Mexico that desire may be coupled with a yearning for "real" revolutionary culture in the Chiapas region. Drawing on research in the two areas and examining initiatives in cultural tourism, I assess gendered outcomes that are also deeply marked by racial or ethnic difference; although unequal social relations are often in play, I will show that this is not always and everywhere the case in just the way we might expect.

Travel Snapshots

CUZCO, PERU. A friend of mine, a retired gay man from the United States, was touring Peru with his partner. After visiting Machu Picchu and the Sacred Valley, they found transport back to the historic city of Cuzco. Along the way, they stopped to visit several communities, and then, as my friend wrote to me by e-mail, they were introduced to the Inca fortress and heritage site known as Sacsayhuamán:

> We ended by going to those ruins outside Cusco that sound like "sexy woman." In fact, the first days in Cusco our taxi drivers kept asking us if we wanted sexy woman and we thought they meant that literally. We were a bit amazed that they all wanted to line us up with a woman! Not until Sunday when we took the CROWDED local public bus to Pisac did I see a sign for the ruins. And as I tried to sound the word out, I realized our error. (Robert Schanke, personal communication)

Anthropologist Michael Hill, who has carried out research on tourism in the Cuzco region, tells me that some locals are amused by this linguistic misunderstanding and play with it in their interactions with tourists (personal communication). What I find striking here is the improbable sexualization of a leading cultural heritage site and the relationship of such representation, in a broad sense, to the growth in tourism. The story my friend related to me is less surprising when we consider the reliance of Andean tourism on both the region's distinguished cultural history and on its exoticized cultural difference.

CHIAPAS, MEXICO. In 1996, the EZLN held an international gathering that spanned the mountainous and Lacandón forest regions of this state in southern Mexico, billed as an "Intercontinental Encounter Against Neoliberalism and for Humanity" but popularly dubbed the *intergaláctica* to underscore its broad reach. Over three thousand people from more than forty countries met to strategize forms of resistance modeled on the Zapatista movement (Harvey 1998a:158). Ten years later, an international gathering I attended in the Zapatista cultural center in Oventic, officially called the "Gathering of the Zapatista People with Peoples of the World," was also referred to as an intergalactic encounter.

Thus, I was struck when reading Patty Kelly's (2008) ethnography of a state-run brothel in Chiapas's capital city, Tuxtla Gutiérrez, to learn that the place is called the Zona Galáctica, this time referring to the broad reach of a very different phenomenon in the region. As Kelly shows, state-regulated prostitution arises from an effort to modernize a part of Mexico that is better known for poverty, conflict, and deep cultural tradition.[3] This odd juxtaposition of initiatives in Chiapas that are light-years apart may appear meaningless until we consider that both the Zapatista gatherings and the state-operated brothel are responses to neoliberalism. The former emerged as a popular-based challenge to neoliberalism's devastating sweep; in contrast, the latter was in sync with the neoliberal current as the state-controlled (yet promoted) sexual commodification in a modern, nearly clinical, environment. Though their objectives were sharply at odds, both emerged to confront conditions of poverty and to counter conflict.

In what follows, I examine how recent developments relating to culture, political economy, and tourism in postconflict Andean Peru and Chiapas are inflected by race and gender; I will note that we find less of the outright sexualization of indigenous women than we see among urban women in some other parts of Latin America and the Caribbean.[4] I discuss ways in which local cultures as well as tourism industries in these regions market indigenous identity and gender difference, sometimes building on historical practices or ideologies, and at times making unabashed use of stereotypes of the Other. I will offer examples of these practices from the Andean community of Vicos as well as in Zapatista and Lacandón communities in Chiapas. This is not to say that more balanced and open exchanges are unknown between local populations and tourists, but rather to suggest that tourism encounters in these regions, as elsewhere, are heavily freighted with layers of difference and power.

Gender, Race, and Tourism in the Peruvian Andes

In Chapter 3, I discussed the changing contours of tourism in Peru since the period of violence and conflict when Sendero militants faced off with the military, leading to suffering and the tragic loss of 69,280 lives.[5] It has only been in the last decade that tourism has returned and, specifically, that cultural tourism has reemerged, enticing visitors with the promise of exposure not only to spectacular settings and archaeological wonders but to intimate encounters with rural and indigenous Andeans themselves. Whereas scholars have usefully considered travelers' romanticization of rural Andeans and their spiritual connection to the natural and supernatural world (Hill 2008; Van den Berghe and

Flores Ochoa 2000), gender differentiation in the Andean tourism encounter is less often examined (Meisch 2002; Zorn 2004).

In contrast to that in Cuba and Nicaragua, sex and romance tourism in Peru is not as prevalent or as widely known; nevertheless, I mention briefly some forms it has taken there. In recent years, I have heard Peruvians express concern about the presence of sex tourism in the highly exoticized Amazon area, especially around the tropical city of Iquitos,[6] and read newspaper accounts of debates on the criminalization of sex with minors.[7] More directly relevant here, young men known as *bricheros* have become commonplace in areas of heavy tourism, especially Cuzco, seeking out female tourists with whom to establish intimate friendships and romance (Vich 2006). These "Andean lovers" perfect the art of seduction of gringas, often by exaggerating qualities of indigenous difference, wearing their hair long, playing traditional flutes, and adopting a dress style evocative of Quechua (Inca) culture.[8] Tourists are said to desire their imagined Andean knowledge and experience and to wish to possess it. In some cases, women attracted to the "authenticity" of bricheros (who actually work hard to speak European languages and adopt a manner that is pleasing to tourists) may invite the men to leave the country with them. Peruvian anthropologist Víctor Vich (2006:191–194) points to the gendered and racialized dimension of these intimate encounters and argues that the postcolonial figure of the brichero stands in for the nation in the contemporary neoliberal world—in which the nation is up for sale. The tourist's desire is for this figure, at once folkloric and romantic, who appears locked in time, even in the modern city of Cuzco.[9]

Australian researcher Irmgard Bauer (2008) examines sexual and romantic relationships in Cuzco, noting that in some cases Andean women too are *bricheras*; these relationships with tourists are generally not an explicit form of sex work, yet they do provide benefits to Andeans. She notes that "mixing the 'exotic' with the 'erotic'" in Cuzco takes the form of mutual attraction to cultural differences: "the Inca look" (for males) or petite and "exotic" (for women) on the one side and the taller fair-haired, blue-eyed appearance of gringos and gringas on the other. She describes the "gringotecas," clubs where locals meet foreign women and men, which often provide opportunities for sexual encounters and material advantage to locals in the form of entrée into more venues, as well as meals, gifts, and travel.[10] For tourists, having a cultural insider as a companion and intimate can be actively sought after and highly desired. The phenomenon is sufficiently well known to be the subject of discussion on various Web sites, including one for expatriates and travelers to Peru (www.expatperu.com).

Several authors consider gender differences in the performance and delivery of more traditional tourism services in Andean Peru. Jane Henrici (2002) examines how tourism development, cultural heritage, and local economy impact women, particularly when the marketing of traditional arts and practices is viewed as a key to modernization. In the case of Pisac (a community near Cuzco that draws tourists to its market), gender, class, and ethnicity conspire to challenge women who would move from the status of vendor to that of artisan. Her case studies of particular women show that artisans must sell not only their crafts but their cultural identities if they are to meet success in the marketplace.[11] Local identity, marked by dress, language, and demeanor, and strongly inflected by gender, is shown to be a critical factor in tourism development. Henrici considers how the "feminine," the "ethnic," and the "exotic" have been key in the branding of tourism in Andean Peru.

That gender and race, or ethnicity, are closely intertwined in the Andes is made clear in Cadena's work in another community near Cuzco, where she reported the perception that "women are more Indian" (1995:329). Although both men and women may acquire "modern" skills and be perceived as less Indian and more mestizo, for women the advantage to be gained is more modest. Cadena writes that "gender intersects with status to structure and legitimate ethnic inequality within the community and even within households." As quoted at the beginning of this chapter, she goes on to say that modernization may underwrite local gender differences and reinforce "the Indianization of women, while opening the option of cultural mestizaje to most men" (1995:343). Recently, however, Cadena and Starn (2007) take into account the emergence of new cultural and political subjectivities, noting that "although poverty, discrimination and second-class citizenship very often shape indigenous lives today, notable exceptions also undercut any simple association of indigeneity with misery and marginalization" (2). This recognition of the need to question long-held analytical frameworks might be extended to consideration of *gendered* indigeneity as well.

Elayne Zorn's (2004) long-term research on Taquile Island in Peru offers a rare case study of community-based tourism that met with some early success. Interestingly, while men were centrally involved in transporting tourists to the island, women had an equally important role as the main producers of their celebrated textiles on sale to visitors. Women were prominent in social and economic exchanges with tourists, even when this contributed to tensions that emerged between Taquile men and women over access to tourism's benefits. In the end, however, competition from mestizo transporters led to local men's displacement from the business of tourism, eroding this communitarian project.

My research on Peruvian tourism, as seen in Chapter 3, has focused on cultural and experiential tourism in the Callejón de Huaylas, an Andean region best known for adventure travel and mountaineering. Responses to my interview questionnaires indicated that a majority of travelers come to the area for cultural and ecotourism. As one U.S. Spanish teacher wrote, she was most surprised "that it is relatively authentic—though I've only been in the north so far. The campesinos aren't what I expected—posing in their quaint dress for a *sol*. Instead they seem to patiently deal with our tourist presence spying on their customs—which are not staged." An Israeli man who came to Peru, as many from his country do, following his military service, captured the elements that drew him to the country: "Beautiful scenery, amazing people, and as a backpacker, it's rather cheap." Many are struck by what a French woman described as "the kindness of people and how helpful they are. The way they're living with the strict minimum and seem to be happier than people like us, who have everything so easily." Similarly, a man from the Netherlands appreciated "the endless solidarity and *cariño* [affection] of the poor people."[12]

While I have been based in the city of Huaraz, capital of the department of Ancash, I have observed travel throughout the Callejón region. The Andean community of Vicos is well known in the history of applied anthropology and has recently undertaken its small tourism project with the assistance of several NGOs. I have made brief visits to Vicos over three decades but was a guest there for several days in 2006 in order to learn more about how a handful of families with support to build guest lodges scattered over rugged terrain has fared in launching this project. Those well acquainted with the Cornell-Peru Project of the 1950s and 1960s might recognize the enterprise as a logical extension of development initiatives of the past. By now, however, Vicosinos themselves are seeking to manage the business of drawing travelers, largely from the United States, for stays of one or a few days during which they participate in the everyday activities of the rural, agricultural community. A selling point for potential visitors is the opportunity to get to know about the lives and culture of a traditional, indigenous Quechua-speaking people.[13]

Having conducted archival research on gender relations in Vicos during the time of the Cornell-Peru Project (Babb 1985), I was eager to see how Vicos was approaching tourism as a new means for economic development and what effect this was having on women and men there. In Huaraz, I visited the NGOs

Women and men in traditional finery for a gathering with international visitors in Vicos

that were supporting Vicos's tourism project and assisting in arranging my travel to the community. The attractive brochure on Vicos tourism, mentioned earlier, serves to orient prospective and current visitors for their stay in "the Peasant Community of Vicos." The images and text offer a brief history of Vicos from the time when it was "a typical Andean hacienda" (1611–1952) to the time of the Cornell-Peru Project; the present is described by reference to the continuing biodiversity and traditional culture in the region.[14] What most caught my attention, however, was the gender-specific focus of the photos and descriptions of the hosts of tourist homestays and of other residents of Vicos. The hosts and local specialists featured are exclusively men; the photos in a few cases include women, wives of the hosts, but the descriptions all emphasize what tourists will experience by staying with or meeting a craftsman, a beekeeper, a musician, a weaver, or a toolmaker (all men). Women are strikingly absent from this portrayal of everyday life in Vicos. Thus, I was prepared to ask some questions about how women were involved in the tourism project and to seek the opportunity to meet and talk with Vicosinas themselves.

As I emphasize here, my visit to Vicos brought to light the gendered and racialized nature of the community tourism experience. I suggest that the social vectors of gender and indigeneity continue to be salient and that tourism development efforts have differential consequences for women and men in Vicos. In part, this may result from the greater difficulty women have in speaking Spanish, given past practices of sending sons to school or the military while daughters remained at home. It may also stem from the perception identified by Cadena (1995) that rural women are "more Indian" and less modern—less able to fulfill key responsibilities in tourism development—though I have shown that in Vicos and elsewhere in the Callejón de Huaylas women play active roles in the local economy (Babb 1985, 1998).

I learned that only Vicosino men attend the *talleres*, tourism workshops, in Huaraz. There, they are given advice on how to receive guests and interact with them, for example, the suggestion that family members should all eat together, using the time to tell guests how things were done in the past and how traditions are continuing in the present. My host, "Tomás," explained that relating to tourists was very new to them, and for his wife, "Dora," it produced considerable anxiety, since her Spanish was very limited and she was not sure how she would manage. Although it might be said that women are the principal conservators of culture and tradition in Vicos, the men are the ones who were expected to pass on such knowledge to their guests. This reflects a private-public gender division that has a long history in the Andes, but it is no doubt reinforced by outsiders who expect and encourage men to take on more of the responsibility in the tourism project. Tomás spoke frequently and reverentially of the time of *the abuelos* (grandparents) and, even as the radio or TV played loudly, he emphasized that things are much the same now as in the past. As the male head of household, he played host while Dora provided the critical, labor-intensive services of preparing the guest quarters and meals.

During my visit, the couple was attentive to my needs, but Dora remained largely behind the scenes while Tomás interacted with me directly. He called me to meals that she had prepared, except in the case of the pachamanca on my last day, which was prepared by Vicosino men and then served by the women. He escorted me to a local wedding, and she joined us only after carrying out work at home. While he delivered a speech at the time of my departure, she was shy and remained apart, along with several other women. Both were kind and hospitable, but Tomás performed the role of gracious host and family spokesperson. This led me to question whether the Vicosinos and those who have assisted them in the tourism project might have integrated women of the community to a greater degree. Are women in Vicos simply too busy with household responsibilities to be more active participants in the tourism project, or is the androcentrism of the tourism project repeating past practices of interventions in Vicos that singled out men for economic development projects?[15] These questions have remained with me since my time there.

A few days after my stay in Vicos, I returned for an afternoon to see the much longer-standing visitor attraction operated by the Vicos community, the thermal baths and hotel at Chancos. Vicosinas are much more in evidence in the Chancos enterprise, playing a significant part in the operation of the baths, hotel, small restaurants, and market stalls that are concentrated along the quiet road that leads into Vicos. The women vendors and restaurant workers I spoke to were comfortable in Spanish and told me they were not familiar with the tourism project, though they were interested in hearing about it. I was particularly impressed by the active role of these women in contrast to those connected to the tourism project. The women at Chancos were no doubt regarded as cholas, having adapted to the world of urban commerce and interacting with a wider social network. Was the tourism project seeking to represent Vicos women as occupying a more domesticated, nonmarket world, even in the face of their longstanding participation in decision making in a market economy?

Tourists make their way to Vicos to see campesinos leading traditional lives, not to see savvy women bargaining with buyers in the market (unaware that rural women have long sold in regional markets); then the same travelers go on to larger towns and cities like Huaraz to see busy marketplaces and to haggle over prices.[16] In such towns, there is a more diverse cross section of society, and social differences stand out in sharp relief. In Vicos, however, cultural commodification is better concealed, and there is little need for cash during a tourist's stay unless it is to give a host a small amount to purchase coca leaves for an Andean ritual, until the end of the visit when there is a quick accounting of the payment due. Tourists are spared from learning of families' urgent need for cash for children's school supplies, household items, or transportation into nearby towns, and of women's central role in managing household budgets.

It remains to be seen how well men and women will collaborate in the tourism initiative in Vicos. Although men are the designated hosts and play the leading public role in experiential tourism in the community, women are critically important to its success. This is evident from the work of women in preparing guest quarters for visitors and in the labor-intensive work of preparing meals.

The complementarity of gender roles in Vicos is arguably as apparent today as it was thirty years ago.[17] Just as the significant part of women in the community eluded the applied anthropology project some decades back, I would suggest that external supporters (NGOs and travel companies) of the tourism initiative may also be overlooking the key part played by women. When Tomás told me of his wife's nervousness about his becoming a socio of the project, he was signaling his own anxiety that without her full support he could not make a go of it. He was surely aware of Dora's value to the family's participation in the tourism initiative, even if those external to the community were not fully cognizant of the key part that women play.

At a conference on gender and Andean culture held in the Callejón de Huaylas several years ago, Peruvian researcher Rosa Mendoza (2003) addressed the need to broaden our conception of development to embrace new knowledge about gender. She drew on recent gender and development critiques in her remarks regarding the last half century: "During the 1950s and '60s, the development model was from the rich countries. To become like them, the tools were modernization and industrialization. The emphasis was on economic growth. In this model, women were not perceived as economic agents but as housewives" (my translation). I would agree with Mendoza that as analysts consider gender and development, "the problem is not the difference of expectations and accomplishments, but the 'naturalization' of inequality . . . the different valorization of roles assumed by women and men." Going beyond the economic to other dimensions of social life suggests that what is taken for granted by many outsiders as women's secondary status in Vicos is actually something more complex. Recognizing women's key participation would allow researchers, Vicosinos, and their advocates to engage in a productive exchange that in the long run could benefit women and men in the community in ways that go beyond the tourism project.

Race, Gender, and Tourism in Chiapas

Since the Zapatista rebellion fifteen years ago there has been renewed international attention to the state of Chiapas in southern Mexico—although anthropologists like June Nash and those in the Harvard Chiapas Project focused close attention on its cultural history beginning a half century ago (Nash 2001; Vogt 1994). Journalists and activists were the first to arrive on the scene in 1994, but mainstream tourism returned later in the decade; today there is a busy tourism season, and visitors come throughout the year. Scholarship on the international impact of the Zapatista social movement (Bob 2005; Hayden 2002; Olesen 2005) and on tourism (Martín 2004) in the region by and large is not overlapping, though researchers in both areas acknowledge the important impact of travel to the area.

As in the case of Andean Peru, the state of Chiapas is well known for its rural and indigenous population. Cultural or ethnic tourism (Van den Berghe 1994) is a response to the broad appeal of traditional Mayan people and culture, and many travelers make the circuit (Ruta Maya) that includes the Yucatán, Oaxaca, Chiapas, and, across the border, Guatemala. The fact that rebels in Chiapas made headlines when NAFTA was put into effect on January 1, 1994, adds to the allure for some who wish to see the place where indigenous people rose up in opposition to free-trade measures they claimed would further marginalize them in Mexican society. A visit there offers the diverse prospects of quaint colonial towns, traditional communities, archaeological and jungle tours, and a politicized climate in which market vendors offer the ubiquitous Zapatista merchandise. What tourists do not often recognize is the diversity of indigenous peoples who live in the region (Stephen 2002; Eber and Kovic 2003; Gil Tébar 1999; Rovira 1997), viewing them instead as essentialized Indians. This is seen in the desires of solidarity tourists to have intimate encounters with idealized indigenous Zapatistas, and of other tourists to purchase textiles made by authentic Indians whose specific cultural identities remain unknown to them.

Researchers and some tourists, however, have discovered the gender differences that are manifest in Chiapas, and some have noted indigenous women's audible voice in the region. Many women have been empowered through organizing artisan cooperatives, in which they control production and marketing. Mayan women who have become involved in Zapatista activism have spoken up about the extra burdens they shoulder at home and in society, with heavy family responsibilities and often lacking equal access to education and other resources. They have addressed domestic abuse, reproductive rights, and the social discrimination they face as both women and indigenous people—asserting their individual and collective rights (Speed et al. 2006). Their organizing as women and as Zapatistas is now widely known, and several comandantas have become celebrated figures in the social movement. The Zapatista call for indigenous rights includes particular attention to women's rights, and the "Women's Revolutionary Law" is one of the cornerstones of their political platform (3–4).

Over the course of research in the region, I joined several groups of solidarity tourists in the cultural center Oventic in Zapatista territory. We met with

A Zapatista community meeting space in Oventic with mural showing a Zapatista woman flanked by men bearing arms, a Zapatista soldier, and Emiliano Zapata (The sign reads "There is no more effective weapon than truth.")

members of the EZLN's Good Government Council, and each time there was at least one woman present among the indigenous leadership, even if she was a quieter member of the group (having less fluency in Spanish). In this way, although they were outnumbered by men in public and political venues, women were visible to tourists and broke with traditional gender divisions in Chiapas. The encuentros I attended along with numerous international activists also made gender issues a central feature on their agendas. In workshops and panels, indigenous women and their supporters discussed matters relating to women and health, education, and economic livelihood.

The iconic Zapatista women in braids and bandannas adorn the most popular items sold to both solidarity and mainstream tourists, including T-shirts, posters, and even ashtrays. Also in abundant supply are the male and female dolls wearing wool tunics and masks symbolizing their resistance; both genders carry rifles and have androgynous forms. Female Zapatistas are represented as different from males by the addition of long braids tied with colorful yarn, and in some cases by small, wrapped bundles (for babies) attached to their backs, often with masked infants peeking out. A newer invention is the "nursing" mother dolls created by Zapatista women of the regional Mujeres por la Dignidad (Women for Dignity) collective; these artisans use Mayan textiles designed in their communities to dress larger plush figures that feature arms that snap together to hold babies, which in turn can be snapped to each round breast. Along with braids and masks, the clever innovation of representing lactating motherhood seems to draw considerable interest from tourists intrigued by women's place in Zapatista political culture.

In areas with the heaviest concentration of tourism, as in San Cristóbal de las Casas, indigenous women whose weavings and other handicrafts are sought after in rural communities may themselves get little notice as they move through the city selling small craft items to make a livelihood. Part of the passing scene, they are viewed at once as folkloric and as bothersome, when they assertively approach travelers. As Walter Little (2004) showed for Antigua, Guatemala, women in their indigenous dress are viewed as the repositories of cultural tradition and may be the preferred vendors of items that tourists desire. Nevertheless, many tourists bypass street vendors and pay higher prices in city shops where they judge that the quality of weavings and traditional articles of clothing may be higher. What they rarely know is that the piles of women's blouses and other items in these appealing shops are often made by indigenous women who are hidden from view, working out of their cramped homes in the *colonias*, poor neighborhoods located away from the historic district known to tourists. When I visited families in one colonia, I spoke with a woman who shared a single room with her husband and five young children, seated together on a broad platform used as a bed; she talked about sewing garments for long hours on her machine and calling on family members to help with the embroidery before the items were sold by the dozens at low cost to wholesalers who acted as intermediaries. She had little knowledge of the markets and shops where tourists would come to purchase what she labored to make at home.

Some women, however, have organized their production of items destined for sale to tourists by forming cooperatives and have greater autonomy over their work process. During one visit to San Cristóbal, as I walked through the shops that ring the café TierrAdentro, I encountered an example of gender and indigenous difference on display, yet nearly invisible in plain sight. I came across a shop I had not noticed before, where, in a space with a small quantity of textiles, embroidered blouses, purses, pencil cases, EZLN wall hangings and T-shirts for sale, two women in Mayan dress were sitting on the floor talking quietly while one wove on a backstrap loom. There was little movement through this area, and I wondered if the women were working as part of the artisan cooperative Women for Dignity or if they were stationed there as a sort of "living history" cultural performance for the rare tourist who wandered into the shop from the cyber café. For me, this recalled the way that women and children pose on roadsides for tourists on Andean Peruvian circuits and baby alpacas are brought to high-end boutiques in Lima to boost sales of clothing. A year later, however, I returned to the same space and found colorfully painted signage showing that it was indeed Women for Dignity who were working there in the space they rented as a cooperative; members of their group were based in Oventic and took turns coming to the San Cristóbal store, where they kept busy preparing yarn and weaving as they made occasional sales. The women I spoke to used little Spanish but revealed a self-possessed attitude about their work as a collective endeavor.

In contrast to the tranquility of the setting just described, gendered indigene- ity is on proud and public display at a lively restaurant, El Fogon de Jovel, cen- trally located in San Cristóbal. Popular among the local middle class, Mexican tourists, and some international visitors who read about it in their guidebooks, El Fogon offers higher-end variations on regional cuisine, including abundant *parrilladas*, grilled dinners served in piping hot earthenware. Specialty drinks make use of the Mayan cane alcohol posh, with fruit and other ingredients to appeal to non-Mayan tastes; pricey examples included cocktails bearing such names as *Sacrificio Maya* (Mayan Sacrifice) and *Diablito Tzotzil* (Tzotzil Little Devil). The space makes decorative use of thatch awnings and traditional hats, and the male waitstaff wear festive traje, as do the musicians playing marimbas, though it is nearly certain that these employees do not customarily dress this way. One woman dressed in exquisite Mayan finery, with her hair in carefully groomed braids, has pride of place near the entrance to the restaurant, where she works briskly and continuously to prepare tortillas consumed at the restaurant; when her young children accompany her, they are picture-perfect in their pol- ished traditional attire. Her persona captures the idealized indigenous woman sought after by mainstream tourists: a prettified, demure, and hardworking Mayan who is unlikely to be associated with the alternative, Zapatista women quietly at work in cooperative stores.

Universidad Intercultural de Chiapas (UNICH), a new university in San Cristóbal, plays a key role in promoting alternative, indigenous-based tourism and draws more women than men into its program. I met with the head of this program, which had just graduated its first class four years after the university opened. He credited the Zapatista movement with the strongly intercultural orientation of the UNICH, which caters to the needs of Mayan students and their communities. The university's 80 percent indigenous student body is encouraged to speak Mayan languages on campus and to train in areas that contribute to communitarian development in Chiapas. The alternative tourism program advocates for the revalorization of Mayan culture and sustainable development and expects its graduates to seek external support for viable initiatives to take back to their communities. The director acknowledged that so far their students have not had great success in securing funding for such initiatives, but the academic program represents a significant way in which indigenous people, and particularly women, are playing an active part in advancing new tourism options in the region. Given the increasing number of Mexicans among tourists coming to Chiapas, these communitarian options may have an impact on national, as well as international, attitudes toward indigenous peoples in the region. If successful, the program's efforts may serve to counter what some critics in the area have called *turismo lite* and a Disneyfied cultural experience in Chiapas.

Before I turn to gender and racial identity in other parts of Chiapas, it is worth noting that some young indigenous women and men living in urban areas are adopting new hybrid forms of dress and bodily adornment that incorporate elements of Mayan tradition along with those of a more global youth culture. Young women, for example, embrace indigenous identity by wearing clothing in the style of their grandmothers but adopt trendy hairstyles and use makeup as references to a more sophisticated, hip cultural identity. Young men wear their hair long, get tattoos and piercings, and may even adopt an "indigenous goth" style, favoring black jeans and T-shirts and studded belts.[18] Such self-conscious fashion statements may not yet be commonplace, but they hint at a changing gender and indigenous sensibility that may, in its way, be linked to the more readily identifiable political current of Zapatismo—this, I suggest, insofar as a social space has opened and a discourse of indigenous rights has given Mayans a newfound sense of ownership of their cultural practices, meanings, and desires.

Little has been written about women and gender in the Lacandón jungle area, site of early civilization and cradle of Zapatista political organizing. Theresa Ortiz (2001) presents narratives of women throughout Chiapas, including those living in settlements in the Lacándon rainforest area; she focuses on the challenges facing those who migrated from the highlands to acquire land to farm in the tropical lowlands, and on women who became involved in political organizing in recent decades. On the population indigenous to the Lacandón area, however, there has been even less attention to gender questions. Travelers go to the area principally to visit archaeological sites and the jungle, where local men are generally the ones who transport and guide visitors. As in the case of Vicos, women are busy behind the scenes while men have greater public presence and interaction with tourists.

In contrast to the self-conscious inclusion of women in Zapatista tourism, my travel to the Lacandón jungle area, including my stay in a local community catering to tourism, revealed men to be the featured hosts. Women, meanwhile, were out of view as they prepared meals, attended to lodging needs, and created handmade souvenirs for visitors to buy and take home. In this respect, I found similarities to community-based tourism in Vicos, Peru. Yet in comparison with my hosts in Vicos, the Lacandón hosts seemed to present a more commodified package to tourists, with less individualized attention to guests. The jungle tour I took, led by a young man as guide, was the most sustained period for more intimate acquaintance with a member of the Lacandón community; women, I was told, rarely serve as guides. As a researcher, I needed to seek out a few women to talk to, something that would be difficult for travelers who do not speak Spanish.

During my stay at the camp at Lacanjá, I spoke with a small group of women of the community who were relaxing with their children in hammocks outside their home. All were part of the same large family that had several campamentos, including Tomás's and his brother's across the road. The women told me that tourism had helped them, as they made and sold artesanía in the campamento shops. However, an older woman among them lamented that younger women were no longer wearing traditional dress, suggesting that this was due to the influence of outsiders and their cultural practices. When I made my way over to the local Internet café, I met a young couple who operate it, a Lacandón man and his wife, who is from Oaxaca and nonindigenous. She told me that she had difficulty as one of only a few non-Lacandón women in the community because people generally spoke the Mayan language and not Spanish, making her feel like an outsider there. She was nonetheless part of the socially diverse fabric of the community, which increasingly is marked by differences relating to language use, gender, and economic opportunity.

There is little sex and romance tourism at present in Chiapas. The prostitution that exists is directed mainly to local men or to soldiers (Kelly 2008), who during the region's recent militarization have been known to draw local women into commercialized sex. Previously unknown in many indigenous communities, prostitution may contribute to family violence and abuse of alcohol (Eber and Kovic 2003:12). A Mayan woman friend called my attention one afternoon to an older indigenous man who appeared to have been drinking and was in the street with a young indigenous woman; my friend, who works with an NGO aiding street children and youth, thought it might be an instance of prostitution, something that would have escaped my notice. Of course, romantic relationships sometimes form between travelers and local men and women, and I heard one account from a European woman who came for a few days, then met a man she married; she has lived in San Cristóbal for some years now, working along with her husband as a tour guide in a leading tourism office. However, as a travel destination Chiapas does not attract the sort of sex or romance tourism found in Mexico's resort locations.

As in Andean Peru, the intertwining of gender and race in the lives of indigenous women in Chiapas is complex and contradictory. Generations of subordination to those of higher socioeconomic class and racial status and, often, to men of their own communities have resulted in these women's historical disadvantage in relation to education, employment, and social position. Higher-status mestizos in both regions continue to look down on campesinos and indigenous peoples and on the in-between category of "modernizing" Indians; women among these groups can be the subject of particular scorn. Tourism may reproduce discriminatory practices even when, in some cases, the figure of indigenous women is rebranded as desirable in marketing traditional societies in transition. The iconic woman spinning yarn in the Andes or weaving on a backstrap loom in Chiapas can be a selling point, and a particularly reassuring image of cultural continuity in places recently marked by conflict. These women are aware of the power of representation in tourism and may seek to get ahead by enhancing their image as authentic indigenous women, in some cases using Web sites and other marketing devices to encourage tourism or the sale of craft items.[19] In contrast to a short time ago when it was safer to conceal indigenous identity (in Peru, the term "Indio" was replaced by "campesino"), it is now a point of pride for some, at least in the realm of tourism.[20] In Chiapas, the indigenous struggle for human rights is characterized by women activists playing a significant role in challenging local- as well as national-level injustices (Speed 2008).

Indigenous Women and Tourism

When Cadena (1995) described Andean women as "more Indian," she parted ways with analysts who earlier found only harmony and "complementarity" among Andean women and men. She acknowledged that those women who gained experience as marketers were already acquiring the modern, urban skills that might enable them to appear less indigenous and more mestizo, but she claimed that local men and women devalued such activity as "not really work."[21] How does the rise of tourism, and particularly cultural tourism, affect the balance of gender relations among indigenous peoples in the Andes and in Chiapas? Is work in tourism regarded as meaningful and worthy? We have seen that indigenous women are often viewed as the most culturally authentic members of their communities and as such may have an economic advantage in tourism when they produce items and sell to the public or interact in other ways with tourists. Does this result in their higher status in local cultures? Does marketing their identity as traditional or indigenous benefit them in other ways?

Ethnographic research in the Cuzco area supports the view that women are finding new ways to market their cultural heritage and indigenous identities as well as their products in the tourism economy. Beatrice Simon (2009) has considered women and children who pose for photos in the town of Pisac, using folkloric dress and sometimes iconic alpacas to cater to tourist preferences. This practice has become commonplace enough that individuals serving as models are referred to as sacamefotos. However, like men performing as bricheros who seek women's affection on the tourism market, these women gain new sources of income without necessarily gaining respect in family and community; the work is not regarded as worthy in the way that the work of artisans in the region is considered to be honorable. Gender and racial identity are put to work in ways that result in deeply ambivalent outcomes at the local level.

Elsewhere in Peru, Amanda Stronza (2008) has carried out long-term research at an ecolodge in the southeastern Amazon area where competition for tourism revenues has resulted in local concern to manifest indigenous identity and culture. In this case, gender appears to be less significant than ethnic identity, in an area characterized by mixed "native communities." Stronza, like many tourism researchers, leaves us to assess to what degree tourism is a benefit, offering new economic resources and validation for indigenous identity, and to what degree it may promote new inequalities, as both potential income and ethnic identity are contested sites. In an ironic twist found in some of the cases

Young girls known as sacamefotos posing for tourist photos and tips near Cuzco

I examine as well, while the community seeks "modern" progress, it is "considering the possibility that a return to the past [reclaiming traditions, retention of language and dress] may be the best path to a prosperous future" (251).

Recent research on indigenous women in the Latin American region suggests that women's position may undergo the greatest change in regions where they participate in local women's movements or in indigenous movements that offer substantial attention to gender injustice and seek to overcome it (Speed et al. 2006). This could account for the greater visibility of women in Zapatista communities than in other areas of Chiapas or in Andean Peru.[22] It may also help to explain their active part in organizing artisan cooperatives that direct their sales to the tourist market (Ortiz 2001). In times and places where women recognize the need to assert their own rights, they clearly tend to have a more prominent role, both in local politics and in tourism development. Tourists themselves often seek opportunities to interact with indigenous women, and this may serve to draw women into more active engagement with tourism. To be sure, as women's participation in tourism grows, they may lose some of the apparent authenticity that serves to attract tourists in the first place. My work presented here supports the view that even though tourism may result in deeply ambivalent outcomes, it is critical to sort through the ways that identities are shifting in response to both new challenges and new opportunities for those who have been marginalized historically. For indigenous women whose full citizenship rights have been denied in the past, even short-term gains may be used strategically to advance their individual and collective interests.

Peoples and nations that increasingly look to tourism for economic and political stabilization frequently refashion their cultural identities and histories to draw travelers.[23] The emergence of indigenous social movements in southern Mexico and Guatemala, as well as in countries like Ecuador and Bolivia, bordering Peru, have the double advantage of asserting rights at the national level and of capturing the interest of international travelers and supporters. Chiapas and the Andean region thus have a higher profile among those considering their options for travel destinations. They hold the cachet of having made recent international headlines and the security of having emerged from deeper conflict. Women, whether exoticized for their cultural difference or simply admired for their artisan skills and newfound activism, are beginning to play a more important part in the tourism encounter in these postconflict and transitional societies. Being "more Indian" can emerge as something other than a social liability and become a source of cultural capital. These women's growing visibility, their social and political participation—and even their marketing of Zapatista dolls and chola Barbies to tourists—suggest that in some cases under the new terms of engagement with tourism, women are taking gradual steps from the margins toward the center.[24]

Conclusion

Posttourism and Nationhood

THE TOURISM ENCOUNTER began by addressing the recent trend in travel to post-socialist and postconflict nations in transition, celebrated in features in the *New York Times* and other widely read publications. A rather different world beckons as I complete this work, one in which a global recession challenges tourism industries and local community-based outfits alike to entice consumers into putting ever-scarcer resources into what is clearly nonessential: costly travel to distant places. As I write this concluding chapter, the *New York Times* 2009 Summer Travel supplement has just appeared, informing readers that travel must now have a clear sense of purpose, and that purpose should be "the experience you take away with you": "Hedonistic holidays are out: cultural sojourns are in" (12). The apparent buzzword is *experiential*, and the quest is for meaning (29). Fortunately for the four nations discussed in this book and others that recently have revived tourism after internal conflict or social revolution, the same places that have enjoyed a shift from off-limits to desired travel destination are finding that they can market their offerings in cultural tourism. Indeed, Cuba, Mexico, Nicaragua, and Peru are all staking claims in diverse travel markets, including eco-, cultural, and experiential tourism.

Like travel itself, advertising and writing about tourism are of course driven by global market forces. The current turn is a reminder that changing fashions in travel are inevitable and that destinations in the global South may experience the same vulnerability to world market conditions and trends that they did in the past as producers of monocrops for colonial powers. This is so even when nations have pursued postcolonial and revolutionary projects since that time. My research has shown that embracing anticapitalist or antiglobalization political ideologies is no guarantee that regions and nations will not make strategic marketing decisions to promote tourism and advance broader plans for stabilization and development. Yet I have argued that there are some specific ways in which these transitional regions and nations market or brand themselves, either by calling on their histories of rebellion or by concealing conflict and creating alternative histories (or sometimes, present-oriented revisions) that may be reassuring to visitors.

Has anything really changed? Or has the pendulum simply swung toward more global austerity before it will swing back again toward more indulgence for travel, including to recently forbidden places? Arguably, transitional societies that have refashioned themselves for tourism will need to seek new sources for sustainable growth and for pursuing programs of social transformation. However, I would judge it unlikely that such a dramatic change in orientation is on the horizon for these nations that have discovered that their peoples, cultures, and histories, along with their natural and built environments, can be calling cards for tourism. In order to consider the question further, I will reflect on what I have observed most currently in my research sites, where there have been some notable national-level developments.

What Has Changed, and What Has Remained the Same

In conclusion, I consider how recent developments in Cuba, Mexico, Nicaragua, and Peru support or challenge my argument that tourism has taken up where social transformation left off, and I question how long the allure of these areas that were previously off-limits may last. I explore some comparative dimensions of my study of postrevolutionary and postconflict tourism and the ways in which gender, race, class, cultural identity, and national heritage are being refashioned in the transitional societies examined in this book. I assess the analytical power of the lens of tourism in shedding light on the often contentious struggles of those who have a stake in the terms of cultural and historical representation and inquire into postcolonial and postmodern conditions of travel. In closing, I look toward the future as I consider how well tourism may serve, as industry and as analytical prism, to shape and interpret the experience of these Latin American and Caribbean nations as they make their way through a time of neoliberal globalization.

In the cases I have presented, postconflict and postrevolutionary nations have turned to tourism to put out the welcome mat and showcase societies in transformation as well as to build economies. Following periods when few trav-

elers approached their shores, these regions and nations have capitalized on desires of world-weary travelers to discover new places that have been "made safe"
for tourism yet still have the allure of the recently off-limits (Goldstone 2001).[1]
Whereas earnest solidarity travelers told me of their "love" for the Zapatistas
or the Cuban revolution, tourists in Nicaragua were sometimes perplexed by
the Sandinista government's revolutionary past and its present authoritarian
practices, and those traveling to Peru were frequently unaware or only dimly
aware of the violent conflict in the recent past. We are entering an age when
postcolonial desires of the toured and postmodern sensibilities of tourists are
shifting the terms of engagement in the tourism encounter. Before considering
this further, I will offer a brief discussion of current developments in the areas
where I have carried out my research.

All four nations discussed here have seen transitions to new government
leadership since I began this work. In Cuba, Fidel Castro gradually turned over
control to his brother Raúl Castro, from 2006 until the latter was named head
of state in 2008. The smooth transfer meant that there was little immediate
change, though it became clear that some new forms of governance were under
way. The opening up of tourist hotels and restaurants to Cubans themselves
signaled a desire to reduce the appearance of "tourism apartheid"; nevertheless,
few Cubans have the ability to pay the prices charged to tourists, rendering this
change a symbolic gesture. Travel to Cuba grew to 2 million visitors per year
by mid-decade and then declined in 2006 and 2007, leading some analysts to
predict that tourism might have had its day. Many attributed losses to poor services, deteriorating infrastructure, the declining value of the dollar, and the violent hurricane season in 2005. However, the number of tourists rebounded after
2007, and during the first quarter of 2009 alone, nearly nine hundred thousand
visitors arrived, setting a new record for the high tourist season despite the
world economic crisis.[2]

My trip in late December 2008–early January 2009 coincided with the fiftieth
anniversary of the Cuban revolution, a time when it was difficult to find available hotel rooms and the streets of Old Havana were filled with travelers. Despite
the global recession, the atmosphere was festive, with Christmas trees on display
for tourists and celebrations of the New Year, as well as of the anniversary. Yet I
couldn't help noticing the poor value of my tourist dollars, the many lackluster
hotels and restaurant meals, and the increased presence of Cuban women and
children begging near tourist markets. As I accompanied a Canadian group in
the cities of Havana and Trinidad, it was evident that their dollars offered a

much better exchange rate than the U.S. dollar and that their nation might well retain its status as the largest supplier of travelers to Cuba. This situation could change as a result of a significant political shift in the United States and the willingness of President Barack Obama to ease restrictions on travel by Cuban Americans visiting family members in Cuba; there is already a growing number of passengers on charter flights from Miami to Havana.[3] Notwithstanding Cuba's unreliable offerings to foreign tourists, there will likely be an increase in travel from the United States to Cuba in the years ahead.

Nicaragua, too, ushered in new leadership in 2006. In this case, there was the surprising return of Daniel Ortega, the Sandinista head of state who had lost the 1990 elections and had tried repeatedly to make a comeback. When he finally succeeded, he revealed the opportunism that defined him since he lost power, by continuing to make deals with the corrupt former president Arnoldo Alemán and with the right-wing Catholic cardinal Obando y Bravo. He tried desperately to hold on to personal power in office, going so far as to bar key opposition parties from participating in municipal elections in 2008. During my visit that year, I observed protests involving some of those Sandinistas who had parted ways with Ortega and the FSLN; among them was the highly regarded Comandante Dora María Téllez, who went on a twelve-day hunger strike alongside the busiest traffic circle in Managua and brought international attention to the government's injustices. During the decade of Sandinista revolutionary government it would have been unimaginable that Daniel Ortega would eventually be compared with the despised dictator Somoza, over whom he had triumphed. Yet banners at the site proclaimed "Ortega and Somoza are the same thing," and the protesters had clearly had enough. The government's populist rhetoric and antipoverty programs could not conceal the profoundly antidemocratic measures Ortega was putting in place.

In his return to power, Ortega had not overlooked the potential of tourism to support his initiatives. Indeed, when he called on John Lennon's "Give Peace a Chance" as his campaign anthem, he sent a message not only to Nicaraguans but to the world, suggesting that the nation was safe for tourism—lest potential visitors still associate the small Central American country with conflict and danger. Once installed as president, he called for an eradication of poverty, a tall order for the nation still ranked second most impoverished in the hemisphere. His aspirations were closely linked to tourism promotion, which had approached the million-visitor mark by the end of 2007.[4] INTUR stated in its annual report for that year that President Ortega "trusts in tourism as a motivating force for the national economy and [endorses this activity to support] the poorest, so they will move ahead and transform their standard of living" (Instituto Nicaragüense de Turismo 2007:5, my translation). This emphasis on "transformative potential" speaks directly to the position I have taken in this book, that postrevolutionary governments may seek to further agendas for change, no longer through armed struggle but through tourism development. As the Nicaraguan case illustrates, although ideological orientations may shift, it is useful to observe the (sometimes ambivalent) connection between the past and present rather than simply to view tourism development as an aberration, a break from past revolutionary practice.

Tourism in Nicaragua may well continue to gain ground, though there appears to have been a setback after the violence following the November 2008 municipal elections, which many judged to be rigged. Figures for tourism in the first quarter of 2009 suggested a slight decline, whether due to domestic problems or to worldwide recession. Even so, the growing attention to eco-, sustainable, and cultural tourism that I discovered during my latest visit to Nicaragua seems to be giving prominence to the sort of wholesome travel opportunities described to me by Comandante Tomás Borge some years ago. It remains to be seen if sexual commerce will persist alongside more respectable attractions like the water and coffee tours featured in 2009, "Year 30 of the Revolution."[5]

When I returned to Peru in 2006 after nine years away, a controversial national election had just pitted a past president, Alan García, who won, against an indigenous-identified candidate who carried much of the Andean region—but not, critically, Lima. With the country still recovering from civil war and violence, the contest resonated with the deep differences that have continued to divide Peru by race and indigenous identity—corresponding to the striking demographic and geographic differences between the rural Andes and urban coast. As Peru underwent its transfer of power, unsettling even to the majority who voted for García but recalled his earlier failed presidency, tourism development was one of the few areas that would garner wide support across political and social sectors. Peruvians' pride in their cultural heritage and their hopes that renewing tourism would benefit a host of stakeholders, from impoverished informal workers to industry giants, could provide the foundation for a united front in this domain.

Nonetheless, long-standing tensions remained, including those between national interests based in Lima and major players located in Peru's main tourist destinations, Cuzco and nearby Machu Picchu, who felt entitled to a substantial role in setting the agenda for tourism development. Moreover, recent protests have emerged in opposition to the government's heavy promotion of investment in tourism at the leading sites, as local residents claim that they do not stand to share in the benefits from this development. In 2008, protesters chanting "Cuzco is not for sale!" shut down the airport in Cuzco and prevented access to the rail line to Machu Picchu. These local protesters are not the only ones who are unhappy with the promotion of higher-end tourism that serves larger, and often foreign, interests. Backpacker tourists see the steeply rising cost of travel and often complain of the further cultural commodification in Peru.[6] The transformation under way as Peru refashions itself for tourism has drawn a number of critics.

Peru received unwanted media attention in 2009 when there were reports of Sendero Luminoso reappearing in parts of the country and causing isolated episodes of violence. In addition, government efforts to dispel attention to past and present conflict, even when linked to reconciliation efforts, were made public internationally. An offer from the German government to donate two million dollars to build a national memory museum in Lima was initially rejected by Alan García, who said that reviving the memory of violence was not a priority when the country was facing immediate problems of poverty, health, and access to education. When international media joined Peruvians across the political spectrum in suggesting that García was trying to bury his own past complicity in human rights abuses and that the country needed to have a national memory museum, he accepted the donation and appointed a commission to head the effort.

In Mexico, there was still another transition to a new president in 2006, from Vicente Fox to Felipe Calderón, who was declared the victor after an extremely close election in which he ran against a candidate of the left. As in the case of Peru, the losing candidate received more support in the rural sector, in this case southern Mexico, including Chiapas—but also in Mexico City, making the outcome especially contentious. The Zapatistas had made it clear that they would not participate in the electoral campaign but would instead launch what they called "The Other Campaign," which they announced on January 1, 2006, twelve years after the public emergence of their social movement. They toured throughout Mexico, taking the opportunity to promote the EZLN alternative, which was not to run for elected office but to establish a network of groups that shared their support for indigenous rights and their opposition to neoliberal capitalism. Their objective was to build the movement for support of other, more inclusive, popular-based social and economic practices.

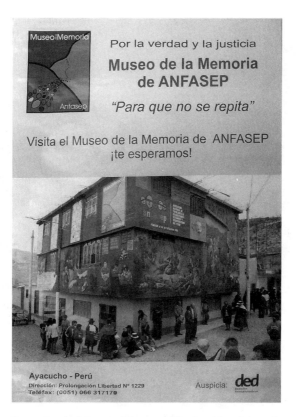

Poster for the Memory Museum, "So that [the violence] is not repeated," in Ayacucho

As in the other three cases discussed here, there has been no dramatic change in the outlook for tourism, which remains one of the leading industries in Mexico. However, a recent challenge to tourism development at the national level has been the upsurge in and media attention to drug cartels and violence and the fears of a global flu epidemic, which was first identified in Mexico. Although some analysts were beginning to consider Mexico a failed state, the government's handling of its crises won it more positive support. Indeed, following a short downturn in travel to leading resorts, special incentives to travel to Mexico were quickly on offer, drawing tourists back to the country.

Periodic problems continue to emerge along with tourism development. A violent clash of local indigenous people with police at a Chiapas tourism site in 2008 suggested the sort of discontent and conflict expressed by protesters in

Zapatista banner announcing "The Other Campaign" at the 2006 global encuentro in Oventic

Cuzco, Peru. In both places, local populations are expected to endorse tourism initiatives at cultural heritage sites but find that they have little say in how initiatives will be implemented or benefits will be distributed. In the Mexican case, hundreds of community members had occupied the entrance to a Mayan archaeological site to protest high admission fees and a failure to invest in the region. During the occupation, the community members allowed archaeologists to keep working and charged tourists a lower entry fee, promising that the revenue collected would be used to repair roads and make other improvements. As in the case of the Zapatista uprising in 1994, tourists were shown consideration and were assured of their safety. Nevertheless, when three hundred state police were sent in to confront the more recent protest, six indigenous protesters were shot and killed as they fought back with sticks and machetes; other villagers and police were injured, and twenty-eight protesters were arrested.[7]

As these four nations made transitions to new governments since 2006, some controversies shaped the political landscapes within which tourism development occurred. Race and indigenous identity marked differences among candidates in the Peruvian election, and class politics drove a wedge between voting groups in the Mexican election. Both Nicaragua and Peru saw the return of former presidents, and Cuba saw the transfer of power from Fidel to Raúl Castro. Gender politics may not appear to have been central to these transitions of power, yet we can discern aspects of gender identity playing a part, even if that identity (not surprisingly) is a masculine one. Daniel Ortega notoriously performed as a caudillo as he campaigned for office and opportunistically took a harsh stand on reproductive rights. In contrast, when Raúl Castro took office, Cubans knew him as a man of fewer words and a less macho style than that of his brother; his late wife, Vilma Espín, was prominent in the revolution and headed the Cuban Federation of Women; and his daughter Mariela Castro is well known as a gay and transgender rights activist, for which she has the support of both her father and her uncle.

Having pointed to recent developments in these nations, I next consider some significant ways in which shifting political climates may set the stage for related changes in tourism practices.

The Cultural Turn: Postmodern or Postcolonial?

The turn toward cultural and experiential tourism described in the opening of this chapter is notable in these four nations. I have presented narratives from my forays into experiential travel in Andean Peru and Chiapas, Mexico, where visitors stay in communities to learn about their cultural practices, foodways, and worldviews. Backpacker, solidarity, and mainstream tourists are increasingly turning to such community-based travel opportunities in these regions and elsewhere. In Nicaragua, there has been a dramatic turn toward what is referred to as communitarian tourism, often involving travel to rural communities where guests participate in light work on coffee plantations or assist artisans in their craft. And Cuba has for some time offered people-to-people exchanges in tourism, aiming to acquaint visitors with Cuban culture and politics; solidarity travelers have often been hosted at parties by neighborhood block committees (Committees for the Defense of the Revolution, or CDRs), staged performances of ideological commitment and community sociality.

We might ask whether this turn (or return) to cultural tourism signals a move away from more historically engaged tourism in postrevolutionary and postconflict sites, and whether the tendency I identified earlier of evoking nostalgia for the past is now, itself, a thing of the past. This may be so to a degree, but we have seen that when tourists journey to places that are racially or culturally different, where people's lives seem only remotely similar to their own, they frequently find that the way they make these others' lives legible is to imagine them as living history.[8] Most notably, visitors to Cuba often imagine that they are in a museum of peoples and artifacts that have remained unchanged since the advent of the revolution, and this nostalgic appeal is a leading attraction there. Similarly, in Vicos, Peru, many travelers believe they are going back to a simpler time and place, before the onset of modernization; in part, this reflects Vicosinos' pronounced emphasis on cultural tradition and the time when their grandparents lived. I have contended that, in contrast to the notion that the community is unchanging, the development of experiential tourism is another in a series of initiatives that Vicosinos themselves regard as making progress toward modernity. In Chiapas, the connection between indigenous lives and the region's recent history is hard to miss, as the Zapatista presence calls attention to past as well as contemporary injustice. Likewise, the Nicaraguan turn toward communitarian tourism is a development strategy for diversifying the economy and allowing rural producers to enhance their incomes during difficult times, yet it has embedded in it a sense that both local peoples and tourists will benefit from a recuperation of "the cultural identity and historical memory of the people" (Cañada et al. 2006:13).

We may consider the degree to which travelers to these societies in transition bring with them an increasingly postmodern sensibility about the world and their own place in it, that is, to what extent they might be described as posttourists. On the other hand, we may examine the growing postcolonial sensibility among the toured and local purveyors of tourism, who find ways to reverse historical relations and benefit from their newfound ability to attract travelers on their own terms. The two are not mutually exclusive, of course, but let us consider each in its turn. I have drawn attention in previous chapters to the sometimes ironic way that travelers, self-conscious about their status as tourists, may resist conventional touristic practices even while engaged in a number of them. I noted the jaded attitudes of some solidarity travelers in Chiapas who come to view the Zapatista communities as a sort of theme park for international activists, as one traveler put it, "like an activist Disneyland." Some travelers are happy to purchase Zapatista kitsch in the form of dolls and other paraphernalia, even as they reject what they view as the consumerist, packaged experience itself.

Yet, Chiapanecos themselves offer a twist on representations of Zapatista culture and politics. During my trip with Global Exchange over the 2006 Christmas and New Year holidays, I was amused to discover in the café TierrAdentro a nativity scene populated with Zapatistas. Figures on donkeys and the baby Jesus in the manger, wearing tiny ski masks and holding miniature wooden rifles, seemed to reflect the cosmopolitan, often playful, approach for which the Zapatistas—and particularly Marcos—have become well known. Although I cannot be certain of the intended irony, I suspect that the artisan behind the installation felt some amusement as well.[9] An irreverent, postcolonial outlook and empowering gaze upon the tourism encounter are no doubt behind such a local initiative and creative endeavor.

We may also recall the theater production in San Cristóbal, *Palenque Rojo*, which presented a dramatic, exotic narrative of Mayan culture and history, as well as a postcolonial perspective on European archaeologists' arrival on the scene. The gringos in their cargo pants and excessive gear contrasted with the indigenous hunters in their loin cloths and noble primitive ways. The jungle setting itself contrasted with the astonishing "discovery" of the scientists, the sites of Palenque and Toniná, and the Popol Vuh. The remarkable achievement of the local population and their predecessors was surely not lost on the audience, though many may have missed the layers of meaning in this representation of the colonial encounter—and of the contemporary and parallel *post*colonial encounter with tourism.

In the Peruvian case, among the examples I offered was that of a young traveler to Vicos who reflected afterward on her experience, telling me how meaningful it was for her. She went on to relate her self-conscious amusement and nostalgia thinking back to the time when she and a friend found themselves "at this saloon . . . two gringas dancing with the Indians." Travelers to urban centers like Cuzco and Huaraz frequently step outside themselves as tourists and reflect on the ironies of their travel experiences. I have overheard a number of conversations in which traveling companions compared notes on the consumer value of different destinations and then chided themselves for their complicity in cultural commodification.

Locals, in Peru as elsewhere, have had more time to study tourists than tourists have typically spent studying them, and this may account for innovative local responses to the tourist presence. The Vicosinos who have trained in workshops to prepare as hosts, for example, encourage their guests to try on their culture by experiencing it, through food, music, beliefs, and even dress, as they invite tourists to don a pollera and hat for a photograph. Elsewhere in the Callejón de Huaylas, it may have been local women entrepreneurs' keen observation of tourists' fascination with cultural difference that inspired some to begin knitting garments for knockoff Barbies. I would venture that travelers from the global North where Barbie has a fifty-year history are intrigued when they recognize the familiar doll in unfamiliar dress. While the Barbies "de Lima" might attract some interest, the "*cholita*" Barbies in full skirts and tiny hats most certainly would hold greater appeal for travelers experiencing the frisson of recognizing their own self-conscious "trying on" of culture in the Andes. The clever and skillful artisans who market the dolls in areas where tour buses stop regularly are able to capitalize on such posttourist desires.

Two more examples from Peru, discussed earlier, reveal a postcolonial sophistication emerging from a region that is toured. The posttourism outlook I

Procession in Cuzco featuring a large papier-mâché Pachamama, sacred kantuta flower and hummingbird springing from her genitals, with her entourage of dancing foods and beverages

discovered in the comic strip tracking the exploits and mishaps of "Backpack-ing Pat" features a gringo tourist who bumbles his way through the Callejón. The cartoonist playfully calls attention to the cultural difference of this clueless traveler in his trekking apparel, effectively reversing the gaze in the tourism encounter. Likewise, the procession I observed just before Inti Raymi in Cuzco made gentle fun of Peruvian cultural emblems, including the giant Pachamama and her dancing entourage of culinary offerings, and of tourists who come to consume these emblems and cultural practices. As a float passed with perform-ers dressed as trekkers laden with backpacks and cameras that were trained on the spectacle and its viewers, both Peruvians and international visitors laughed in recognition.

Cuba and Nicaragua have attracted tourists of revolution over the last sev-eral decades, but more recently they have promoted cultural tourism to appeal to a broader range of travelers. Thus, it is instructive to observe the changing uses of cultural and political icons, notably Che and Sandino, which are still extremely popular on T-shirts, postcards, and other merchandise. Cuba has also embraced Hemingway and old American cars as its own brand, market-ing nostalgia in a way that suggests ambivalent yearnings on the part of both Cubans and tourists. In these nations, John Lennon has emerged as a cultural icon symbolic of hopes and dreams. In the case of Cuba, this is an appropria-tion that breaks with the past, when the Beatles were banned as emblematic of bourgeois culture (seen in the movie *Strawberry and Chocolate*). Now the images of Che and Lennon appear side by side in the tourist market, and there is a life-size figure of Lennon in a Havana park named after him. In Nicaragua, Ortega's adoption of Lennon's "Give Peace a Chance" as his own (Nicaraguan) anthem was apparently without a trace of irony. Current government figures are rarely fodder for kitsch, but "Fidelitos," small painted replicas of Fidel Cas-tro in military dress and smoking a cigar, made their way into market stalls in Havana while the leader was still in power, suggesting a tolerance for a certain degree of humor, particularly if it attracts tourists.

The aging city of Havana is grappling with a slow restoration of its historic area, and the crumbling ruins of many buildings are served up as a melancholy reminder of days gone by. In a poetic documentary by German filmmakers Florian Borchmeyer and Matthias Hentschler, *Havana: The New Art of Making Ruins* (2006), the city is filmed affectionately but searingly, as buildings that are on the verge of collapse are shown to be inhabited by individuals with nowhere else to live. In addition to the unfortunate residents of these spaces, the video features the dissident writer José Antonio Ponte (author of *An Art of Making Ruins and Other Stories*), who offers critical commentary on the decaying city and what he regards as the decaying nation and its politics. Watching it, I remembered a conversation some years ago with Ponte, in which he described the peculiar amalgamation of travelers' nostalgia for the crumbling city and the harsh everyday experience of many Cubans who live there.[10]

During my most recent trip to Cuba, the fiftieth anniversary of the revolution was to be celebrated by the Cuban political elite in Santiago de Cuba, the historically important city at the eastern end of the island. On New Year's Eve, I was with the Canadian group mentioned previously that had traveled earlier in the day from Havana to Trinidad, a colonial city and UNESCO World Heritage Site. We stayed at an all-inclusive resort outside Trinidad, located on a white sand beach and attracting tour groups from many countries.[11] The resort threw an open-air party for its guests that night, staging a variety show with musical performances and presenting guests with festive bags of party favors. Resort employees constructed an elaborate tower of glasses and poured champagne for guests near midnight, at which time fireworks were set off. There was a solitary banner that announced "Fifty Years of the Revolution," but perhaps in deference to the broad political spectrum of visitors to the island and to the generally apolitical nature of tourism at the resort, nothing was said of the anniversary that evening. The next day, January 1, 2009, the formal event was televised to the nation, and I watched from my hotel room. Raúl Castro gave a speech honoring the history of the revolution, an official spoke of women in the revolution, and a young girl from the communist youth group, the Pioneers, spoke passionately and patriotically, ending with the group's slogan, "We will be like Che!"

The difference was striking between the experience of tourists on holiday and the official Cuban political culture during those days of celebration. Our group was a mix of fairly liberal individuals, couples, and families, though differences in outlook were expressed (and sometimes suppressed). Our guide was often candid in his assessments of Cuban politics, revealing his doubts to us. On this trip, I was impressed by the ambivalence of Cubans at the revolution's historic conjuncture and of tourists who appeared to enjoy a cultural experience with political overtones, without unsettling many ideas they had formed before traveling to Cuba. Of the nations I have discussed in this book, it was harder to discern the sort of posttourist sensibility I found in Andean Peru and Chiapas in postrevolutionary Nicaragua and Cuba. The closest I found was in some dissident voices in Nicaragua and in the innuendos of Cuban tour guides willing to comment on national political culture, letting visitors in on their jokes, whether they understood them or not.

Fashioning Nations, Decolonizing Travel

In the tourism encounters that I have examined in Latin America and the Caribbean, political landscapes are in transition, and drawing on global tourism is expected to further stabilization and economic development. I have argued that initiatives to promote tourism can be understood as continuing processes of transformation that were begun earlier in times of revolution or social upheaval. As this occurs, regions and nations are reimagined as safe, if still-edgy, tourist destinations. Other world regions have seen such developments, in some cases dramatically. Rebecca L. Stein offers an account of Israeli national tourism during the time of the Middle East peace process, which drew on desires for the Arab Other and turned places that had been feared into popular tourist attractions. She shows that tourism was instrumental in forging "new notions of national identity befitting the altered regional landscape" (2008:3). In another context, a journalist writes of the transformation of the eastern Congo from "epicenter of the deadliest conflict since World War II, into a tourist attraction," as travelers are enticed by "the untrammeled beauty as a result of the country's long isolation" (Polgreen 2008:A10). Camping out along the edge of a still-active volcano is currently popular and is helping create jobs for Congolese tour operators, guides, and porters. One local tour operator offered the pertinent, if exaggerated, remark that "tourism can end war here in Congo. If people are working, they are too busy to fight."

These examples of tourism in places still overcoming histories of prolonged conflict resonate with the cases I have presented. Although Cuba, Mexico, Nicaragua, and Peru have by and large been more stable in recent years than the examples just cited, they have nonetheless experienced periods of dramatic transition and national reconstruction; with transfers of power in all four nations since 2006, outbreaks of conflict and social dissent continue to mark their political landscapes. At its best, tourism may contribute to furthering not only postconflict stabilization and economic transformation but decolonizing projects that challenge imbalances of power by race, class, gender, and nationality. We have seen instances of this in community-based tourism in Andean Peru and southern Mexico, where indigenous peoples set the terms as hosts welcoming visitors, and it is also seen in emergent Afro-Cuban tourism and in Nicaragua's rural-based communitarian tourism. These examples of cultural tourism often have as an objective that tourists themselves may undergo a transformation, though to be sure, travelers often come away with very incomplete new knowledge or even reconfirmed stereotypes of culturally different peoples.

Gender nearly always figures significantly in tourism encounters, laden as these encounters are with differences of power, as analysts in tourism studies and feminist cultural studies have shown (Kinnaird and Hall 1994; Sinclair 1997; Kaplan 1996). In some cases, gender differences appear quietly and behind the scenes, as in the Vicos and Lacandón communities where women often provide labor-intensive services while men play more prominent roles as hosts interacting with tourists. As I showed in the comparison of Nicaragua and Cuba, women participate in a range of tourism-related activities, as artisans and service providers, and sometimes as sex workers. Those who engage in sex tourism range from young girls pressed into sexual commerce in Nicaragua to Cuban women who have alternatives but find that their earning power is far greater when they seek sexual intimacy with foreign men. All these women are social actors with the potential to get ahead by looking to tourism, even if many of them find that their opportunities are narrowly limited as a consequence of their race, class, and gender. When women are regarded within their own societies or by tourists as more Indian, more exotic, or more sexual than their male counterparts, this form of objectification can work both for and against them under changing conditions of tourism development.

Among indigenous women in highland Chiapas and, especially, those in the Zapatista communities, there is more evidence of self-assertion and collective identity formation. Women artisans and others who cater to tourism have shown independence in their creative endeavors and have found ways to better their own lives as well as those of their families and communities. While young girls selling dolls and friendship bracelets in San Cristóbal sometimes receive tips from tourists taking their pictures, a group of Mayan women has acquired the skills they need to take photographs of their everyday lives at home and at work, thus challenging the tourist gaze with their own. Their Indigenous Photography Archive has had a broad reach, traveling to nearby schools and international exhibitions. Also emerging from productive collaborations between global North and South, the Chiapas Media Project has given indigenous women and men the technical skills to document their experience and represent themselves, as an alternative to the prevailing representations of tourists, researchers, and other outsiders.[12]

My work has considered the powerful allure of the once forbidden in draw-ing tourists to postconflict and postrevolutionary travel destinations. This attraction, based in part on the notion that places formerly shunned by tour-ists have been protected from overexposure and are likely to be "natural" and "undiscovered," may last only until the recently discovered is overcrowded and overdeveloped. The turn toward cultural tourism and sustainable tourism re-sponds to redefined desires of tourists who, even on tighter budgets, wish to travel, know other peoples and cultures, and in some cases, offer something back—beyond payment for services rendered—to the communities that host them.[13] This adaptation of tourism in transitional societies to meet changing market demands, I have argued, does not necessarily mean rejecting all pros-pects of social transformation, and it may in fact enable such a process to con-tinue under altered global conditions.

With new challenges facing Latin America and the Caribbean, I want to conclude with a cautionary note. The profound disappointments experienced by regions and nations that staked so much on far-reaching processes of so-cial and political transformation are well known. Tourism is hardly a panacea, and it often conspires with forms of social inequality and injustice to rein-force representations of cultural difference in ways that add insult to injury in already-oppressive relations at the local, national, and global levels. I have no quarrel with those who argue that tourism can in fact reproduce past colonial relationships and contribute to deeper inequalities as new national and inter-national elites benefit from its spoils.[14] Yet, as both development strategy and analytical lens, tourism has proven to be particularly fruitful for exploration of the dynamics of change in these transitional societies, and although it is neither innocent nor benign, tourism can at its best offer opportunities to advance transformative programs in the interests of wider sectors of society. What I have found most revelatory in my research in Cuba, Mexico, Nicaragua, and Peru is the degree to which—despite all manner of obstacles—actors at every level reimagine histories of conflict, shift the terms of engagement, and struggle to pursue futures that build upon what is most auspicious in their encounters with tourism.

Reference Matter

Notes

Introduction

1. However, it may take some time before Iraq is ready to welcome tourists. Recently, the arrival of a single tourist threw the country into upheaval (Farrell and Rubin 2009:A6).

2. See Babb (2005) for more discussion of tourism promotion in postconflict and postrevolutionary nations worldwide. There, I mention some of the following popular accounts of tourism in areas previously shunned. One recent *New York Times* article describes the positive economic impact on Laos following UNESCO's decision to name a town a World Heritage Site, calling it the "Best Preserved City in Southeast Asia"—with the result that "tourism has rescued the town." Another article touts South Africa, and Johannesburg in particular, as revived and ready for visitors. Whereas in the past tourists have often flocked to game parks, in post-1994 democratic South Africa, many wish to discover the country's national museum of apartheid atrocities and to visit Nelson Mandela's prison cell. Still another article invites readers to consider the advantages of travel to Libya, long viewed as a despotic nation and now a "must-see destination." The writer points out that much of the appeal is the attraction of the forbidden, at least for U.S. residents, who were banned from travel there for twenty-three years, and that Libya's reputation as a dangerous place actually serves to draw some travelers.

In Chiapas, Mexico, site of the Zapatista uprising a decade ago, San Cristóbal de las Casas has garnered a record number of tourists, and a *New York Times* reporter states that the rebels have served as a "radical-chic" attraction. Similarly, El Salvador has emerged from civil war in the 1980s to postconflict tourism, which relies not only on the country's lush natural landscape but also on its rich cultural heritage. And the movie *The Motorcycle Diaries*, based on the journal of a young Che Guevara as he traveled through South America, has sparked more travel in that region, so much so that to enhance tourism, the Bolivian government has recently promoted the "Che Trail" taken by the older, seasoned revolutionary. China and Vietnam have also experienced tourism booms, and the cachet of Mao and Ho Chi Minh helps lure visitors to discover what was once off limits.

3. See also Degregori and Sandoval (2008:152) on the field of anthropology's emergence in Peru "from an encounter with the Other" going back to colonial times.

4. I am not the first to make such claims for tourism, and indeed scholars dating back to Dean MacCannell (1999:1) have discussed tourism as offering one of the best frameworks for understanding the modern condition.

5. Little (personal communication) points out that such "reinvention" in Guatemala is really window dressing and indigenous people continue to face exclusion and discrimination. See Little and Smith (2009) and Hale (2006) for more on cultural identity and the state in Guatemala. Persistent social inequality is found in the regions I examine as well.

6. As this book goes to press, two new collections are appearing that give some attention to tourism in postconflict areas of Latin America. See Baud and Ypeij (2009) on cultural tourism in Latin America, with contributions on Peru, Ecuador, Mexico, and Guatemala. Although they do not expressly focus on tourism, see Bilbija and Payne (2011) on the marketing of memory in Latin America, with contributions on trauma tourism, memory museums, commemorative sites, and the commodification of violence in Argentina, Brazil, Chile, Mexico, Peru, and Uruguay.

7. Luisa Campuzano, at Havana's Casa de las Americas, brought this work to my attention in 2005, for which I am grateful.

8. Peter Rosset, former director of Food First, whom I met at a gathering of scholars at the San Cristóbal home of June Nash in 2008, commented that Naomi Klein's provocative work had been the focus of some discussion since she visited Chiapas.

9. Later chapters will discuss the work of others in more detail, but here I would cite the ongoing and important research of Walter Little in Guatemala and of Elayne Zorn, who has written on tourism in Peru and is carrying out research in the present-day Bolivia of Evo Morales.

10. I borrow this notion of "ethnographic partners" from Judith Farquhar, who usefully describes her own use of different genres of source material on China as forming "a kind of cosmopolitan or itinerant ethnography" (2002:5).

11. See Goldstone (2001) for discussion of the reengineering of danger zones for tourism and the prospects for democratization. Chambers (2000) discusses tourism's potential to bring nations together, commenting that it alters the way we understand the world and each other.

Chapter 1

Material from this chapter is forthcoming in "Che, Chevys, and Hemingway's Daiquiris: Cuban Tourism as Development Strategy in a Time of Globalization" in a special issue on island tourism in the *Bulletin of Latin American Research*.

1. This was the palace of Cuban dictator Fulgencio Batista.

2. Espino discusses the introduction of this program in 1991 at the Fourth Communist Party Congress, when tourism was promoted as "an important source of revenue for economic development" (2000:360). She notes that a decade later the tourism industry had emerged as the leading performer of the Special Period.

3. These figures are from http://www.usatoday.com/travel/destinations/2009-01-13-cuba-record-tourism_N.htm. See *Digital Granma Internacional*, the Internet version of Cuba's official newspaper, for frequent updates on tourism in the country (available at www.granmai.cubasi.cu).

4. See Pérez (1999) and Schwartz (1997) for discussion of Cuban tourism earlier in the twentieth century when the island was presented as an exotic location for recreation and urban pleasures. The latter gives brief attention to changes brought about by postrevolutionary tourism.

5. See Chávez (2005) and Sanchez and Adams (2008) for discussion of the impact of tourism on Cuban society and politics.

6. In their masterful work, *Havana: Two Faces of the Antillean Metropolis*, Scarpaci et al. (2002) examine the abundance of features in Cuba's capital city that date from both before and after the revolution.

7. See Boym (2001) for a fruitful discussion of Russian nostalgia in the postcommunist era. The Russian and Cuban cases may be similar insofar as "nostalgia became a defense mechanism against the accelerated rhythm of change and the economic shock therapy" (64). Moreover, she might be writing of Cuba when she states, "Russian nostalgia was made not only for domestic but also for tourist consumption, and thus has to be easily digestible and convertible" (67).

8. Hernández (2002:61) discusses the Buena Vista Social Club as "a narrative of an ahistorical nostalgia for a pre-Revolutionary Cuba."

9. My five trips to Cuba averaged about three to four weeks for a total of about four months spent there. I discuss my latest trip, during December 2008–January 2009, in the Conclusion.

10. In 1993 and 2003 I took part in Global Exchange "Reality Tours" (the first trip, in 1993, focused on women's issues and was headed by writer and feminist Margaret Randall, who lived for some years in Cuba as well as in Nicaragua), and in 2008–2009 I joined a Canadian group with Cuba Education Tours.

11. It is arguable whether "precapitalist" is the best way to describe these strategies for surviving the economic crisis, but the reliance on nonmarket ways of coping was notable during this period. Interestingly, ecotourism in the form of bicycle tours and

attention to the environment emerged during this time, though this goes beyond the scope of this chapter.

12. Other writers have similarly commented on "Cuba's venture into a sort of never-never land between communism and capitalism . . . [as] the island has drifted between two opposing economic systems" (Chávez 2005:1).

13. Berger (2006) offers a related perspective on tourism in Mexico, where tourists enjoy "pyramids by day, martinis by night." However, Walter Little usefully notes (personal communication) that such iconic figures as Guevara and Hemingway may have become "disarticulated" from their previous meanings and "resignified" by tourists.

14. Padilla and McElroy (2007:654).

15. See Sanchez and Adams (2008:1) for a discussion of "Janus-faced tourism in Cuba." The authors consider the return of pre-revolutionary "ills" even as the Cuban government seeks to advance its political ideology through tourism development. Some travelers appreciate that Cuba is one of the few places where U.S. tourists are not plentiful. One commented in a recent *USA Today* blog that "the fact that Cuba is not Americanized is very appealing for travelers from Canada and Europe" (www.usatoday.com/travel/destinations/2009-01-13-cuba-record-tourism_N.htm).

16. Jorge Duany, personal communication.

17. See Scarpaci (2005) for discussion of heritage tourism in Old Havana and Trinidad, two UNESCO World Heritage Sites in Cuba.

18. This is with the exception of Cuban American visits, which amounted to over 140,000 in 1999 (see Eckstein and Barberia 2001:12).

19. As mentioned, two of my four trips to Cuba were tours arranged by Global Exchange (http://globalexchange.org/), in 1993 and 2003. My trip in 2001 was with a group of faculty and students from the University of Iowa and Grinnell College, and my trip in 2005 was made independently with assistance from Marazul Charters. In 2008–2009 I traveled with Cuba Education Tours. Such trips are now practically impossible under more restrictive policies in the United States. I traveled with a general license on all five visits.

20. Jorge Duany notes that a sort of tourism without travel to Cuba is made possible in the United States through the commodification of nostalgia. Cuban retail outlets such as Café Nostalgia and Little Havana To Go on Calle Ocho in Little Havana in Miami are examples of this (personal communication).

21. Questionnaires that I gave tourists in Cuba revealed such generational differences. Whereas middle-aged and older visitors might recall seeing Desi Arnaz as Lucille Ball's Cuban American husband on TV's *I Love Lucy*, as well as hearing news of the revolution, visitors under the age of thirty were familiar with Cuba as a wedding destination, the site or subject of recent movies, and a place for ecotourism.

22. Now a joint venture with Spain, the hotel has been renamed the Hotel Tryp Habana Libre, but it is better known as the Habana Libre.

23. Among these companies, Gaviota is controlled by the armed forces and now dominates the tourism industry. See the *Economist*, "Cuba Returns to the Command and Control Economy," July 31, 2004.

24. Modest though the cost is for many tourists, fifteen dollars is what many Cubans earn in a month on government salaries. Note that throughout this book, all dollar amounts are in U.S. dollars unless otherwise noted.

25. See Palmié (2002) for a discussion of the historical fascination (and its modern expression) with Afro-Cuban religious tradition. See Hagedorn (2001) for a rich ethnography of the performance of Santería and its marketing for tourism. Notably, the Cuban government has capitalized on the popularity of the tradition, despite continued race discrimination, by promoting religious tourism.

26. Although better known to select visitors who are "in the know," Cuba has become a significant player in the international art and music world. Hip-hop, like other kinds of music in Cuba, is appreciated for its independent, noncommercial form; the annual Havana Film Festival draws filmmakers and connoisseurs from around the world who recognize Cuba as a leading center for film production; and the arts in general in Cuba receive strong support, with events like the Havana Biennial Art Exhibitions drawing many visitors to the country.

27. Several years ago, dollars were still circulating along with Cuban pesos and convertible pesos, but today tourists are required to use convertible pesos, which are tied to foreign currencies.

28. A photo of Ernest Hemingway and Fidel Castro, who appear to be intimate friends though they met just once, is on display around Havana.

29. José Quiroga brought this to my attention, for which I am grateful.

30. There is a large literature on sex and romance tourism in Cuba, including Cabezas (1998, 2004); Davidson (1996); Elizalde (2002); Fernandez (1999); and Fusco (1998).

31. Gropas (2007) has recently described the revolutionary billboards that dot the Cuban landscape but not their odd juxtaposition and ironic presence in touristic settings.

32. Baseball figures as an iconic pastime of Cubans despite (or because of) its association with the United States. See Carter (2008) for a cultural analysis of the sport in Cuban society.

33. More research is needed on ordinary Cubans' response to the fashioning of their nation for tourism. I often spoke with workers in the tourism industry, but not systematically with other citizens, about how Cuba is marketed. See Hernández (2003) and Prieto (2004) for discussion of insiders' and outsiders' reflections on Cuba that are shaped in part by travel to and from the island.

34. Two years later, in 2005, I went on a similar city tour with the same basic format. However, the guide was not so inclined to make jokes and kept a serious tone for

the most part. This makes me think that there is some leeway in the narratives and perhaps in their political content, at least within reasonable bounds.

35. See Quiroga (2005:83–84) for discussion of this "pretense of antiqueness" and the "unwritten rule that Havana be stuck in time: Those old cameras somehow correspond to the old Chevys on the streets."

36. By way of contrast, see the work of Rafael Hernández (2003), which offers a Cuban assessment of Cuba rather than presenting outsiders' perspectives.

37. This same image is used on the cover of an edited collection of pieces written by travelers to Cuba spanning three centuries, evoking nostalgic images of the island long before the revolution (Jenkins 2002). There is an abundance of travel writing on Cuba, which could be the subject of another work.

38. Little has been written about tourism from 1959 until the 1990s, but see Schwartz (1997); and for a view that is critical of solidarity travel in Cuba and Nicaragua, see Hollander (1986).

39. However, see Scarpaci (2005) for a discussion of the Disneyfication of Old Havana as it is turned into a living museum for tourists to experience the past in the present. To some extent Miami and Havana developed in complementary fashion before the revolution (Pérez 1999). And it is worth noting that Havana does have its own fast-food chain restaurants.

Chapter 2

This chapter is an updated version of "Recycled *Sandalistas*: From Revolution to Resorts in the New Nicaragua," published in *American Anthropologist* 106, no. 3 (2004):541–555.

1. All translations from the Spanish are my own. In Spanish, Borge said "¿Y por qué hay que estimular el turismo en este país desgraciado? Porque es la tabla de salvación de la economía nacional" (interview, June 30, 2003).

2. I carried out research in Nicaragua in 1989, 1990, 1991, 1992, 1993, 1996, 1998, 2000, 2002, 2003, 2004, and 2008. Funding was provided by the Fulbright Foundation, the Wenner-Gren Foundation, the University of Iowa, and the University of Florida.

3. It is also illustrative of the politics of location in a time of globalization. See Appadurai (2001); Gupta and Ferguson (1997).

4. I discuss the work of these writers and others who made the pilgrimage to revolutionary Nicaragua in Babb (2001a).

5. Note that by 2007 the number of international travelers to Nicaragua had close to doubled that figure, rising to 978,330, with 82 percent designated as tourists, according to INTUR's Boletín de Estadísticas de Turismo, 2007 (www.intur.gob.ni/DOCS/ESTADISTICAS/estadisticas2007.pdf).

6. See www.intur.gob.ni/.

7. See Liechty (1996) for discussion of the making of Kathmandu, Nepal, as a tourist destination and the influence of a Lonely Planet guidebook in that process.

8. See Gould (1998) for discussion of Nicaraguan indigenous peoples and the myth of mestizaje. Field (1999) examines the foundational narrative of Güegüense in relation to artisans and national identity in contemporary Nicaragua. T. M. Scruggs (personal communication) notes that in the town of Masaya and the community of Monimbó indigenous identity and artisanship draw tourists.

9. See Wilk (2006) for discussion of efforts in Belize to market to tourists, including Peace Corps volunteers training local people to make handicrafts that would later be sold to American tourists. In Managua, I observed several Peace Corps volunteers attempting to help women start a tie-dye microenterprise, an effort that failed.

10. In November 2001, a French biker broke the world record for mountain biking by flying down the volcanic slopes of Cerro Negro at over 130 kilometers per hour. Tour operator Pierre Gédéon of Nicaragua Adventures promoted the event in Europe and invited a French film crew.

11. Nicaraguan males are often the providers of services to female travelers, but the gendered politics generally have a different and less sexual character, as noted in a recent travel article in the *New York Times* (Klein 2003:15). However, my observations in Cuba and those of others elsewhere (Phillips 1999) suggest that women tourists, too, may seek sexual liaisons with "locals" when traveling. See also Bolles (1997) on women and tourism in Jamaica, and Rojek and Urry (1997:16–18) on gendered differences in the "tourist gaze."

12. I discuss popular accounts of Nicaragua in the 1980s in Babb (2001a). Celebrated authors of memoirs of visits to Nicaragua include Ferlinghetti (1984) and Rushdie (1987).

13. Although the telephone book currently lists some forty tourist agencies in the country, a number of them are devoted to foreign travel rather than to Nicaraguan tourism.

14. Visitors to Munditur's Web site are informed quite candidly, "Our goal through these past few years has been to eradicate any negative perception the rest of the world has of Nicaragua" (www.munditur.com).

15. The 2005 edition of *Moon Handbooks: Nicaragua* offers more attention to the history of conflict. In fact, a few years after I had a conversation with one of the writers, Joshua Berman, about the possibility that a Sandinista revolution tour would become popular, I was interested to see a couple of pages devoted to a two-week self-guided tour tracing "the path of Sandino."

16. Here again I should note that most of my research was conducted before Daniel Ortega and the Sandinista Party returned to power in 2006. I returned to Nicaragua in 2008 and observed the fraught politics of that period, with those on both the Right and the Left critical of the government's populist rhetoric in the face of its increasingly autocratic practices. I discuss recent change in my concluding chapter.

17. The photograph, taken by Orlando Valenzuela, became a defining image of the

Sandinista period, inspiring artist Chico Emery to paint a mural entitled *Sandinista Woman and Child* on a wall in central Managua in 1985. The mass women's organization AMNLAE (Luisa Amanda Espinoza Association of Nicaraguan Women) used the image in a poster, and it is now found on postcards in hotel gift shops and markets. Kunzle (1995) notes that this photograph has been copied in images as far away as Belfast, Ireland.

18. Erika Moreno (personal communication) has suggested that the safe reappearance of images and narratives of revolution might also be possible because of the decline of the revolutionary Left in Latin America, even if there is a new leftward turn. In Nicaragua, the Sandinista Party remained a significant political force but was no longer perceived as a threat to national security—thus its past could be romanticized.

19. I refer to the Wisconsin Coordinating Committee on Nicaragua, based in Madison, and to Global Exchange, an organization I have traveled with in Cuba and Chiapas, Mexico.

20. There is one such reenactment that takes place every year in June, when in 1979 the Sandinistas made a tactical retreat from Managua to Masaya before their triumphant return to take power. Old and young Sandinistas make the long walk and are joined by internationalists in solidarity with them. This is a show of political strength and a commemoration, however, and no organized tour has been designed to follow the course of the insurrection.

21. In the prologue to Sheesley's (1991) work on representations of Sandino in Nicaraguan public culture, artist and poet Ernesto Cardenal comments that the national hero may be unique in being recognized by his silhouette alone. Indeed, just the sketch of his hat, with a sort of sideways figure 8 for the brim and a triangular line for the top, is instantly familiar to any Nicaraguan and to many others who have spent time in the country.

22. I am grateful to Aynn Setright for details about these monuments. Managua's mayor had another "worker's" monument erected across the street from the "Rambo" statue, depicting a man with a jackhammer and a woman picking through metal scraps. Both are hunched over and appear downtrodden—in contrast to the Sandinista virile worker/combatant. See Craven (1989) for detailed discussion of art and popular culture during the revolutionary period.

23. The Sandinista Party became "safer" with the New Age refashioning of Daniel Ortega for the 2001 elections; in the post–September 11 climate, however, the United States again helped turn the tide toward the Liberal Party candidate. It was only in 2006 that Ortega was again the victor.

24. See Mallon (2003) for discussion of the popularity of Che in Allende's Chile and his image of revolutionary masculinity. Che's image now appears around the globe as a kitsch symbol of cultural opposition; nonetheless, in Nicaraguan political culture there is a deeper connection between Che and ideas of revolution.

Chapter 3

1. The video *Miss Universe in Peru* documents this event and critically contrasts the glamour of the pageant with the everyday realities of most Peruvian women (see Grupo Chaski 1986).

2. The final report of the Truth and Reconciliation Commission is available online at http://www.cverdad.org.pe/ingles/pagina01.php. For a local perspective from Ayacucho, see DED (2005).

3. See Council on Hemispheric Affairs (2008) for an article detailing the rise and fall and the possible return of Sendero Luminoso.

4. For a brief reflection on the history of tourism in Peru, see Van den Berghe and Flores Ochoa (2000). The authors note the early travelers from the sixteenth through the nineteenth centuries, including illustrious individuals such as Alexander von Humboldt and Charles Darwin, and the much higher volume of tourism made possible by air travel in the twentieth century.

5. Walter Little (personal communication) points out that separating location from history has been a strategy in Guatemala for decades to divert attention from memories of war and violence though it has not always been successful.

6. Another image used by PromPerú shows a bird emerging in flight out of its own imprint, taken from the famous Nazca line drawings, evoking both the archaeological past and the natural environment, recurring themes in tourism promotion in Peru.

7. In fact, Adventures by Disney offers family vacations to Peru that promise, "From traveling to Inca ruins to rafting remote rivers, there is something for everyone!" (http://abd.disney.go.com/abd/en_US/destination?name=PeruLandingPage).

8. In Lima in December 1996, members of the Túpac Amaru Revolutionary Movement took hundreds of hostages at the home of Japan's ambassador to Peru. Most were soon released, but the remaining dignitaries were held until April 1997, when the Peruvian Armed Forces raided the home and freed them. The international media followed the developments.

9. An article in *Condé Nast Traveler* (Glowczewska 2008:206) on travel to Rwanda notes that the Kigali Memorial Center, which documents the 1994 genocide, is "frequently (and appropriately) the first stop on any visit to Rwanda." Perhaps the magnitude of the events in that country make it harder for tourists to overlook the horrific past. The recent Peruvian violence is more often concealed.

10. For further discussion of the ANFASEP Memory Museum, see Milton and Ulfe (2011), who offer an analysis of the uses of memory in Peru; they found that the museum was beginning to appear on tourist maps of Ayacucho. See also the work of Joseph Feldman (2010), who has carried out ethnographic research on the museum as commemorative site.

11. The scholarly literature on the period of violence in Peru has grown in recent years and includes political analyses, psychological appraisals, and, to offer but one

recent contribution, a riveting collection of photographs centering on the experience of orphans, violence, and memory (Larrabure 2007).

12. See Bode (1989) and Oliver-Smith (1986) for anthropological accounts of the aftermath of the earthquake in the Callejón de Huaylas and its social consequences. The city of Huaraz was being rebuilt when I carried out my doctoral research there in 1977.

13. See contributions to Baud and Ypeij (2009) on Peru's *sacamefotos* (literally, "take my photos"), street vendors, and other service providers who interact with tourists.

14. See also http://www.vivencialtours.com/.

15. Over three decades ago, I wrote my master's thesis on gender and power in the Cornell-Peru applied anthropology project in Vicos based on archival materials (later published in several versions, Babb 1985, 1999b). Since that time, I have made a number of brief trips to Vicos, but I did not stay there until I participated in the tourism program.

16. See interviews with Miriam Torres of the Mountain Institute and Tammy Leland of Crooked Trails for discussion of how their NGOs came to work with Vicosinos on the tourism project (http://instruct1.cit.cornell.edu/courses/vicosperu/vicos-site/ecotourism_page_1.htm). Torres remarks, "We identified a work process that started with pilot projects. We said, 'Let's do relatively small projects to test our hypothesis and that especially can empower peasant leaders'"—an approach reminiscent of the Cornell-Peru Project's applied social change. Leland, who cofounded her nonprofit travel company, comments that she has observed the increasing confidence and openness of Vicosinos who work with tourists, adding, "I don't even know if it is normal for Quechua families to kiss people on the cheek"—a practice that is in fact strikingly new in the community.

17. See the Web site for Vicos: A Virtual Tour (http://courses.cit.cornell.edu/vicosperu/vicos-site/) for a video stream showing a tearful tourist expressing how moved she was by her visit to the community. I was told travelers going to Vicos with Crooked Trails rarely leave without such an emotional response to their experience.

18. During my trip to Vicos in 2007, I was honored to join a small group of distinguished visitors who included Allan Holmberg's son and daughter, David and Anna Holmberg, Barbara Lynch, and others who were there for a reunion with members of the community. The Vicosinos had planned a mass followed by a pachamanca and speeches, celebrating the work of Allan Holmberg and Mario Vazquez a half century ago with the Cornell-Peru Project. Elders in the community well remember the work and continuing support of Cornell University.

19. See Bruner (2005), Little (2004), and others who discuss the common misperception of tourists that they are observing cultures preserved from the past. Of course, even anthropologists held a fairly static view of the community until recently. There have been many critiques of ahistorical approaches to cultural analysis in much of the twentieth century. Scholars working in Vicos were no exception. A common percep-

tion was that social scientists in the Vicos Project were launching campesinos from their sixteenth-century mode of life into the modern age. Jason Pribilsky's current research has taken a historical approach to the interventions in Vicos.

20. Barbara Kirshenblatt-Gimblett (1998) discusses the construction of culture as a hallmark of modernity, something that may be pertinent in the case of Vicos and other tourist destinations in Peru.

21. See Rosaldo (1989) on imperialist nostalgia and Pratt (1992) on imperialism and travel. Some postmodern travelers may be implicitly critiquing nostalgia as it manifests in the quest for the Other.

22. See Femenías (2005:292–295) for discussion of similar dolls in southern Peru, dressed in embroidered clothing typical of that region. She found, interestingly, that some Ken dolls were similarly dressed, as is culturally appropriate for transvestite men in the area (known as Witite). The phenomenon of "transnational Barbie" is discussed by Grewal (1999), who documents the marketing success the doll has had as she travels the globe in varying ethnic attire to meet new consumer desires.

Chapter 4

1. I borrow this formulation from the subtitle of Berger's (2006) book. See also Daniel Cooper Alarcón (1997) for discussion of the production of Mexicanness through Mexico's tourism industry. He describes the promotion of multiple Mexicos, whereby tourists experience "'exploring' ancient ruins in the morning, bartering with natives at noon, sipping piña coladas in the afternoon, being serenaded by mariachis in the evening" (182).

2. It is worth noting that tourism in Mexico, like the other cases I discuss, has been influenced not only by national developments but by trends in global travel during the past century.

3. Nonetheless, some in Nicaragua, as in all the nations examined here, are beginning to plan ahead by promoting sustainable tourism. And even places that are well trodden can be reconstructed by capitalist interests as new and exciting.

4. The relatively higher number of tourists from Europe than from the United States may in fact contribute to the perceived unspoiled character of the area.

5. The Zapatista uprising has been discussed by many writers, including, for example, Harvey (1998a), Hayden (2002), and Stephen (2002).

6. Kathleen Adams (2006a:205) cites a similar case in Jakarta, Indonesia, reported in a 1961 issue of *National Geographic* by travelers who were addressed by a commandant, "'Forgive us,' he said, 'but Indonesia is in a state of emergency.'"

7. Martín presents an interesting analysis of the use of the rhetoric of tourism by Subcomandante Marcos and the Zapatistas.

8. For a review essay on Olesen's book and interesting commentary on the global Zapatismo phenomenon, see Stahler-Sholk (2007).

9. My research in Chiapas was carried out during four fairly short trips between 2005 and 2009; I also draw on my longer-term experience elsewhere in Mexico, including summer 1976 in Cuernavaca, summer 1981 in Mexico City and Jalapa, and a number of shorter visits since then.

10. Herbert Buchsbaum (2004) wrote in a *New York Times* article that a decade after the Zapatista uprising, tourism had rebounded and San Cristóbal had become "radical-chic" even to mainstream travelers.

11. See Flusty (2006) for a discussion of traveling Zapatista dolls, including blue-eyed Subcomandante Marcos and Comandanta Romona, with dark braids and a baby on her back. These have become, as he writes, "the most prominent artifact within the proliferating commodity landscape of Zapatista tie-in merchandise" (191).

12. Mexico currently receives over 20 million tourists each year, and up to 80 percent of them come from the United States (http://www.spanish-mexico.com/tourism-mexico/).

13. A new road opened during the time of research in Chiapas, cutting the driving time between Tuxtla and San Cristóbal almost in half. During later visits, it took about an hour to make the drive.

14. Journalist and writer Naomi Klein visited café TierrAdentro in December 2007 and described the place as "ground zero" for internationalists and Zapa-tourism.

15. For classic anthropological studies of these communities, see Gossen (1999) and Vogt (1969).

16. See Nash (2007) for discussion of the aggressive marketing of Coca-Cola in Chiapas, where the company has gone so far as to buy up local groundwater supplies, selling bottled water back to indigenous communities.

17. During a visit to the Bar Revolución the following year, in 2009, the bartender told me that the bar's owners were fans of both the Cuban revolution and of cinema, and that the name of the bar actually referred to the "revolution" of reels of film; those in the know might appreciate the double meaning. On that recent visit, I also discovered a new Burger King restaurant across the street from the bar in this prime location for tourists and locals to pass by, showcasing radical chic on the one hand and global capitalism on the other.

18. See www.globalexchange.org/tours/712.html.

19. The Zapatistas have made efforts, though not entirely successful, to build a social movement that is committed to gender justice.

20. In San Cristóbal during this time, there was a photograph displayed at the café TierrAdentro showing a wall in Oaxaca with graffiti reading in English, "Tourists: Oaxaca is temporarily closed. Will open as soon as there is justice." Like San Cristóbal, Oaxaca's colonial city is a leading tourist destination, but the violence that followed a teachers' strike in 2006 discouraged travel there.

21. This seemed to be a conflation of memories of the past and experience in the

present—referencing high points in this woman's personal life history but also suggesting that the past may be reimagined as a foreign country (see Lowenthal 1985).

22. See www.globalexchange.org/tours/712.html.

23. The increasing number of seekers may be due in part to the notion that the Mayan calendar will expire on December 21, 2012, leading some to question what the future (if any) will hold.

24. The Rainbow gathering refers to a free-spirited group from around the world who convene to build community based on nonviolence, environmentalism, and alternative lifestyle. A number of their beliefs and practices are loosely based on Native American traditions.

25. At the risk of oversimplifying, the Lacandón may represent an attempt at apolitical cultural tourism, whereas the Zapatista sites discussed in this chapter embrace the political movement and its market advantage.

26. Oakes (2006:235) discusses the reaction of American tourists to what they perceive as commercialized and indifferent village tourism, as tourists "needed to believe that their encounter would be genuine and meaningful for the villagers."

27. This reserve is one of the largest areas of tropical forest in Mexico and comprises a mix of federal, communal land and private land. Tzeltal, Chol, and Lacandón Mayan communities see the Montes Azules reserve as a buffer against outside threats to their land. In recent years, there has been exploitation of chicle and mahogany, and the military has made incursions in the reserve.

28. As Kathleen Adams (2001, 2006b) has shown so well, a certain strain of tourism is directed precisely to "hot spots" before they are widely viewed as safe to visit. She discusses "danger tourism" in areas of Southeast Asia. Flusty (2006:196) comments that in Chiapas "the uprising has only served to enlarge Chiapas's appeal as a tourist destination."

Chapter 5

1. Cuban sociologist Marta Núñez Sarmiento (2000) discusses sexism in tourism promotion in the country and the use of images of women that suggest their sexual availability to foreign men.

2. In Chapters 1 and 2, I examine solidarity tourism as a precursor to contemporary tourism in Cuba and Nicaragua. The only other writer I am aware of who has compared tourism in the two nations is Hollander (1986), who offers a right-wing assessment of "political" tourism in Cuba and Nicaragua.

3. This distinction between sex and romance tourism is made particularly clear in the work of Cabezas (2004).

4. On women tourists seeking local men for sex and romance tourism elsewhere in the Caribbean, see Joan L. Phillips (1999). On gay male sex tourism in Cuba, see Fosado (2005) and Hodge (2001). Hodge makes the salient point, which is echoed here,

that sex workers express in their very bodies "the contradiction of the Cuban revolutionary regime inviting capitalism to do its work on the bodies and souls of its people" (21). Up until now, there has not been much work on gay romance tourism. In the future, we may hope to see the sort of approach taken by Mark Padilla (2007) in the Dominican Republic directed toward longer-term gay relationships that may involve many return trips to Cuba.

5. The Associated Press recently reported that the Spanish airline Iberia withdrew a cartoon ad "that depicts a baby boy frolicking on a beach with buxom black Cuban ladies after consumer groups complained it is insulting to women and encourages sex tourism." After the ad was removed from Iberia's Web site, it appeared on YouTube. (*The Alligator*, Gainesville, FL, May 24, 2007:8).

6. See also Campuzano (2004) for essays offering a feminist perspective on Cuban literature and culture, including the phenomenon of jineterismo that emerged during the Special Period.

7. A year later, Codrescu (a commentator on National Public Radio) published his travel memoir, *Ay, Cuba! A Socio-Erotic Journey* (1999).

8. See Brennan (2004) for discussion of this question in the case of sex tourism in the Dominican Republic.

9. Given the terms of contemporary tourism in Cuba, in which there is a strict separation between ordinary Cubans (those not in the tourism industry) and international visitors, any interaction may be regarded as suspect. My relationship with Claudia, who was a friend and research collaborator, often drew attention, particularly because she was Afro-Cuban, a racially marked identity.

10. See Cabezas (2004) for discussion of moral panics and the imprisonment of women sex workers (and even women who are simply unaccompanied in public) in Cuba and the Dominican Republic. She very usefully addresses the implications for sexual citizenship rights.

11. Berg (2004a) discusses the police repression of Cubans, particularly Afro-Cubans, suspected of being involved with jineterismo. I observed this myself in working with Claudia, who was approached by police and asked for documentation simply because she was talking with me in a place generally reserved for tourists.

12. Notably, see Fernández Robaina (1998). See also Elizalde's (2002) work in a series published by Cuba's National Center for Sex Education (CENESEX).

13. See the Digital *Granma Internacional* (May 10, 2006), the online version of Cuba's official newspaper, which carries frequent updates on tourism in the country. Available at http://www.granmai.cubasi.cu.

14. See Sanchez and Adams (2008) for discussion of the contradictions of tourism in Cuba that nonetheless allow for a rapidly growing industry.

15. But see Whisnant (1995) for attention to travel to Nicaragua dating back to the nineteenth century.

16. In Spanish, the theme is "Por una Nicaragua limpia y segura." The II Convención de Turismo drew participants from throughout Central America, including the well-known Rubén Blades, who had recently been named minister of tourism in Panama.

17. This recalls the well-known lyrics to the song "Managua, Nicaragua," written during the early years of the Somoza dictatorship. There, the evocation of hot temperatures was accompanied by the notion that tropical real estate could be had for a pittance at that time—something repeated in a recent article in *Condé Nast Traveler* (Wilson 2002:98–112), which relates that islands in Lake Nicaragua may now be purchased "for a song."

18. I later had a chance to speak with this woman's boss, who said that there was discussion in INTUR regarding the bikini-clad moment in the ad. She and other women convinced the advertisers to make the moment briefer, saying that the ad must appeal to women viewers since they are the ones making vacation decisions for their families.

19. In June 2008, when I was in Nicaragua, the celebrated and revered Dora María Téllez (a comandante in the revolution and leading voice in politics) went on a hunger strike to protest the FSLN attempt to keep the MRS and another party out of upcoming municipal elections. Ortega was compared to Somoza, the dictator he helped topple in 1979.

20. In Managua in 2004, I met with Josh Berman, coauthor of the Moon Handbook on Nicaragua and asked him if he had come across interest in anything like "revolutionary tourism." He told me he might include a suggested circuit in the forthcoming second edition of his guidebook. Indeed, the new edition offered a "path of Sandino" tour (Wood and Berman 2005:14–15).

21. Besides these publications, the Fundación Luciérnaga has produced videos that explore both the potential and the risk of new initiatives in tourism development in Nicaragua: *Turismos* (Zurita 2005) and *Turismo Rural Comunitario* (Zúniga 2006). Rural and communitarian tourism is often viewed as an alternative to the more exploitative forms of tourism in the country.

22. Nicaraguan culture is highly politicized between Sandinistas and anti-Sandinista neoliberals. The successful owner of a high-end tour company told me that Borge opposes casinos only because they are not found in Cuba. This same man blamed the Sandinista revolutionary government for having allowed prostitution and homosexuality in exchange for votes. Coming from a family whose tourism company was expropriated by the Sandinistas, he felt that problems in tourism development dated to the revolution (Adan Gaitán, Menditur, interview, July 7, 2004). Others in the tourism industry, however, claim that tourism is indebted to the revolution for protecting the country from overdevelopment.

23. When I searched the Internet for one of these strip clubs, I came across one

man's detailed discussion of nine venues in Managua, evaluating their women and the services they provide, as well as his assessment of which tourist hotels in the city are "guest-friendly," i.e., will allow men to take prostitutes to their rooms.

24. Many writers have discussed this transition. See Babb (2001a) for my discussion of the neoliberal turn and its gendered consequences in Nicaragua.

25. I am very grateful to the late Grant Gallup, in whose home I often stayed in this barrio, for sharing rich stories of his neighbors' lives with me. A wonderful friend and keen observer of the human condition, he is greatly missed.

26. I met a Nicaraguan couple from Masaya, a dental surgeon and lawyer, who were visiting San Juan del Sur and expressed to me that tourism is entirely positive, as all good things come from outside Nicaragua. Class privilege was very evident in their views of the benefits of tourism.

27. There are not many studies of rural women's sexuality in Nicaragua, but see Montoya (2002) for a useful account of women's ability to maneuver in heterosexual contexts in the western part of the country.

28. This NGO is one of the most active in Managua, and its lesbian feminist founders have given substantial attention to same-sex sexuality. See Babb (2003) for more discussion of lesbian and gay culture and politics in Nicaragua. Montenegro (2000) writes on Nicaraguan sexual cultures more generally.

29. See Adrienne Rich's groundbreaking essay on the politics of location, written after she made a trip to revolutionary Nicaragua. She famously wrote that "a place on a map is also a place in history" (1986:212).

Chapter 6

1. I and others have discussed the multiple layers of social subordination experienced by rural women in Peru (Babb 1998:60–65), but Cadena's work is particularly rich and poignant on rural women's status and has received considerable attention. Thus, I find it useful to discuss here in light of tourism's alteration of the social landscape.

2. Pierre Bourdieu (1984) introduced discussion of "cultural capital" in the field of anthropology.

3. I want to note that in the case of this brothel, clients were not sex tourists but local men for the most part and the sex workers included a good number of Central American immigrants. My point, however, is to highlight the mix of responses in the Chiapas region, from indigenous cultural resistance and revolutionary politics to sexual commerce, during a time of rapid neoliberalism and globalization.

4. But see Weismantel (2001) for rich discussion of the sexualization of Andean women, especially cholas, and Nelson (1999) on the sexualization of as esteemed a figure as the Mayan Nobel laureate Rigoberta Menchu.

5. This figure comes from the report of Peru's Commission on Truth and Recon-

ciliation (2003). At the time of this writing, Sendero Luminoso has reappeared and been held responsible for more deaths of citizens and members of the military.

6. In Iquitos, there is also "shamanic tourism" focused around the use of the hallucinogenic brew *ayahuasca* for healing and spiritual growth (Fotiou 2008).

7. Interestingly, even though President Alan García has supported criminalization of those having sex with minors, some feminists have opposed moral and legal sanctions because they feel these may be used against young people expressing their sexual agency.

8. Although they cultivate a somewhat different image, bricheros may be compared with Caribbean men known as "beach boys" who seek out the attention of women tourists (Pruitt and LaFont 1995; Phillips 1999).

9. See also Fernando Pomareda (2007) for selections written about bricheros in Cuzco, relating stories of cultural encounters and gendered performance. Interestingly, contributors note the hybridity of bricheros who in order to represent their cultural difference sometimes adopt dreadlocks and other non-Andean attributes.

10. See Meisch (2002) for discussion of some similar cases in Ecuador, where female tourists attracted to Andean artisans and musicians form intimate relationships. The men cultivate iconic indigenous looks, utilizing the cultural capital of long hair and traditional dress. She calls this a "noble savage trope" (215).

11. Little (2004) had a similar finding in his research on cultural tourism in Guatemala.

12. From interviews conducted June–July 2006 during day trips from Huaraz to the Pastoruri glacier and to Lake Llanganuco.

13. It is interesting that in Vicos economic development initiatives have shifted from emphasizing modernization under the Cornell-Peru Project to emphasizing cultural difference to promote tourism. I thank Joe Feldman (personal communication) for this insight and for noting that this may reflect a shift in the global economy.

14. See Vicos: A Virtual Tour (2006), a Web site developed by Billie Jean Isbell of Cornell University in collaboration with the community of Vicos, Peru. The site includes attention to tourism and to women's role in helping the community preserve its biodiversity.

15. My earlier work on Vicos found that although women and men in Vicos shared household decision making, men were treated as family spokespersons and were the favored recipients of new technologies, training, and agricultural opportunities (Babb 1985).

16. Even so, marketing in Andean towns and cities may be viewed as quaint in comparison to modern markets—and they often attract sellers from small communities like Vicos.

17. At a gathering on gender and Andean culture, Beatriz Rojas (2003) presented the testimonies of women and men of Vicos as they described the gender division of

labor, decision making, and family relations in the contemporary context. Her recent work reminded me of very similar commentaries offered by Vicosinos and Vicosinas that I read years earlier in the Cornell-Peru Project archives at Cornell University, reflecting on everyday life a half century ago.

18. I want to thank Jan Rus (personal communication) for his insights on changes in Chiapas youth culture and style. He noted as well the changing musical preferences of indigenous youth and their greater freedom of expression, for example, young women and men holding hands in public.

19. For example, collectives such as Women for Dignity work with various international organizations to market items they produce through Internet sales.

20. Of course, tourist valorization of indigenous cultures may also lead to new or more subtle forms of racism and sexism, as when indigenous women are viewed as "unmodern" and resistant to change.

21. Cadena (1995:330) generously cited my work on Peruvian market women (Babb 1998) as contesting earlier views of gender complementarity. I would add that my work revealed that in many cases market women were regarded as more modern than their husbands, who devoted much of their time to farming on family plots of land.

22. I do not wish to overlook or underestimate examples of Peruvian women's successful participation in community-based tourism (Zorn 2004). Nevertheless, it is arguable that more sustainable successes are made possible when social movements incorporate women's interests and when women themselves participate more fully in those movements.

23. See Benavides (2007) for discussion of the historical reproduction of an Indian past in Ecuador as a form of historical legitimization that can revolutionize understanding and serve as political capital for changing lives.

24. Here I paraphrase bell hooks (2000), whose book *Feminist Theory: From Margin to Center* has been influential in thinking about women's place in society as well as feminist theory in the academy.

Conclusion

1. On the subject of making the world safe for tourism, it is notable that entrepreneurs in Iraq envision that they will soon bring back foreign visitors, who have been kept away since the U.S. invasion in 2003. The *New York Times* (September 21, 2008:8) ran an article entitled "Promoting a Vision of Tourist Bliss in Baghdad's Dusty Rubble," describing plans for high-end tourism.

2. "Cuba Tourism Grows Despite World Crisis," *Digital*, newspaper of Sancti Spiritus province, Cuba, May 8, 2009. The figure given for the first quarter in 2009 was 809,937 tourists.

3. See *New York Times*, May 20, 2009, reporting on the growing number of char-

ter flights to Cuba since the White House announced a new policy allowing Cuban Americans to visit relatives and send remittances as often as they wish.

4. In its annual *Bulletin of Tourism Statistics*, the Instituto Nicaragüense de Turismo (2007) gives 978,330 as the number of international visitors to the country in 2007.

5. Billboards in Managua called 2009 "Year 30 of the Revolution," suggesting the continuity of Sandinismo since 1979 (Rosenberg 2009:26).

6. "Tourism Booms amid Concerns in Peru" (April 17, 2008) describes the contradictions in recent years as tourism has made significant gains, but poverty persists (www.msnbc.msn.com/id/24164980/).

7. Manuel de la Cruz, "Clash with Police at Mexico Mayan Ruins Kills 6 Villagers" (Associated Press, October 4, 2008).

8. See Little (2004) for discussion of this phenomenon in Guatemala.

9. A year later, Naomi Klein (2008) observed this or a similar nativity scene in café TierrAdentro and wrote of it in the *Nation*, describing the "local twist" given to the traditional holiday display.

10. In Nicaragua, there is also talk of the nation in ruins. Many consider Daniel Ortega's leadership a betrayal of the revolution they had supported so passionately. A recent struggle has emerged over property rights to the music of Carlos Mejía Godoy, who was closely associated with the Sandinista struggle and a favorite among many visitors to the country. The conflict has pitted the president and his wife against those, including Mejía Godoy, who condemn the direction taken by the current FSLN government. Writer and former Sandinista vice president Sergio Ramírez used the metaphor of ruins to describe "the decayed sets, the ragged curtains, the moth-eaten stages" and the lost "ideals of a revolution of which now only ruins are left" (2008:3–4).

11. For a recent study that includes attention to Cuba's all-inclusive resorts, see Cabezas (2009), an important ethnography of sex and tourism in Cuba and the Dominican Republic.

12. See Ortiz (2001:75–79) for discussion of the Chiapas Photography Project and its impact on young women. The Chiapas Media Project (Promedios), based in San Cristóbal de las Casas, provides information on their work, including video productions made by and focusing on indigenous women's experience, which have had a broad impact (http://www.promediosmexico.org/eng/index.html). See also the work of Ruperta Bautista Vázquez, an indigenous playwright from San Cristóbal who has written a play based on the everyday lives of children who experience "racism and paternalism that mark the relationships between the children and mestizos and foreigners, including tourists, government officials, and wealthy residents of the city" (2003:71–79). Her work has been performed at a local venue where tourists often gather so that it may serve as a corrective to essentialized thinking about indigenous experience.

13. See Vivanco (2006) for valuable discussion of environmentalism and "green" tourism in Costa Rica. His work offers a useful view of tourism encounters that

"reflect specific world-historical conditions in which the boundaries between the 'local' and 'global' are also in flux" (8).

14. See contributions to Hall and Tucker (2004) for recent discussion of tourism and postcolonialism, and Fuller (2009) for an overview of the consequences of tourism in the global South, including growing inequalities as benefits are shared among the few in host countries.

References

Adams, Kathleen M. 2001. Danger-Zone Tourism: Prospects and Problems for Tourism in Tumultuous Times. In *Interconnected Worlds: Tourism in Southeast Asia*. P. Teo, T. C. Chang, and K. C. Ho, eds. Pp. 265–281. New York: Pergamon.

———. 2006a. *Art as Politics: Re-crafting Identities, Tourism, and Power in Tana Toraja, Indonesia*. Honolulu: University of Hawai'i Press.

———. 2006b. Terror and Tourism: Charting the Ambivalent Allure of the Urban Jungle. In *Travels in Paradox: Remapping Tourism*. Claudio Minca and Tim Oakes, eds. Pp. 205–228. New York: Rowman and Littlefield.

Agosín, Marjorie, and Julie H. Levison, eds. 1999. *Magical Sites: Women Travelers in 19th Century Latin America*. Buffalo, NY: WhitePine Press.

Algo queda (Something Remains). 2001. Luciano Capelli and Andrea Ruggeri, dirs. 51 min. Rio Nevado Productions.

Andrews, Abigail. 2007. Touring the Revolution: U.S. American Activist-Tourists and the Zapatista Movement. Unpublished manuscript.

Appadurai, Arjun, ed. 2001. *Globalization*. Durham, NC: Duke University Press.

Aquino, Erick. 2005. Hacia un verdadero turismo vivencial / Towards a Genuine Vivencial Tourism. *Peripheria*, December:20–21.

Asad, Talal, ed. 1973. *Anthropology and the Colonial Encounter*. London: Ithaca Press.

Avila Molero, Javier. 2005. Los dilemmas del desarrollo: Antropología y promoción en el Perú. In No hay país ás diverso: Compendio de antropología Peruana. Carlos Iván Degregori, ed. Lima, Peru: Instituto de Estudios Peruanos.

Babb, Florence E. 1985. Women and Men in Vicos: A Peruvian Case of Unequal Development. In *Peruvian Contexts of Change*. William W. Stein, ed. Brunswick, NJ: Transaction Publishers.

———. 1998. *Between Field and Cooking Pot: The Political Economy of Marketwomen in Peru*. Rev. ed. Austin: University of Texas Press.

————. 1999a. "Managua Is Nicaragua": The Making of a Neoliberal City. *City and Society* 1–2:27–48.

————. 1999b. *Mujeres y hombres en Vicos, Perú: Un caso de desarrollo desigual.* Género y Desarrollo II. Lima, Peru: Pontificia Universidad Católica del Perú.

————. 2001a. *After Revolution: Mapping Gender and Cultural Politics in Neoliberal Nicaragua.* Austin: University of Texas Press.

————. 2001b. Nicaraguan Narratives of Development, Nationhood, and the Body. *Journal of Latin American Anthropology* 6(1):60–93.

————. 2003. Out in Nicaragua: Local and Transnational Desires After the Revolution. *Cultural Anthropology* 18(3):304–328.

————. 2005. Post-revolutionary Tourism: Heritage Celebrated or Forgotten? *Anthropology News* 46(5):11–12.

————. 2008. *Entre la chacra y la olla: Cultura, economía política y las vendedoras de mercado en el Perú.* Lima, Peru: Instituto de Estudios Peruanos.

Barbassa, Juliana. 2005. The New Cuban Capitalist. In *Capitalism, God, and a Good Cigar: Cuba Enters the Twenty-first Century.* Lydia Chávez, ed. Pp. 17–30. Durham, NC: Duke University Press.

Baud, Michiel, and Annelou Ypeij, eds. 2009. *Cultural Tourism in Latin America: The Politics of Space and Imagery.* Leiden, The Netherlands: Brill.

Baud, Michiel, Annelou Ypeij, and Annelies Zoomers. 2006. Introducción: El turismo como estratégia para el desarrollo sostenible. In *La Ruta Andina: Turismo y desarrollo sostenible en Perú y Bolivia.* Annelou Ypeij and Annelies Zoomers, eds. Pp. 9–36. Quito, Ecuador: Ediciones Abya-Yala.

Bauer, Irmgard. 2008. Understanding Sexual Relationships Between Tourists and Locals. *Desarrollo, cultura y turismo desde la Peripheria* 11(4):8–11.

Bautista Vázquez, Ruperta. 2003. Indigenous Children: We Are Not to Blame. In *Women of Chiapas: Making History in Times of Struggle and Hope.* Christine Eber and Christine Kovic, eds. Pp. 71–79. New York: Routledge.

Behar, Ruth. 2002. While Waiting for the Ferry to Cuba: Afterthoughts About Adio Kerida. *Michigan Quarterly Review* 41(4):651–667.

Benavides, O. Hugo. 2007. Historical Disruptions in Ecuador: Reproducing an Indian Past in Latin America. In *Cultural Heritage and Human Rights.* Helaine Silverman and D. Fairchild Ruggles, eds. New York: Springer Publishers.

Berg, Mette Louise. 2004a. "Sleeping with the Enemy": Jineterismo, "Cultural Level" and "Antisocial Behaviour" in 1990s Cuba. In *Beyond the Blood, the Beach, and the Banana.* Sandra Courtman, ed. Pp. 186–204. Kingston, Jamaica: Ian Randle Publishers.

————. 2004b. Tourism and the Revolutionary New Man: The Specter of *Jineterismo* in Late "Special Period" Cuba. *Focaal: European Journal of Anthropology* 43:46–56.

————. 2005. Localizing Cubanness: Social Exclusion and Narratives of Belonging in

Old Havana. In *Caribbean Narratives of Belonging: Fields of Relations, Sites of Identity*. Jean Besson and Karen Fog Olwig, eds. Oxford: Macmillan Caribbean.

Berger, Dina. 2006. *The Development of Mexico's Tourism Industry: Pyramids by Day, Martinis by Night*. New York: Palgrave.

Berman, Josh, and Randy Wood. 2002. *Moon Handbooks: Nicaragua*. Emeryville, CA: Avalon Travel Publishing.

Bilbija, Ksenija, and Leigh A. Payne, eds. 2011. *Accounting for Violence: The Memory Market in Latin America*. Durham, NC: Duke University Press.

Bob, Clifford. 2005. *The Marketing of Rebellion: Insurgents, Media, and International Activism*. New York: Cambridge University Press.

Bode, Barbara. 1989. *No Bells to Toll: Destruction and Creation in the Andes*. New York: Scribner.

La Boletina. 2007. *Cuando te roban la vida: La compra-venta de sexo con adolescents, niñas y niños*. Managua, Nicaragua: Puntos de Encuentro.

Bolles, Lynn. 1997. Women as a Category of Analysis in Scholarship on Tourism: Jamaican Women and Tourism Employment. In *Tourism and Culture: An Applied Perspective*. Erve Chambers, ed. Pp. 77–92. Albany: State University of New York Press.

Bourdieu, Pierre. 1984. *Distinction: A Social Critique of the Judgment of Taste*. Richard Nice, trans. Cambridge, MA: Harvard University Press.

Boym, Svetlana. 2001. *The Future of Nostalgia*. New York: Basic Books.

Bradsher, Keith. 2003. Vietnam, Poor but Orderly, Is Now Tourists' Safe Haven. *New York Times*, January 5:8.

Bravo, Gerardo. 2004. Casinos: Una industria en crecimiento. *La Prensa*, June 30:4A.

Brennan, Denise. 2004. *What's Love Got to Do with It? Transnational Desires and Sex Tourism in the Dominican Republic*. Durham, NC: Duke University Press.

Brooke, James. 1990. Cuzco Journal: Drumming Up Tourism Is Aim of "the Safe Peru." *New York Times*, November 17.

Bruner, Edward M. 2005. *Culture on Tour: Ethnographies of Travel*. Chicago: University of Chicago Press.

Buchsbaum, Herbert. 2004. Emerging from the Mist. *New York Times*, September 5. Available at nytimes.com.

Cabezas, Amalia L. 1998. Discourses of Prostitution: The Case of Cuba. In *Global Sex Workers: Rights, Resistance, and Redefinition*. Kamala Kempadoo and Jo Doezema, eds. Pp. 79–86. New York: Routledge.

———. 2004. Between Love and Money: Sex, Tourism, and Citizenship in Cuba and the Dominican Republic. *Signs* 29(4):987–1015.

———. 2009. *Economies of Desire: Sex and Tourism in Cuba and the Dominican Republic*. Philadelphia: Temple University Press.

Cadena, Marisol de la. 1995. "Women Are More Indian": Ethnicity and Gender in a Community near Cuzco. In *Ethnicity, Markets, and Migration in the Andes: At the*

Crossroads of History and Anthropology. Brooke Larson and Olivia Harris, eds. Pp. 329–343. Durham, NC: Duke University Press.

———. 2000. *Indigenous Mestizos: The Politics of Race and Culture in Cuzco, Peru, 1919–1991.* Durham, NC: Duke University Press.

Cadena, Marisol de la, and Orin Starn. 2007. Introduction. In *Indigenous Experience Today.* Marisol de la Cadena and Orin Starn, eds. Pp. 1–30. New York: Berg.

Campuzano, Luisa. 2004. *Las muchachas de la Habana no tienen temor de Dios . . . Escritoras Cubanas (s.XVIII–XXI).* Havana, Cuba: Ediciones Unión.

Cañada, Ernest, Leonor Delgado, and Helena Gil. 2006. *Guía turismo rural comunitario— Nicaragua.* Managua, Nicaragua: Fundación Luciérnaga.

Cañada, Ernest, and Jordi Gascón. 2006. *Turismo y desarrollo: Herramientas para una mirada crítica.* Managua, Nicaragua. Fundación Luciérnaga.

Canessa, Andrew, ed. 2005. *Natives Making Nation: Gender, Indigeneity, and the State in the Andes.* Tucson: University of Arizona Press.

Carter, Thomas. 2008. *The Quality of Home Runs: The Passion, Politics, and Language of Cuban Baseball.* Durham, NC: Duke University Press.

Castañeda, Quetzil E. 1996. *In the Museum of Maya Culture: Touring Chichen Itza.* Minneapolis: University of Minnesota Press.

Chambers, Erve. 2000. *Native Tours: The Anthropology of Travel and Tourism.* Long Grove, IL: Waveland Press.

Chávez, Lydia, ed. 2005. *Capitalism, God, and a Good Cigar: Cuba Enters the Twenty-first Century.* Durham, NC: Duke University Press.

Clifford, James. 1997. *Routes: Travel and Transformation in the Late Twentieth Century.* Cambridge, MA: Harvard University Press.

Codrescu, Andrei. 1998. Picking the Flowers of the Revolution. *New York Times Magazine,* February 1:32–35.

———. 1999. *Ay, Cuba! A Socio-Erotic Journey.* New York: St. Martin's Press.

Cohen, Jeff. 1991. Cuba Libre. *Playboy,* March:69–74, 157–158.

Colantonio, Andrea, and Robert B. Potter. 2006. *Urban Tourism and Development in the Socialist State: Havana During the "Special Period."* Hampshire, UK: Ashgate.

Comunidad Campesina de Vicos. 2005. Memorias de la Comunidad Vicos: Así nos recordamos con alegría. Florencia Zapata, coord. Huaraz, Peru: The Mountain Institute and Asociación Urpichallay.

Coombes, Annie E. 2003. *Visual Culture and Public Memory in a Democratic South Africa.* Durham, NC: Duke University Press.

Cooper Alarcón, Daniel. 1997. *The Aztec Palimpsest: Mexico in the Modern Imagination.* Tucson: University of Arizona Press.

Cortés, Guillermo. 2007. Marca turística y la construcción de la identidad-país. In *Industrias culturales: Máquina de deseos en el mundo contemporáneo.* Santiago López Maguiña, Gonzalo Portocarrero, Rocío Silva Santisteban, Juan Carlos Ubilluz, and

Víctor Vich, eds. Pp. 301–311. Lima, Peru: Red para el Desarrollo de las Ciencias Sociales en el Perú.

Council on Hemispheric Affairs. 2008. The Rise and Fall of Shining Path. Council on Hemispheric Affairs, May 6. Available at http://www.coha.org/2008/05/06/the-rise-and-fall-of-shining-path/.

Craven, David. 1989. *The New Concept of Art and Popular Culture in Nicaragua Since the Revolution in 1979*. Lewiston, NY: Edwin Mellen Press.

Davidson, Julia O'Connell. 1996. Sex Tourism in Cuba. *Race & Class* 38(1):39–48.

DED (Deutscher Entwicklungsdienst). 2005. *Six Days in October 2005: The "Museum of Memory" in Ayacucho and the International Conference on "Remembering the Past and Moving Towards a Peace Culture" from 16th–21st of October 2005 in Ayacucho and Lima*. Lima, Peru: DED Country Office.

Degregori, Carlos Iván, and Pablo Sandoval. 2008. Peru: From Otherness to a Shared Diversity. In *A Companion to Latin American Anthropology*. Deborah Poole, ed. Pp. 150–173. Malden, MA: Blackwell.

Dobyns, Henry F., Paul L. Doughty, and Harold D. Lasswell, eds. 1971. *Peasants, Power, and Applied Social Change: Vicos as a Model*. Beverly Hills, CA: Sage Publications.

Duany, Jorge. 2005. Revisiting the Cuban Exception: A Comparative Perspective on Transnational Migration from the Hispanic Caribbean to the United States. In *Cuba Transnational*. Damián J. Fernández, ed. Pp. 1–23. Gainesville: University Press of Florida.

Durante. 2005. Backpacking Pat: First Trip to Huaraz. *Development, Culture and Tourism from the Peripheria* (October and December):31.

Eber, Christine, and Christine Kovic, eds. 2003. *Women of Chiapas: Making History in Times of Struggle and Hope*. New York: Routledge.

Eckstein, Susan. 2003. From Communist Solidarity to Communist Solitary. In *The Cuba Reader: History, Culture, Politics*. Aviva Chomsky, Barry Carr, and Pamela Smorkaloff, eds. Pp. 607–622. Durham, NC: Duke University Press.

Eckstein, Susan, and Lorena Barberia. 2001. Cuban-American Visits: Public Policy, Privacy Practices. Mellon Report Series. Available at http://web.mit.edu/cis/www/migration/pubs/mellon/5_cuba.pdf.

Economist. 2004. Cuba Returns to the Command and Control Economy. *Economist*, July 31:33.

Elizalde, Rosa Miriam. 2002. Crimen o castigo? Tres mitos acerca del comercio sexual: Un acercamiento desde el caso cubano. *Sexología y Sociedad* 8(20):32–38.

Escobar, Arturo. 1995. *Encountering Development: The Making and Unmaking of the Third World*. Princeton: Princeton University Press.

Espino, María Dolores. 2000. Cuban Tourism During the Special Period. *Cuba in Transition* 10:360–373.

Esta Semana. 2001. Inocencia en venta (Innocence for Sale). Television segment, February 23.

Eviatar, Daphne. 2003. Bored with Sand and Sun? Try One of the Growing Number of Hands-On Tours to the World's Trouble Spots. *Newsweek International*, May 26. Available at www.globalexchange.org/tours/697.html.pf.

Facio, Elisa. 1998–1999. *Jineterismo* During the Special Period. *Global Development Studies* 1(3–4):57–78.

Farquhar, Judith. 2002. *Appetites: Food and Sex in Post-socialist China*. Durham, NC: Duke University Press.

Farrell, Stephen, and Alissa J. Rubin. 2009. The Alert Is Sounded in Iraq: A Tourist Is Entering Falluja. *New York Times*, February 7:A6.

Feldman, Joseph. 2010. Exhibiting Conflict? History and Politics and the Museo de la Memoria de ANFASEP in Ayacucho, Peru. Master's thesis, University of Florida.

Femenías, Blenda. 2005. *Gender and the Boundaries of Dress in Contemporary Peru*. Austin: University of Texas Press.

Ferlinghetti, Lawrence. 1984. *Seven Days in Nicaragua Libre*. San Francisco: City Lights Books.

Fernández, Damián J. 2000. *Cuba and the Politics of Passion*. Austin: University of Texas Press.

———, ed. 2005. *Cuba Transnational*. Gainesville: University Press of Florida.

Fernandez, Nadine. 1999. Back to the Future? Women, Race, and Tourism in Cuba. In *Sun, Sex, and Gold: Tourism and Sex Work in the Caribbean*. Kamala Kempadoo, ed. Pp. 81–89. Lanham, MD: Rowman and Littlefield.

Fernández Robaina, Tomás. 1998. *Historias de mujeres públicas*. Havana: Editorial Letras Cubanas.

Field, Les. 1999. *The Grimace of Macho Ratón: Artisans, Identity, and Nation in Late-Twentieth-Century Western Nicaragua*. Durham, NC: Duke University Press.

Flusty, Steven. 2006. Portable Autonomous Zones: Tourism and the Travels of Dissent. In *Travels in Paradox: Remapping Tourism*. Claudio Minca and Tim Oakes, eds. Pp.185–204. Lanham, MD: Rowman and Littlefield.

Fosado, Gisela. 2005. Gay Sex Tourism, Ambiguity, and Transnational Love in Havana. In *Cuba Transnational*. Damián J. Fernández, ed. Pp. 61–78. Gainesville: University Press of Florida.

Fotiou, Evgenia. 2008. Shamanic Tourism and the Commercialization of Ayahuasca. *Desarrollo, cultura y turismo desde la Peripheria* 11(4):12–15.

Fuller, Norma. 2009. *Turismo y cultura: Entre el entusiasmo y el recelo*. Lima, Peru: Fondo Editorial, Pontificia Universidad Católica del Perú.

Fusco, Coco. 1998. Hustling for Dollars: *Jineterismo* in Cuba. In *Global Sex Workers: Rights, Resistance, and Redefinition*. Kamala Kempadoo and Jo Doezema, eds. Pp. 151–166. New York: Routledge.

Gardner, James, ed. 2000. *Let's Go Central America*. Cambridge, MA: Let's Go.

Gascón, Jorge. 2005. Gringos como en sueños: Diferenciación y conflicto campesinos en los Andes peruanos ante el desarrollo del turismo. Lima, Peru: Instituto de Estudios Peruanos.

Ghodsee, Kristen. 2005. *The Red Riviera: Gender, Tourism, and Postsocialism on the Black Sea.* Durham, NC: Duke University Press.

Gil Tébar, Pilar R. 1999. *Caminando en un solo corazón: Las mujeres indígenas de Chiapas.* Málaga, Spain: Universidad de Málaga.

Glowczewska, Klara. 2008. The Week of (Not) Living Dangerously. *Condé Nast Traveler*, September:206–211, 270–273.

Gold, John R., and Margaret M. Gold. 2003. Representing Culloden: Social Memory, Battlefield Heritage, and Landscapes of Regret. In *Mapping Tourism*. Stephen P. Hanna and Vincent J. Del Casino Jr., eds. Pp. 108–131. Minneapolis: University of Minnesota Press.

Goldstone, Patricia. 2001. *Making the World Safe for Tourism.* New Haven, CT: Yale University Press.

Gossen, Gary H. 1999. *Telling Maya Tales: Tzotzil Identities in Modern Mexico.* New York: Routledge.

Gould, Jeffrey L. 1998. *To Die in This Way: Nicaraguan Indians and the Myth of Mestizaje, 1880–1965.* Durham, NC: Duke University Press.

Graburn, Nelson, ed. 1976. *Ethnic and Tourist Arts: Cultural Expressions from the Fourth World.* Berkeley: University of California Press.

Granma Internacional. 2006. Cuba, the Country That Many People Want to Know. Digital *Granma Internacional*, May 10. Available at http://www.granmai.cubasi.cu.

Greenhouse, Carol J., Elizabeth Mertz, and Kay B. Warren, eds. 2002. *Ethnography in Unstable Places: Everyday Lives in Contexts of Dramatic Political Change.* Durham, NC: Duke University Press.

Grewal, Inderpal. 1999. Traveling Barbie: Indian Transnationality and New Consumer Subjects. *Positions* 7(3):799–826.

Griest, Stephanie Elizondo. 2004. *Around the Bloc: My Life in Moscow, Beijing, and Havana.* New York: Villard Books.

Gropas, Maria. 2007. The Repatriotization of Revolutionary Ideology and Mnemonic Landscape in Present-Day Havana. *Current Anthropology* 48(4):531–549.

Grupo Chaski. 1986. *Miss Universe in Peru.* Women Make Movies.

Gupta, Akhil, and James Ferguson, eds. 1997. *Culture, Power, Place: Explorations in Critical Anthropology.* Durham, NC: Duke University Press.

Hagedorn, Katherine J. 2001. *Divine Utterances: The Performance of Afro-Cuban Santería.* Washington, DC: Smithsonian Institution Press.

Hale, Charles R. 2006. *Más que un Indio: Racial Ambivalence and Neoliberal Multiculturalism in Guatemala.* Santa Fe, NM: School of American Research Press.

Hall, C. Michael, and Hazel Tucker, eds. 2004. *Tourism and Postcolonialism: Contested Discourses, Identities and Representations.* New York: Routledge.

Hanna, Stephen P., and Vincent J. Del Casino Jr., eds. 2003. *Mapping Tourism*. Minneapolis: University of Minnesota Press.

Harvey, Neil. 1998a. *The Chiapas Rebellion: The Struggle for Land and Democracy*. Durham, NC: Duke University Press.

———. 1998b. The Zapatistas, Radical Democratic Citizenship, and Women's Struggles. *Social Politics* 5(2):158–187.

Hayden, Tom, ed. 2002. *The Zapatista Reader*. New York: Thunder's Mouth Press / Nation Books.

Henrici, Jane. 1997. Promoting Peruvian Crafts and Selling Culture. *In Peru: Beyond the Reforms*. Lima, Peru: PromPerú.

———. 2002. Calling to the Money: Gender and Tourism in Peru. In *Gender/Tourism/ Fun(?)*. Margaret Swain and Janet Momsen, eds. Pp. 118–133. Elmsford, NY: Cognizant Communication.

Hernández, Rafael. 2003. *Looking at Cuba: Essays on Culture and Society*. Gainesville: University Press of Florida.

Hernández, Tanya Katerí. 2002. The Buena Vista Social Club: The Racial Politics of Nostalgia. In *Latino/a Popular Culture*. Michelle Habell-Pallán and Mary Romero, eds. Pp. 61–72. New York: New York University Press.

Hill, Matthew J. 2007. Reimagining Old Havana: World Heritage and the Production of Scale in Late Socialist Cuba. In *Deciphering the Global: Its Scales, Spaces and Subjects*. Saskia Sassen, ed. Pp. 59–77. New York: Routledge.

Hill, Michael. 2007. Contesting Patrimony: Cusco's Mystical Tourist Industry and the Politics of Incanismo. *Ethnos* 72(4):433–460.

———. 2008. Inca of the Blood, Inca of the Soul: Embodiment, Emotion, and Racialization in the Peruvian Mystical Tourist Industry. *Journal of the American Academy of Religion* 76(2):251–279.

Hodge, G. Derrick. 2001. Colonization of the Cuban Body: The Growth of Male Sex Work in Havana. Special issue on The Body Politic: Gender in the New World Order. *NACLA Report on the Americas* 34(5):20–28.

Holgado Fernández, Isabel. 2000. *No es fácil: Mujeres cubanas y la crisis revolucionaria*. Barcelona: Icaria Editorial.

Hollander, Paul. 1986. *Political Hospitality and Tourism: Cuba and Nicaragua*. Washington, DC: Cuban American National Foundation.

hooks, bell. 2000. *Feminist Theory: From Margin to Center*. London: Pluto Press.

Hulme, Alan, Steve Krekel, and Shannon O'Reilly. 1990. *Not Just Another Nicaragua Travel Guide*. Chico, CA: Mango Publications.

Instituto Nicaragüense de Turismo. 2001. *Plan de Acciones 2002–2006*. Managua, Nicaragua: INTUR.

———. 2007. *Boletín Estadísticas de Turismo*. Managua, Nicaragua: INTUR.

Isbell, Billie Jean. 1992. Shining Path and Peasant Responses in Rural Ayacucho. In *Shining Path of Peru*. David Scott Palmer, ed. Pp. 59–82. New York: St. Martin's.

Jenkins, John, ed. 2002. *Travelers' Tales of Old Cuba*. New York: Ocean Press.

Joseph, Gilbert M., Catherine C. Legrand, and Ricardo D. Salvatore, eds. 1998. *Close Encounters of Empire: Writing the Cultural History of U.S.–Latin American Relations*. Durham, NC: Duke University Press.

Kalman, Rowenn B. 2005. Image-Making in the Andes: How Homestay Tourism in Vicos, Peru Creates Photographic Interactions. Master's thesis, Western Washington University.

Kaplan, Caren. 1996. *Questions of Travel: Postmodern Discourses of Displacement*. Durham, NC: Duke University Press.

Kelly, Patty. 2008. *Lydia's Open Door: Inside Mexico's Most Modern Brothel*. Berkeley: University of California Press.

Kincaid, Jamaica. 1988. *A Small Place*. New York: Farrar, Straus and Giroux.

Kinnaird, Vivian, and Derek Hall, eds. 1994. *Tourism: A Gender Analysis*. Chichester, UK: Wiley.

Kinzer, Stephen. 2002. A Faded City Brightens in Nicaragua. *New York Times*, February 17:10–12.

Kirshenblatt-Gimblett, Barbara. 1998. *Destination Culture: Tourism, Museums, and Heritage*. Berkeley: University of California Press.

Klein, Debra A. 2003. A Woman Alone, Except for the Men. *New York Times*, August 24:15.

Klein, Naomi. 2002. The Unknown Icon. In *The Zapatista Reader*. Tom Hayden, ed. Pp 114–122. New York: Thunder's Mouth Press / Nation Books.

———. 2007. *The Shock Doctrine: The Rise of Disaster Capitalism*. New York: Metropolitan Books.

———. 2008. Zapatista Code Red. *The Nation*, January 7. Available at http://www.the nation.com/doc/20080107/klein/print.

Kunzle, David. 1995. *The Murals of Revolutionary Nicaragua: 1979–1992*. Berkeley: University of California Press.

Lacayo, Rossana, dir. 2005. *Verdades ocultas* (Hidden Truths). Vanguard Cinema. DVD. 90 min.

Lacey, Marc. 2006. Hold the Mojito and Margarita, Nicaragua Has el Macuá. *New York Times*, International section, October 5.

Larrabure, Cecilia. 2007. *Ciertos Vacíos: Un ensayo fotográfico sobre orfandad, violencia y memoria en el Peru*. Lima, Peru: Fondo Editorial de la Pontificia Universidad Católica del Perú.

Leonardi, Richard. 2001. *Footprint Nicaragua Handbook*. Bath, UK: Footprint Handbooks.

Liechty, Mark. 1996. Kathmandu as Translocality: Multiple Places in a Nepali Space. In *The Geography of Identity*. Patricia Yaeger, ed. Pp. 98–130. Ann Arbor: University of Michigan Press.

Lima, Lázaro. 2005. Locas al Rescate: The Transnational Hauntings of Queer *Cubanidad*. In *Cuba Transnational*. Damián J. Fernández, ed. Pp. 79–103. Gainesville: University Press of Florida.

Linarte, Maricely. 2004. Foro sobre explotación sexual commercial. *El Nuevo Diario*, August 5:13B.

Little, Walter E. 2004. *Mayas in the Marketplace: Tourism, Globalization, and Cultural Identity*. Austin: University of Texas Press.

Little, Walter E., and Timothy J. Smith, eds. 2009. *Mayas in Postwar Guatemala: Harvest of Violence Revisited*. Tuscaloosa: University of Alabama Press.

Lopez Torregrosa, Luisita. 2005. Waiting for Havana. *New York Times*, November 27, section 5:1, 8–9.

Lowenthal, David. 1985. *The Past Is a Foreign Country*. New York: Cambridge University Press.

MacCannell, Dean. 1999. *The Tourist: A New Theory of the Leisure Class*. Foreword by Lucy R. Lippard. Epilogue by Dean MacCannell. Berkeley: University of California Press.

Mallon, Florencia E. 1995. *Peasant and Nation: The Making of Postcolonial Mexico and Peru*. Berkeley: University of California Press.

———. 2003. *Barbudos*, Warriors, and Rotos: The MIR, Masculinity, and Power in the Chilean Agrarian Reform, 1965–74. In *Changing Men and Masculinities in Latin America*. Matthew C. Gutmann, ed. Pp. 179–215. Durham, NC: Duke University Press.

Managua en mi corazón (Managua in My Heart). 1997. Video. Clemente Guido, dir. Managua, Nicaragua: Instituto Nicaragüense de Cultura, Mántica Waid y Cia.

Mancillas, Jorge. 2002. The Twilight of the Revolutionaries? In *The Zapatista Reader*. Tom Hayden, ed. Pp. 153–165. New York: Thunder's Mouth Press / Nation Books.

Marrero, Teresa. 2003. Scripting Sexual Tourism: Fusco and Bustamante's STUFF, Prostitution and Cuba's Special Period. *Theatre Journal* 55:235–250.

Martín, Desirée A. 2004. "Excuse the inconvenience, but this is a revolution": Zapatista Paradox and the Rhetoric of Tourism. *South Central Review* 21(3):107–128.

Martin de Holan, Pablo, and Nelson Phillips. 1997. Sun, Sand, and Hard Currency: Tourism in Cuba. *Annals of Tourism Research* 24(4):777–795.

Meisch, Lynn A. 2002. *Andean Entrepreneurs: Otavalo Merchants and Musicians in the Global Arena*. Austin: University of Texas Press.

Meiselas, Susan, Richard P. Rogers, and Alfred Guzzeti, dirs. 1992. *Pictures from a Revolution: A Memoir of the Nicaraguan Conflict*. Video. 93 min. New York: GMR Films.

Mendoza, Rosa. 2003. La dimensión de género el desarrollo. Paper presented at Taller Internacional [International Workshop], Genero y Cultura Andina. Marcará, Ancash, Peru: Asociación Urpichallay.

Milton, Cynthia E., and María Eugenia Ulfe. 2011. Promoting Peru: Tourism and Postconflict Memory. In *Accounting for Violence: The Memory Market in Latin America.* Ksenija Bilbija and Leigh Payne, eds. Durham, NC: Duke University Press.

Ministerio de Turismo. 1995. *Plan Maestro para el Desarrollo Turístico de le República de Nicaragua.* Managua, Nicaragua: Gobierno de Nicaragua.

Montenegro, Sofía. 2000. *La cultura sexual en Nicaragua.* Managua, Nicaragua: Centro de Investigaciones de la Comunicación (CINCO).

Montoya, Rosario. 2002. Women's Sexuality, Knowledge, and Agency in Rural Nicaragua. In *Gender's Place: Feminist Anthropologies of Latin America.* Rosario Montoya, Lessie Jo Frazier, and Janise Hurtig, eds. Pp. 65–88. New York: Palgrave.

The Mountain Institute. N.d. *Experiential Tourism: The Peasant Community of Vicos.* Huaraz, Peru: TMI.

Nash, Dennison. 1989. Tourism as a Form of Imperialism. In *Hosts and Guests: The Anthropology of Tourism.* 2nd ed. Valene L. Smith, ed. Pp. 37–52. Philadelphia: University of Pennsylvania Press.

Nash, June. 2001. *Mayan Visions: The Quest for Autonomy in an Age of Globalization.* New York: Routledge.

———. 2007. Consuming Interests: Water, Rum, and Coca-Cola from Ritual Propitiation to Corporate Expropriation in Highland Chiapas. *Cultural Anthropology* 22(4):621–639.

Nelson, Diane. 1999. *A Finger in the Wound: Body Politics in Quincentennial Guatemala.* Berkeley: University of California Press.

New York Times. 2002. Sandalista. Barneys New York advertisement, April 14:7.

Nicaraguan Institute of Tourism. 1988. *This Is Nicaragua.* Santo Domingo, Dominican Republic: Editora Alfa and Omega.

Noel, Pamela. 2004. South America Calls. *New York Times,* March 28:10, 17.

Núñez Sarmiento, Marta. 2000. Dos ideas para crear una imagen publicitaria de Cuba no sexista. *Apuntes* 4:12–16. Havana: Escuela de Altos Estudios de Hoteleria y Turismo.

Oakes, Tim. 2006. Get Real! On Being Yourself and Being a Tourist. In *Travels in Paradox: Remapping Tourism.* Claudio Minca and Tim Oakes, eds. Pp. 229–250. Lanham, MD: Rowman and Littlefield.

Obejas, Achy. 2000. Cuba Fever. *Playboy,* December:82–88, 220–233.

Olesen, Thomas. 2005. *International Zapatismo: The Construction of Solidarity in the Age of Globalization.* New York: Zed Books.

Oliver-Smith, Anthony R. 1986. *The Martyred City: Death and Rebirth in the Andes.* Albuquerque: University of New Mexico Press.

Orlove, Benjamin S. 1993. Putting Race in Its Place: Order in Colonial and Postcolonial Peruvian Geography. *Social Research* 69(2):301–336.

Ortiz, Teresa. 2001. *Never Again a World Without Us: Voices of Mayan Women in Chiapas, Mexico.* Washington DC: Epica.

Padilla, Art, and Jerome L. McElroy. 2007. Cuba and Caribbean Tourism After Castro. *Annals of Tourism Research* 34(3):649–672.

Padilla, Mark. 2007. *Caribbean Pleasure Industry: Tourism, Sexuality, and AIDS in the Dominican Republic.* Chicago: University of Chicago Press.

Palmié, Stephan. 2002. *Wizards and Scientists: Explorations in Afro-Cuban Modernity and Tradition.* Durham, NC: Duke University Press.

Penland, Paige R., Gary Chandler, and Liza Prado. 2006. *Nicaragua and El Salvador.* Oakland, CA: Lonely Planet.

Pérez, Fernando, dir. 2003. *Suite Habana.* Video. 80 min. Havana, Cuba: El Instituto Cubano de Arte e Industria Cinematográficos (ICAIC).

Pérez, Louis A. 1999. *On Becoming Cuban: Identity, Nationality, and Culture.* New York: HarperCollins.

Perna, Vincenzo. 2005. *Timba: The Sound of the Cuban Crisis.* Burlington, VT: Ashgate.

Phillips, Joan L. 1999. Tourist-Oriented Prostitution in Barbados: The Case of the Beach Boy and the White Female Tourist. In *Sun, Sex, and Gold: Tourism and Sex Work in the Caribbean.* Kamala Kempadoo, ed. Pp. 183–200. Lanham, MD: Rowman and Littlefield.

Pitts, Wayne J. 1996. Uprising in Chiapas, Mexico: Zapata Lives—Tourism Falters. In *Tourism, Crime and International Security Issues.* Abraham Pizam and Yoel Mansfeld, eds. Pp. 215–227. New York: John Wiley and Sons.

Polgreen, Lydia. 2008. Some Congolese See Hope in a Caldron of Fire. *New York Times,* September 23:A10.

Pomareda, Fernando. 2007. *Pachamama Club.* Lima, Peru: Editorial Estruedomudo.

Poole, Deborah, ed. 1994. *Unruly Order: Violence, Power, and Cultural Identity in the High Provinces of Southern Peru.* Boulder, CO: Westview Press.

Poole, Deborah, and Gerardo Rénique, eds. 1992. *Peru: Time of Fear.* London: Latin America Bureau.

Pratt, Mary Louise. 1992. *Imperial Eyes: Travel Writing and Transculturation.* New York: Routledge.

Prieto, Alfredo. 2004. *El otro en el espejo.* Havana, Cuba: Ediciones Unión.

Pruitt, Deborah, and Suzanne LaFont. 1995. For Love and Money: Romance Tourism in Jamaica. *Annals of Tourism Research* 22(2):422–440.

Quiroga, José. 2005. *Cuban Palimpsests.* Minneapolis: University of Minnesota Press.

Ramírez, Sergio. 2008. Nicaragua: Heartbeat of Protest. Open Democracy News Analysis, September 2. Available at www.opendemocracy.net.

Randall, Margaret. 1981. *Sandino's Daughters: Testimonies of Nicaraguan Women in Struggle.* Vancouver, BC: New Star Books.

Rich, Adrienne. 1986. Notes on a Politics of Location. In *Blood, Bread, and Poetry, Selected Prose, 1979–1985.* Pp. 210–231. New York: W. W. Norton.

Ripley, C. Peter. 1999. *Conversations with Cuba.* Athens: University of Georgia Press.

Rivers-Moore, Megan. 2007. Untouchable Gringos and 20 or 30 Girls: The State, NGOs and the Costa Rican Sex Trade. Paper presented at the Congress of the Latin American Studies Association, Montreal, Canada.

Rodríguez, Silvio. 2003. Silvio Rodríguez Sings of the Special Period. In *The Cuba Reader: History, Culture, Politics*. Aviva Chomsky, Barry Carr, and Pamela Smorkaloff, eds. Pp. 599–603. Durham, NC: Duke University Press.

Rohter, Larry. 1997. Nicaragua on the Mend. *New York Times*, February 16, section 5:10.

Rojas, Beatriz. 2003. *Pachamamantsic: La mujer es nuestra madre tierra*. Paper presented at Taller Internacional, Genero y Cultura Andina [International Workshop, Gender and Andean Culture]. Marcará, Ancash, Peru: Asociación Urpichallay.

Rojas Pérez, Isaias. 2008. Writing the Aftermath: Anthropology and "Post-conflict." In *A Companion to Latin American Anthropology*. Deborah Poole, ed. Pp. 254–275. Malden, MA: Blackwell.

Rojek, Chris. 1997. Indexing, Dragging and the Social Construction of Tourist Sights. In *Touring Cultures: Transformations of Travel and Theory*. Chris Rojek and John Urry, eds. Pp. 52–74. New York: Routledge.

Rojek, Chris, and John Urry, eds. 1997. *Touring Cultures: Transformations of Travel and Theory*. New York: Routledge.

Rosaldo, Renato. 1989. *Culture and Truth: The Remaking of Social Analysis*. Boston: Beacon Press.

Rosenberg, Tina. 2009. The Many Stories of Carlos Fernando Chamorro. *New York Times Magazine*, March 22:24–29.

Rovira, Guiomar. 1997. *Mujeres de maíz*. Mexico City: Ediciones Era.

Rushdie, Salman. 1987. *The Jaguar Smile: A Nicaraguan Journey*. London: Pan Books.

Safa, Helen I. 1995. *The Myth of the Male Breadwinner: Women and Industrialization in the Caribbean*. Boulder, CO: Westview Press.

Said, Edward W. 2003. *Orientalism*. 25th Anniversary Edition with new preface. New York: Vintage Books.

Salazar de Robelo, Lucia. 2004. A Conversation with Lucia Salazar de Robelo. In *Costa Rica and Nicaragua*. Pp. 4–7. New York: Linblad Expeditions.

Sanchez, Peter M., and Kathleen M. Adams. 2008. The Janus-Faced Character of Tourism in Cuba. *Annals of Tourism Research* 35(1):27–47.

Sánchez Campbell, Gabriel. 2004. Turismo lanza grito de guerra contra la basura. *La Prensa*, Managua, Nicaragua:9A.

Scarpaci, Joseph L. 2005. *Plazas and Barrios: Heritage Tourism and Globalization in the Latin American Centro Histórico*. Tucson: University of Arizona Press.

Scarpaci, Joseph L., Roberto Segre, and Mario Coyula. 2002. *Havana: Two Faces of the Antillean Metropolis*. Chapel Hill: University of North Carolina Press.

Schwartz, Rosalie. 1997. *Pleasure Island: Tourism and Temptation in Cuba*. Lincoln: University of Nebraska Press.

Schweid, Richard. 2004. *Che's Chevrolet, Fidel's Oldsmobile: On the Road in Cuba.* Chapel Hill: University of North Carolina Press.

Scott, Joan W. 1986. Gender: A Useful Category of Historical Analysis. *American Historical Review* 91(5):1053–1075.

Scruggs, T. M. 1999. Nicaraguan State Cultural Initiative and "The Unseen Made Manifest." *Yearbook for Traditional Music* 30:53–73.

Sheesley, Joel C. 1991. *Sandino in the Streets.* Bloomington: Indiana University Press.

Silverman, Helaine. 2002. Touring Ancient Times: The Present and Presented Past in Contemporary Peru. *American Anthropologist* 104(3):881–902.

———. 2005. Embodied Heritage, Identity Politics, and Tourism. *Anthropology and Humanism* 30(2):141–155.

Simon, Beatrice. 2009. Sacamefotos and Tejedoras: Frontstage Performance and Backstage Meaning in a Peruvian Context. In *Cultural Tourism in Latin America: The Politics of Space and Imagery.* Michiel Baud and Annelou Ypeij, eds. Pp. 117–140. Leiden, The Netherlands: Brill.

Sinclair, M. Thea, ed. 1997. *Gender, Work and Tourism.* New York: Routledge.

Speed, Shannon. 2008. *Rights in Rebellion: Indigenous Struggle and Human Rights in Chiapas.* Stanford: Stanford University Press.

Speed, Shannon, R. Aída Hernández Castillo, and Lynn M. Stephen, eds. 2006. *Dissident Women: Gender and Cultural Politics in Chiapas.* Austin: University of Texas Press.

Stahler-Sholk, Richard. 2007. Review of Thomas Olesen, *International Zapatismo: The Construction of Solidarity in the Age of Globalization.* New York: Zed Books. In *A Contracorriente* 4(2). Available at http://www.ncsu.edu/.

Starn, Orin, Carlos Iván Degregori, and Robin Kirk, eds. 1995. *The Peru Reader: History, Culture, Politics.* Durham, NC: Duke University Press.

Stein, Rebecca L. 2008. *Itineraries in Conflict: Israelis, Palestinians, and the Political Lives of Tourism.* Durham, NC: Duke University Press.

Stein, William W. 2003. *Deconstructing Development Discourse in Peru: A Meta-Ethnography of the Modernity Project at Vicos.* Lanham, MD: University Press of America.

Stephen, Lynn. 2002. *Zapata Lives! Histories and Cultural Politics in Southern Mexico.* Berkeley: University of California Press.

Stronza, Amanda. 2001. Anthropology of Tourism: Forging New Ground for Ecotourism and Other Alternatives. *Annual Review of Anthropology* 30:261–283.

———. 2008. Through a New Mirror: Reflections on Tourism and Identity in the Amazon. *Human Organization* 67(3):244–257.

Teo, Peggy, T. C. Chang, and K. C. Ho, eds. 2001. *Interconnected Worlds: Tourism in Southeast Asia.* London: Pergamon.

Tierra mía, Nicaragua (My Land, Nicaragua). 2001. Carlos Mántica Cuadra, dir. Video. Managua, Nicaragua: Producciones Video Arte, Mántica Waid y Cia.

Tree, Isabella. 2005. Travels Among the Zapatistas in Chiapas. In *Mexico OtherWise:*

Modern Mexico in the Eyes of Foreign Observers. Jürgen Buchenau, ed. Pp. 251–259. Albuquerque: University of New Mexico Press.

Tweedy, Maureen. 1953. *This Is Nicaragua.* Ipswich, UK: East Anglian Magazine.

Urry, John. 1990. *The Tourist Gaze.* London: Sage.

Van den Berghe, Pierre. 1994. *The Quest for the Other: Ethnic Tourism in San Cristóbal, Mexico.* Seattle: University of Washington Press.

Van den Berghe, Pierre, and Jorge Flores Ochoa. 2000. Tourism and Nativistic Ideology in Cuzco, Peru. *Annals of Tourism Research* 27(1):726.

Van Es, Guido. 2003. Los Vicosinos: Cultural Barriers in Tourism Development. Master's thesis, International Tourism Management and Consultancy, The Netherlands.

Vich, Víctor. 2006. La Nación en venta: Bricheros, turísmo y mercado en el Perú contemporáneo. In *La ruta andina: Turísmo y desarrollo sostenible en Perú y Bolivia.* Annelou Ypeij and Annelies Zoomers, eds. Pp. 187–197. Quito, Ecuador: Ediciones Abya-Yala.

———. 2007. Magical, Mystical: El Royal Tour de Alejandro Toledo. In *Industrias culturales: Máquina de deseos en el mundo contemporáneo.* Santiago López Maguiña, Gonzalo Portocarrero, Rocío Silva Santisteban, Juan Carlos Ubilluz, and Víctor Vich, eds. Pp. 313–325. Lima, Peru: Red para el Desarrollo de las Ciencias Sociales en el Perú.

Vicos, A Virtual Tour. 2006. Collaboration of Cornell University, The Mountain Institute, Uprichallay Association, and the community of Vicos, Peru. Available at http://instruct1.cit.cornell.edu/courses/vicosperu/vicos-site/.

Vilar, Alysia. 2003. Havana Honey, Parts 1–4. Available at http://www.salon.com/sex/feature/2003/05/20/havana.

Vivanco, Luis A. 2006. *Green Encounters: Shaping and Contesting Environmentalism in Rural Costa Rica.* New York: Berghahn Books.

Vogt, Evon Z. 1969. *Zinacantán: A Maya Community in the Highlands of Chiapas.* Cambridge, MA: Harvard University Press.

———. 1994. *Fieldwork Among the Maya: Reflections on the Harvard Chiapas Project.* Albuquerque: University of New Mexico Press.

Walker, Franklin, and G. Ezra Dane, eds. 1940. *Mark Twain's Travels with Mr. Brown: Heretofore Uncollected Sketches.* New York: Alfred A. Knopf.

Warren, Kay B. 2002. Toward an Anthropology of Fragments, Instabilities, and Incomplete Transitions. In *Ethnography in Unstable Places: Everyday Lives in Contexts of Dramatic Political Change.* Carol J. Greenhouse, Elizabeth Mertz, and Kay B. Warren, eds. Pp. 379–392. Durham, NC: Duke University Press.

Wenders, Wim, dir. 1999. *Buena Vista Social Club.* Video. Road Movies Production in association with Kintop Pictures, ARTE, and ICAIC. Santa Monica, CA: Artisan Entertainment.

Weismantel, Mary. 2001. *Cholas and Pishtacos: Stories of Race and Sex in the Andes.* Chicago: University of Chicago Press.

Whisnant, David E. 1995. *Rascally Signs in Sacred Places: The Politics of Culture in Nicaragua.* Chapel Hill: University of North Carolina Press.

Wilk, Richard. 2006. *Home Cooking in the Global Village: Caribbean Food from Buccaneers to Ecotourists.* New York: Berg.

Wilson, Jason. 2002. Nicaragua's New Wave. *Condé Nast Traveler,* February 2002:98–112.

Wilson, Tamar Diana. 2008. The Impacts of Tourism in Latin America. *Latin American Perspectives* 35(3):3–20.

Wilson, Wade T. 1998. *Fantasy Islands: A Man's Guide to Exotic Women and International Travel.* 2nd ed. Alameda, CA: Roam Publishing.

Wood, Carol. 1999. *Nicaragua. Ulysses Travel Guide.* 2nd ed. Montreal: Ulysses Books and Maps Division.

Wood, Randy, and Joshua Berman. 2005. *Moon Handbooks: Nicaragua.* Emeryville, CA: Avalon Travel Publishing.

Ypeij, Annelou, and Annelies Zoomers, eds. 2006. *La ruta andina: Turismo y desarrollo sostenible en Perú y Bolivia.* Quito, Ecuador: Ediciones Abya-Yala.

Ypeij, Annelou, and Elayne Zorn. 2007. Taquile: A Peruvian Tourist Island Struggling for Control. *European Review of Latin American and Caribbean Studies* 82:119–128.

Zambrana, Emilio. 2004. Arranca convención de turísmo. *La Prensa,* August 11:7B.

Zorn, Elayne. 2004. *Weaving a Future: Tourism, Cloth, and Culture on an Andean Island.* Iowa City: University of Iowa Press.

Zúniga, Joaquín, dir. 2006. *Turismo Rural Comunitario.* DVD. 12 min. Managua, Nicaragua: Fundación Luciérnaga.

Zurita, Félix, dir. 2005. *Turismos.* DVD. 23 min. Managua, Nicaragua: Fundación Luciérnaga.

Index